*A Centennial History of the State
Historical Society of Missouri, 1898–1998*

Alan Havig

A Centennial History

—— of the ——

State Historical Society of Missouri, 1898–1998

Alan R. Havig

University of Missouri Press
Columbia and London

Copyright © 1998 by
The Curators of the University of Missouri
University of Missouri Press, Columbia, Missouri 65201
Printed and bound in the United States of America
All rights reserved
5   4   3   2   1   02   01   00   99   98

Library of Congress Cataloging-in-Publication Data

Havig, Alan R., 1940–
    A centennial history of the State Historical Society of Missouri,
1898–1998 / Alan R. Havig.
        p.   cm.
    Includes bibliographical references and index.
    ISBN 0-8262-1169-0 (alk. paper)
    1. State Historical Society of Missouri—History.   I. Title.
F461.S73H38   1998
977.8—dc21   97-48912
                                                              CIP

⊗™ This paper meets the requirements of the
American National Standard for Permanence of Paper
for Printed Library Materials, Z39.48, 1984.

Designer: Stephanie Foley
Typesetter: BOOKCOMP
Printer and binder: Thomson-Shore, Inc.
Typefaces: Adobe Garamond and Regency Script

ERRATUM

Page 219 Caption should read H. Riley Bock (right)
served as president . . .

Contents

List of Tables / vii

*Foreword by James W. Goodrich, Executive Director
of the State Historical Society of Missouri / ix*

Introduction / 1

1. The Need and the Beginnings, 1898–1915 / 8

2. The Floyd C. Shoemaker Years, 1915–1940 / 46

3. The Floyd C. Shoemaker Years, 1940–1960 / 97

4. The Society under Richard S. Brownlee II, 1960–1985 / 150

*5. Completing the First Century under
James W. Goodrich, 1985–1998 / 203*

Conclusion / 256

A Note on Sources / 261

Index / 271

Tables

2.1.   The Society's Membership, 1916–1938   56

2.2.   Biennial State Appropriations, 1915–1916 to 1939–1940   79

2.3.   The Membership Fund (Trust)'s Support of the Society's
       Budget in Three Biennial Periods   84

3.1.   State Appropriations for the State Historical Society of
       Missouri, 1941–1942 to 1959–1961   98

3.2.   Membership of the State Historical Society of Missouri,
       1941–1961   100

3.3.   Presidents of the State Historical Society of Missouri,
       1898–1962   105

4.1.   State Appropriations for the State Historical Society of
       Missouri, 1961–1962 to 1985–1986   161

5.1.   Presidents of the State Historical Society of Missouri,
       1959–1998   212

5.2.   New Nonpresidential Members of the Finance/Executive
       Committee, 1960–1997   212

5.3.   Recipients of the Distinguished Service Award and
       Medallion   220

5.4. State Appropriations for the State Historical Society of Missouri, 1985–1986 to 1994–1995   227

5.5. New Members, Fiscal Years 1971–1972 to 1993–1994   230

Foreword

*A*s a part of the State Historical Society of Missouri's centennial observance, its Executive Committee authorized the publication of a volume celebrating and recounting the organization's first century. Stephens College professor Dr. Alan Havig, after a series of discussions, agreed to undertake the assignment. A University of Missouri–Columbia Ph.D., Havig's publications include three books (two on Missouri subjects) and a number of articles, including one contribution to the State Historical Society's quarterly publication, the *Missouri Historical Review.* As a Columbia resident, he had easy access to the society's records and its staff while doing his research for the monograph. In addition, he was able to consult with officers and trustees of the society, plus peruse Floyd C. Shoemaker's semicentennial history for pertinent information.

Havig's narrative naturally mentions the founding of the State Historical Society by the Missouri Press Association in 1898. Throughout its existence, the society has maintained strong and friendly relationships with the state's journalists. The editors and publishers of Missouri weeklies and dailies have assisted the society in many ways, including service as officers and trustees. They have made available to the society copies of their editions, enabling it to house the largest state newspaper collection in the nation. These papers are consulted by thousands of society patrons each year.

When the founders of the State Historical Society in 1898 looked for quarters, they found University of Missouri President Richard Jesse willing to provide the space. Jesse's keen interest in the society, fortunately, has been shared by his successors and their administrations. Two in particular, Elmer Ellis and James C. Olson, have played significant roles in the State Historical Society's existence. Being accomplished historians in their own right no doubt contributed to their deeply felt attachment.

The officers, trustees, members, and staff of the State Historical Society, of course, have been instrumental in the prosecution of its statutory obligations—to collect, preserve, exhibit, and publish the history of Missouri and the Middle West. The tireless work of these individuals has created a specialized research library that holds untold amounts of material covering all aspects of Missouri's history.

Equally important has been the support of state, county, and local elected officials, university and college administrators and staffs, professional and lay historians, genealogists, members of fraternal, civic, and patriotic organizations, and, last but not least, the public. Not only does the public make extensive use of the society's collections, but it also donates books, manuscripts, photographs, and artworks that strengthen the holdings. It would be impossible to mention everyone who has aided the society in its missions, but the governors and the state legislators deserve special mention because they have provided the majority of the society's funding since the turn of the century.

What success the State Historical Society has achieved over the years, then, is directly attributable to the countless men and women who have exhibited a heartfelt commitment to keeping the history of this wonderful state and its resourceful people available for us and future generations. It would be fitting to dedicate this volume to those individuals, past and present, who have accepted the challenge to preserve Missouri's rich history. Alan Havig's rendition, it is hoped, will allow those interested to discover how the State Historical Society of Missouri has gone about doing its part.

James W. Goodrich
August 15, 1997

A Centennial History of the State
Historical Society of Missouri, 1898–1998

Introduction

The centennial of any organization, public or private, is a historic event. It is historic on more than one level when history is the content of that institution's life. The mission of the State Historical Society of Missouri is to preserve and make available to the people the record of their state's past and to awaken citizen interest in and understanding of that past. These citizens may be schoolchildren, specialized scholars, or genealogists. They may contact the society only once in their lives, to simply locate a fact. The careful examination of the society's own history that produced this book clearly demonstrates that Missourians like these have enjoyed a great bargain for the past century, perhaps the greatest bargain purchased by their tax money over that length of time. With sometimes generous, but often inadequate funding, a small staff of dedicated employees and a wider circle of friends have built to prominence and great usefulness one of the nation's leading state historical societies. By telling its story, this study may serve as a monument to the society's first century.

A book's introduction permits an author to speak directly to readers, alerting them to what will follow in the various chapters and highlighting important themes. It is also the place where an author may step briefly out of the anonymity imposed by a narrative style to introduce, in this case, himself. I do not work for the State Historical Society of Missouri nor for any state agency. I am a proud product of the graduate history program of the University of Missouri at Columbia, an equally proud teacher of American history courses at Stephens College in Columbia during the three decades since I left graduate school, and a frequent

1

user of the historical society's collections. In a sense, I am a sympathetic outside evaluator of what I judge to be the society's many achievements and few shortcomings since its founding in 1898.

The life of any institution is a record both of limits recognized and opportunities taken—limits on what may be done, given available resources, and special strengths that represent opportunities grasped and developed over time. Of necessity, the leaders of the State Historical Society of Missouri have made decisions, not only at the beginning but throughout the organization's history, about which tasks and functions it would assume and which it could not. Thus, while a number of state historical societies operate museums, Missouri's owns a notable art collection and galleries in which to display it, but no museum. The society does not operate historic sites around the state, a function performed by some state societies, but it does, together with the University of Missouri, operate an extensive manuscript collection. While some states have constructed separate buildings for their historical societies—often in the capital city—Missouri, since 1898, has provided the society with space in the buildings that have housed the state university's general library. Some state societies continue to erect historic markers along highways or beside buildings, while this society's highway marker experience ended in the early 1960s. State historical societies, in short, display variety and idiosyncrasy.

A major goal of this account is to record the distinctive experience of the State Historical Society of Missouri, a part of which is its rejection of certain activities and acceptance of others. On a number of occasions, Secretary Floyd C. Shoemaker and his finance committee devoted effort to fending off tasks that legislators, other state agencies, or citizen groups wanted the society to assume. With a role carefully defined to fit available resources, the society was simply unable to adopt added functions that others thought appropriate. Financial resources set most of the limits within which the society operated; thus, this book gives considerable attention to the subject of finance.

Some of the topics to which the chapters give extended treatment reach beyond the society's own day-to-day work to touch important aspects of the state's life. From its beginning, the state historical society has developed a unique and unusually positive relationship with its cooperating institution, the University of Missouri–Columbia. The issue of physical space in the library required frequent conversation and adjustment, but beginning in the early 1940s, the two institutions also interacted over such matters as the formation of the Western Historical Manuscript Collection. For many years, key members of the university's history department gave the society crucial leadership and support. Two other themes that appear in this account are the recruitment, assignment, and retention of a professional staff in the society's Columbia quarters and the recruitment of members across the state and beyond its borders.

This narrative gives much attention to the varied activities of the society during its first century of existence. The agency has, for example, participated in a number of historical commemorations, beginning with the 1904 St. Louis World's Fair and continuing through such events as Missouri's centennial celebration in 1920–1921 and the Civil War centennial in the early 1960s. Much of the society's effort has gone into the acquisition and maintenance of its collections. Its assemblage of local newspapers is unmatched in size and comprehensiveness for any state; it also holds a famed collection of George Caleb Bingham paintings, works in various media by Missouri artist Thomas Hart Benton, and rare books and manuscripts on Missouri and nineteenth-century western history. This account discusses the society's collections at some length and makes special note of significant acquisitions, such as the J. Christian Bay Collection of Middle Western Americana in 1941–1942. Publications, which have included the *Missouri Historical Review* since 1906, as well as volumes of documents and narrative history, are one way in which the society has reached out to its members and other readers. Other outreach efforts include the society's relationship with local historical societies, special services provided to the schools of the state, and the erection of historic markers in every one of Missouri's counties. These and other activities find their place in the pages that follow.

Escaping mention so far is a key factor, without which the work of the society cannot be understood: leadership. As the society turns one hundred, it enjoys the leadership of only its fifth chief administrator. (A sixth interim executive, Director Virginia Young, served for two months in 1985 while a search committee chose Richard Brownlee's successor.) While the first secretary, Isidor Loeb, provided a caretaker administration until the finance committee could identify and fund a full-time administrator, each of the four professional directors of the society has given the organization a distinctive voice and personality.

The account that follows assesses the unique contributions of Francis A. Sampson, Floyd C. Shoemaker, Richard S. Brownlee II, and James W. Goodrich, as it identifies the common problems and opportunities with which they dealt.

It is important at the same time, however, to avoid what some might call a top-down history of the State Historical Society of Missouri. Rush H. Limbaugh of Cape Girardeau, who would become the society's president in the 1950s, remarked during World War II that Floyd Shoemaker was "ninety-nine and ten-ninths percent" of the society. While Limbaugh certainly exaggerated for effect, he had a valid point. The society's professional heads have been essential to its success, as have been a few key individuals who have served as elected officers and members of the finance/executive committee (the title has changed). On the other hand, they are not the whole story. It is the responsibility of this centennial history to suggest the contributions made by others: staff, members, visitors to the reading rooms, legislators and governors, authors of articles and reviewers of books for the *Missouri Historical Review*, those who attend the society's annual meeting and luncheon, and all the Missourians, past and present, who daily make the history that the society will preserve so that future generations will know their common past. As fully as the available sources allow, in short, this is a bottom-up as well as a top-down history.

Having made that point, however, I readily admit what the table of contents reveals: that this book adopts as its organizing principle the chronological sequence of administrations provided by the society's directors. Chapter 1 will address the desire for a historical society among newspaper editors organized in the Missouri Press Association. Founded by the editors in 1898, made a legal trustee of the state in the following year, and given its initial state appropriation in 1901, the society acquired its first paid secretary, and the core of its book and manuscript collections, when Francis A. Sampson arrived, also in 1901. Floyd Shoemaker began his fifty-year association with the society when he became Sampson's assistant in 1910.

Shoemaker served as the society's administrator from 1915 to 1960, and the story of that very long tenure fills Chapters 2 and 3. For several reasons, the year 1940 seems the best point at which to break the Shoemaker years into nearly equal halves of twenty-five and twenty years. If austere budgets were by no means a thing of the past in 1940, at least the stringencies of the Great Depression were over, and at the dawn of the 1940s, the society stood on the brink of some remarkable achievements. These included important acquisitions and major publications.

When Shoemaker gave up the helm in 1960, an able replacement was close at hand. Dr. Richard S. Brownlee, a product of the university's history department, had been helping direct its extension division. The announcement of his predecessor's impending retirement came early enough that Brownlee benefited from an apprenticeship during Shoemaker's final months in office. Then, after twenty-five years of advancements on numerous fronts, which Chapter 4 will detail, Dick Brownlee retired in 1985. His successor, James W. Goodrich, the society's associate director in 1985, needed no apprenticeship. Like Brownlee, he was a product of the university's history department and long familiar with the organization's operations; he brought the society through a smooth transition of leadership. For the last thirteen years of the society's first century, Jim Goodrich built a record of achievement on the foundations laid by his predecessors. Chapter 5 discusses that record. While the tenures of administrators do not provide the only useful way to assess the record of the State Historical Society of Missouri, they provide units of time more meaningful than decades or groups of gubernatorial terms or discernable eras in state or national history; thus, they are the organizing principle of this volume.

Among the subjects that this account discusses, one is basic to the others. It is the *raison d'être* of state historical societies and of those persons and institutions who, under any sort of sponsorship, preserve the record of the past. Why should they bother? Why should we pay them to do so? One reason is described in a letter that United States Supreme Court Justice Felix Frankfurter sent Floyd Shoemaker in 1943. The justice wrote to thank the secretary for sending to him volume 1 of the society's latest publication, *Missouri, Day by Day.* Frankfurter, a New Deal Democrat who shared responsibility for a significant growth in federal governmental power during the 1930s, confessed: "I am one of those old-fashioned people who believes in the continued importance—indeed the increasing importance—of our states." The publications of a state historical society make citizens proud of their past, he reasoned, "and therefore zealous to make the future worthy of the past." Shoemaker himself stated the case for historical societies and their important work on many occasions, but perhaps never more effectively than in a tribute to his predecessor, Francis Sampson. In 1918, Shoemaker wrote in Sampson's obituary: "A people who care nothing for their past, will make few records for the future. A state that refuses to preserve her history, will make little history to preserve." For a century, the State Historical Society of Missouri has symbolized Missourians' pride in their past and their determination to build a better future founded on the best of the past.

I wish to single out a few of the many people who assisted me in the preparation of the book. The first is Jim Goodrich, who, as we chatted in the aisle of a supermarket one Saturday morning, first mentioned the possibility of my writing the society's history. At every step along the way, Jim has made my job easier. As I learned many years ago when we both were graduate students, working with Jim Goodrich is a pleasure. Another historian of Missouri whose valued friendship dates from our days in graduate school is Professor Lawrence O. Christensen of the University of Missouri at Rolla. Chris's encouragement and careful reading of an early draft of this study have made the book a better one than it would have been without his help. I also wish to thank Trustee Virginia Young of Columbia for the interview that she granted to me in June 1996.

Members of the historical society's staff have been most helpful, in particular Sandi Wells and Dianne Buffon in the administrative office. In the reference library, where I did considerable reading and note-taking, I owe debts of gratitude to Laurel Boeckman, Linda Brown-Kubisch, and Marie Concannon. I also benefited from the expertise and kindness of these professionals on the Columbia campus staff of the Western Historical Manuscript Collection: Associate Director Nancy Lankford; manuscript specialists Randy Roberts, Diane Ayotte, Cindy Stewart, Kristina Gray Perez, and David Moore; and oral historian Ray Brassieur. Associate Director Lynn Wolf Gentzler and staff members Christine Montgomery, Linda Brown-Byrne, and Fae Sotham also provided important assistance. The society's treasurer, Albert M. Price, and trustees Francis M. Barnes III, John K. Hulston, Emory Melton, Robert C. Smith, and James C. Olson responded to my request for their views, and I thank them. All of these good people share responsibility for the positive features of this book. Its shortcomings are mine alone.

Stephens College offers a comfortable environment in which to teach and write. I wish to acknowledge the assistance of Dr. Andy Walker, my department chairperson in 1995–1996, and Dr. Robert S. Badal, the college's Vice President for Academic and Student Affairs. They approved a reduced teaching load during the fall semester of 1996, which greatly facilitated my completion of this volume's initial draft.

Finally, I recommend that every citizen of Missouri visit the quarters of the State Historical Society of Missouri, located in Ellis Library on the university's Columbia campus. Each citizen should come to enjoy a tour and to sample the unique and fascinating collections found in the newspaper library, the art galleries, the manuscript archive, and the reference library. This is a way to see for oneself that our state government not only assists agriculture, promotes tourism, supports classroom instruction, manages wildlife, maintains highways, conducts foreign trade missions, inspects municipal water supplies, and carries on myriad other functions. It also preserves the record of Missouri's past, making it available to all who would plumb its mysteries and seek its truths, and citizens may observe that function of state government most dramatically and comprehensively at the society's headquarters. When squinting at the page of a 150-year-old newspaper projected on the screen of a microfilm reader, or gazing at a historic painting depicting Missouri's colorful past from a gallery wall, a citizen-visitor may muse that, ultimately, this may be the most valuable of all the state government's services. Who knows? That visitor may be correct.

Columbia, Missouri
June 6, 1997

1

The Need and the Beginnings, 1898–1915

rganizations emerge from a context. Like people, they are born of a heritage that explains their character and the timing and circumstance of their appearance. The first task of this history is to establish the turn-of-the-century context that produced the State Historical Society of Missouri and helps to explain its nature even after a century of growth. While this society shares many traits with other state-supported agencies devoted to historical study, and some characteristics with all those that preserve and disseminate the historical record, it is, at the same time, quite unique.

Two important aspects of the setting that produced Missouri's state historical society deserve emphasis. The first is what some historians call the "historical sense" of Americans and Missourians around the turn of the twentieth century. Citizens of this nation, which possessed a brief but already rich history, observed and used that past in numerous ways. Second, the State Historical Society of Missouri drew upon a dual heritage of more formal efforts, both public and private and in Europe and the eastern United States, to preserve historical materials, open them to interested citizens, and stimulate an interest in the past. The specific model of a publicly funded historical society, the strongest examples of which had developed in the midwestern states since the mid-nineteenth century, was the one that Missouri adopted. But it did so only after a private organization, the Missouri Press Association, had initiated the society in 1898.

I

Prior to the society's appearance, Missouri's schools and colleges offered history instruction. They did so, we may assume, with widely varying degrees of thoroughness and accuracy, given the absence of rigorous teacher-training, statewide educational standards, and adequate text-books. The state university in Columbia, which had opened its doors in 1843, did not teach history as a discipline distinct from political science until the 1890s. According to Frank F. Stephens's *History of the University of Missouri,* during that decade Isidor Loeb became the first faculty member "to give his undivided time to history." In 1902, the university established a separate history department, one of whose earliest members was Dr. Jonas Viles. Both he and Loeb would become leaders of the state historical society.

In Missouri and other states of the Ohio and Mississippi River valleys, as the early settlers aged and towns celebrated the golden anniversaries of their founding, volumes of local history proliferated during the late nineteenth century. Based largely on the memories of longtime residents and the files of early newspapers and often compiled by editors, these county histories were short on analysis but rich with lists of important people and accounts of defining community events. Their purposes were to preserve knowledge about events before death removed the participants and to celebrate individual and collective achievements. A Missouri example of these local histories was a 1,255-page *History of Adair, Sullivan, Putnam, and Schuyler Counties.* Published in 1888 without indication of authorship, the volume announced in a twenty-seven-word subtitle that it included many individual biographies and family profiles. The Central Missouri publisher and editor William F. Switzler published his *History of Boone County, Missouri,* in 1882 through the Western Historical Company of St. Louis. By that date, the firm marketed twenty-two other titles in local and statewide Missouri history, including some intended for school use.

As a young man, Edwin W. Stephens of Columbia had helped Switzler compile his Boone County history. In 1895, Stephens's own paper published *The Columbia Missouri Herald Twenty-fifth Anniversary Historical Edition,* a still-useful collection of community data and biographical information. Walter Williams was the editor of Stephens's *Herald.* Just three years after their volume of local history appeared, these two historically minded journalists helped spearhead the movement that established the state historical society in their town.

As the collections of the state historical society grew in the early twentieth century, they offered researchers a much more reliable foundation for their studies than memory had for the nineteenth-century local histories. In 1898, for example, Switzler related how University of Missouri officials had tried to persuade him to write that institution's history. Such a project, he thought, "ought to be done by somebody personally conversant with the university from its opening in 1843," someone like himself who had known all the school's presidents and participated in many of its landmark events. But when Professor Viles compiled the history that Switzler had not, to mark the university's centennial in 1939, he and his coauthors drew upon library and archival resources. As Floyd Shoemaker, the society's secretary, noted with pride in 1938: "The data on the university from which the history is being written is largely in the collections of the state historical society." The society would provide Missourians with a collective memory that extended far beyond what personal experience could document.

In the wake of the Civil War, Americans found other ways to preserve, narrate, and interpret their shared experience. That conflict, of course, provided the nation with contrasting, even antagonistic, versions of the past's meaning, and both Northerners and Southerners organized after 1865 to preserve and present their perspectives. The erection of monuments to military units in town squares, on battlefields, and in cemeteries; the founding of veterans' groups and patriotic societies such as the Grand Army of the Republic and the United Daughters of the Confederacy; and the formation of study groups such as the Confederate Memorial Literary Society and the Southern Historical Society—all strengthened the appreciation and veneration, if not always the accurate understanding, of history.

Southerners used a cluster of ideas and emotions that contemporaries and historians have called the *Lost Cause* to interpret and cope with the failure of their stillborn nation. Similarly, victorious unionists passed on to their descendants a version of what the events of the 1860s meant. One function that publicly funded, professionally managed historical societies performed, with their charge to serve all of a state's citizens, was the collection and provision of objective data to persons holding widely varying interpretations of past events.

Much of white America's definition of the great struggle between North and South came at the expense of African Americans, during slavery and after. And within a half-century of the Civil War's conclusion, a powerful new medium, motion pictures, visually dramatized an antiblack interpretation of America's racial and sectional history. In 1915, however, when the racist, pro–Ku Klux Klan *The Birth of a Nation* appeared, a few black scholars like W. E. B. Du Bois were already at work documenting an accurate understanding of the African American experience. The Association for the Study of Negro Life and History issued the first volume of the *Journal of Negro History* in 1916, with Carter G. Woodson as editor.

In other ways, too, Americans expressed a sense of history at the close of the nineteenth century. These expressions both of interest and neglect helped form the context in which the State Historical Society of Missouri appeared in 1898. The preservation of historic sites is primarily a twentieth-century phenomenon, but it has important if somewhat attenuated roots in earlier years. The birthplaces, adult homes, and final resting places of venerated national leaders received attention from private preservation groups, for example. George Washington's Mount Vernon and Thomas Jefferson's Monticello exist today because groups of admirers saved them from decay at a time when governments spent no funds on preservation. Shrines to Washington in the capital city named for him and to Abraham Lincoln at his gravesite in Springfield, Illinois, also attest to the importance some Americans attached to physical symbols of the lives of significant leaders.

On the other hand, in both the nineteenth and twentieth centuries, Americans destroyed and neglected countless structures that later generations would consider priceless historic sites. When Academic Hall at the University of Missouri burned in 1892, the sense of loss was not that a fifty-year-old building intimately connected with the entire history of the institution had disappeared. Rather, consternation centered on practical problems of where to hold classes and how to pay for a replacement building. In Columbia, the deepest fear was that the state might relocate the university to another town. Francis A. Sampson of Sedalia, who soon became the historical society's first paid secretary, was one who argued for placing the institution in his city. Slated for leveling along with the remaining walls, the building's six ionic columns survived only because of a fortunate afterthought; a physical link to the past, they have become the symbol of the university. The marking of historic sites awaited the development of a sense that what had occurred in a place might disappear from public consciousness if not visually and verbally labeled significant. The granite markers placed along the Boonslick Trail and other roads by the Daughters of the American Revolution between 1910 and 1917 was one such early effort.

As the State Historical Society of Missouri matured over the next one hundred years, new methods of finding and sharing meaning in the past multiplied. Although museums flourished in the nineteenth century, the sophistication of their presentations near the dawn of the twenty-first century was dramatic. Historical reenactors of Civil War battles learned from their performances as well as taught schoolchildren and others who observed them. Some of these amateur soldiers became amateur actors as well, appearing in historical films like *Gettysburg* (1993). Documentary as well as fictional films shaped viewers' understanding of the past, as did certain radio and television programs. A cable network debuted in the 1990s with exclusively historical programming.

Earlier generations, without such technology, had their own means of reaching masses of people with historical interpretations. Relatively rare today, historical pageantry was once a powerful means of celebrating past events and conveying messages about them. David Glassberg's book on American historical pageantry includes a key case study of "The Pageant and Masque of St. Louis," an event also interpreted by Missouri historian Donald B. Oster. Intended to celebrate the city's 150th anniversary, the pageant cost $125,000, enlisted a cast of thousands, and attracted an audience of over a hundred thousand for four presentations in May 1914. It demonstrated the high degree of interest that some Missourians had in sharing, celebrating, and interpreting their history. Halfway across the state, other Missouri citizens worked through the youthful state historical society to achieve the same result.

American historical societies had developed for a century before Missourians acquired their state society. Many of them were private. Following the example of the earliest such group, the Massachusetts Historical Society (1791), organizations such as the American Antiquarian Society, the Essex Institute, and the Pennsylvania Historical Society arose to nurture the British heritage of the original thirteen states. Other private societies, founded in the nineteenth and twentieth centuries, served the needs of the many ethnic and racial groups that massive immigration had deposited in this nation. Examples include the Norwegian-American Historical Association located in Minnesota and the Chinese Historical Society of America, with its home in San Francisco. In Missouri, the private Missouri Historical Society (1867) was thirty-one years old when the Missouri Press Association formed the State Historical Society of Missouri. Other Missouri societies whose names appeared in a 1905 national directory of historical groups included the Lexington Historical Society, the Missouri Historical and Philosophical Society of Jefferson City, the New England Society of Saint Louis, and the Southern Historical and Benevolent Association, also of that city.

An original purpose of the American Historical Association (AHA), chartered by Congress in 1889, was to act as a clearinghouse of information and a forum for the leaders of the nation's state and local historical societies. In the years surrounding the turn of the century, an annual meeting of societies' representatives and the publication of its proceedings by the AHA demonstrated a growing interest in the systematic preservation and study of state and local history. Especially exciting was the increased willingness of state governments in the Middle West to subsidize historical study. Discussions about the purposes and functions of publicly funded state societies proliferated at the beginning of the twentieth century, and those discussions help a later generation to understand the national setting from which the State Historical Society of Missouri emerged.

The Annual Report of the American Historical Association for the Year 1897 contained advice from two knowledgeable historians that the founders of Missouri's state society would have found useful. In separate papers, J. Franklin Jameson, then a professor of history at Brown University and later the "father" of the National Archives, joined Reuben Gold Thwaites, secretary of the State Historical Society of Wisconsin, in analyzing the goals and paths to success of state historical societies.

The specialists recommended ways that state societies ought to function; the State Historical Society of Missouri would eventually accept some of these and reject others. For example, Jameson and Thwaites suggested that they collect and preserve historical materials, both printed and manuscript sources; certainly, the Missouri society did that from the beginning. While citizens might come forward with collections of letters or books, Thwaites advised that societies' professionals "actively solicit historical material." Both men suggested historical museums as a part of the state society's mission, and Thwaites identified anthropological as well as historical displays as proper. Those who shaped the state society in Columbia rejected both the museum idea and the anthropological emphasis. Thwaites also suggested a portrait gallery in which to display the images of eminent citizens. But Jameson implied, and Thwaites asserted outright, that the library collection, and not portraits or pioneer artifacts, was "the chief strength of the society." From Francis Sampson and Floyd Shoemaker's years with the society, down through the administrations of Richard Brownlee and James Goodrich, that belief has remained central to the mission of the State Historical Society of Missouri.

Even at the beginning of the twentieth century, an interest in genealogy attracted the greatest number of patrons to most societies' collections. But Jameson warned that genealogy must not dominate a society's activities. Both historians encouraged state societies to develop an active publications program, including volumes of edited primary source material as well as monographs and biographies. As types of what he called "field work," Thwaites cited the need to gather oral history; advise local historical societies and tie them to the state organization as auxiliaries; and promote serious historical study among high school teachers. Such efforts would meet Jameson's injunction to "arouse public interest and keep alive a patriotic regard for local history." So, too, would the state society's promotion of and participation in historic observances, such as the state semicentennials celebrated in the Middle West after the Civil War. Finally, prophetic of a special strength of the State Historical Society of Missouri, Thwaites advised history society professionals to maintain "close touch" with newspaper editors, whose historical articles and features would stimulate a popular interest in history.

What formulae for success did the university professor and the society administrator endorse one year before Missouri editors established a state historical society? While he mentioned the obvious—attract members and raise money—Jameson also isolated less predictable criteria. One was to avoid "fussy antiquarianism" by defining the society's mission broadly. For this scholar, all local history was a reflective fragment of national history and must appear in that context to possess meaning. Who could better establish that wider context of content than professionally trained historians? Thus, Jameson thought it natural that college teachers be active members of state societies. The State Historical Society of Missouri's success in attracting the interest and support of the state's college history teachers has been a mixed one. But it also is true that a few of Missouri's professional historians have provided creative and dedicated service to the society.

Thwaites had managed the State Historical Society of Wisconsin for ten years by 1897, and his map of the road to institutional success drew upon that experience. It was remarkably prescient of the experience-to-come of the Missouri society. His suggestion about close ties to the state's newspapers joined with other practical advice. Having successfully "dogged" the Wisconsin legislature for an appropriation and functioned both with and without that public support, Thwaites's conclusion was simple: "The society must look to the state, or die." At least that was essential in newer western states. But, the administrator from Madison warned, state subsidy sometimes brought the curse of political interference in a society's affairs. To blunt such interference, Thwaites thought it essential that a society attract the support of its state's eminent citizens. That such persons would regard the position of trustee or curator as an honor could only strengthen a historical society's political position and its standing with taxpayers. Thwaites cautioned that the existence of a state appropriation must not discourage wealthy friends from donating funds. An endowment, as the finance committee of the State Historical Society of Missouri could one day attest, strengthened public as well as private societies. Finally, Thwaites stated what all public administrators know: their agencies must continually demonstrate their usefulness to a broad sample of the state's citizenry by performing their many functions well.

A 1905 AHA survey yielded useful information about state historical societies in the era when Missouri acquired its own. The questionnaire found that twelve responding societies "own their own halls," five of which exceeded $100,000 valuation. Wisconsin's building, at $610,000, was the most expensive. Thirteen societies occupied space in their state capitols, seven found quarters on state university campuses, and four had homes in other public buildings. Wisconsin was the model for the "strong tendency on the part of Western and Southern historical agencies to associate themselves with their state universities." Missouri's young society was a part of that movement.

Of all the states, legislatures in Missouri's region gave the most generous financial support to their societies. Wisconsin's appropriation in 1905 was $32,000; Minnesota's and Iowa's, $15,000 each. Two private societies, Massachusetts and Pennsylvania, together with Wisconsin, enjoyed the largest endowments: $221,000, $169,000, and $53,000 respectively. The largest libraries were these in 1905: Wisconsin with 275,000 titles, Pennsylvania with 245,000, Massachusetts with 155,000, Kansas with 115,000, and New Hampshire with 100,000. As well as presenting statistics, the survey made qualitative judgments, the most notable of which was advice on the leadership required of successful state historical societies. The ideal administrator must attract scholars by setting an example of learning and an ability to oversee the growth of significant collections while demonstrating to "hard-headed men of affairs" an ability to solve practical problems and manage funds. The 1905 report concluded, "No society has attained its full measure of usefulness without some such personality dominating its affairs. Institutions dependent upon state aid are peculiarly in need of this vigorous personal management." Beginning with Floyd Shoemaker in 1915, and continuing in the administrations of Richard Brownlee and James Goodrich, the State Historical Society of Missouri would demonstrate the truth of that early-twentieth-century insight.

II

Missouri lagged behind many other states in establishing a publicly funded historical society. Although it had gained statehood sooner than neighbors Kansas, Iowa, and Nebraska, by the late 1890s Missouri had not even attempted to match their efforts to collect and preserve the record of the past. The status of records preservation in state government may suggest why the General Assembly had not established a historical society. When Missouri's 1837 capitol burned in 1911, it was the second occasion that a capitol fire had destroyed large quantities of Missouri's public records. The state had expanded the 1837 structure, built on the ashes of its predecessor, in 1887–1889, but even then, crowded quarters and the lack of a systematic archival program meant that the records of state agencies, stuffed into boxes, stood in "ill-lighted rooms in the basement." That is where University of Missouri history professor Jonas

Viles found many of them when he surveyed the quantity and condition of state records in 1907. "There is urgent need of some special official or department to take charge of the archives as a whole and arrange and classify them," Viles concluded.

Less than four years after his survey, the capitol burned, set ablaze by a lightning strike on a Sunday afternoon in February. After the Jefferson City fire department's equipment failed, the fire had its way. Arriving on Monday noon from Columbia, Viles observed the horrifying scene: "I do not remember any more exasperating experience than watching at short range this little fire eating its way leisurely from room to room and destroying records and printed material." State prison inmates rescued some boxes of constitutional convention and legislative documents. Viles delivered "these papers, water soaked, frozen, and covered with dirt," to the State Historical Society in Columbia, but the fire destroyed other records, the extent and nature of which can only be imagined.

Professor Viles reported on Missouri's tragedy to the archival commission of the American Historical Association. He confessed that it was "distinctly humiliating" to admit that his state had so little regard for preserving the historical record. The cause, he believed, was "the innate conservatism of the Missourian," who would not be taxed to fund any but the most fundamental of governmental functions. For whatever reasons, Missouri did not establish its state archives, within the secretary of state's office, until 1965.

If the state of Missouri, through its historical society, did not begin to collect and preserve materials until after 1898, who did? A few private collectors, conscientiously and at their own expense, began assembling Missouriana in the late nineteenth century. William Clark Breckenridge of St. Louis was one of these bibliophiles, and Francis Asbury Sampson of Sedalia another. Collectors did what the state ought to have done and what the private Missouri Historical Society did for St. Louis and vicinity: assemble and protect printed and manuscript sources that reflected the early history of the state and its communities. When Sampson's library became the foundation of the state historical society's collection in 1901, his shelf of official state publications was "far superior to that possessed by the state at the capitol," according to one newspaper report. In a state without a historical society, "Mr. Sampson has in a sense filled the place of such a society."

In county courthouses and city halls across Missouri, the daily business of government had produced decades' worth of records by 1898. It is impossible to generalize about records management in these hundreds of locations when few in public life had yet conceptualized that process. No systematic statewide inventory of local records occurred until New Deal agencies provided funding in the 1930s. Families and businesses, of course, preserved personal and institutional papers in every community. The collecting efforts of Sampson, Shoemaker, and others located many of these collections and brought them to Columbia and other sites for cataloging and preservation. But no one can know how much Missourians discarded prior to 1898 that active state agencies might have saved.

Scholars like Professor Viles were not alone in perceiving the need for a historical society. A newspaper editor is a historian, recording a day's or a week's worth of local history in each paper printed. Although many editors preferred to retain possession of their back issues, others wanted a safe, central repository for bound volumes of old newspapers and a place to send current issues. Several Missouri journalists with an especially acute sense of history took the lead in urging their professional association to found a state historical society.

The historian of the Missouri Press Association, William H. Taft, wrote that an "interest in their own history stimulated a desire among the members of the Association to collect and preserve the materials significant to the history of the entire state." Founded in 1867, the group dedicated itself to more than journalists' professional concerns and "shop talk" about presses and paper. The editors saw themselves as educators and inaugurated their organization in part to dampen the rancor that continued to divide Missourians after the Civil War. Newspapers could set an example for calm and reasoned discussion for citizens, although too few had grasped the opportunity. By 1897, when Edwin W. Stephens first suggested that Missouri follow the lead of other states by acquiring a state historical society through editors' initiative, their press association had thirty years of its own history to preserve. Eighteen ninety-eight, in addition, was the ninetieth anniversary of the first newspaper to publish in the state, the *Missouri Gazette* of St. Louis. Although the press and the state shared a proud past at the turn of the century, no library existed in which to place the records that documented that past.

Surviving sources do not answer all the questions that students of the society's origins wish to ask. As a result, although essentially the same story of the society's founding is told by Floyd Shoemaker in his 1948 history of the society, Taft in accounts published in 1964 and 1966, and Richard Brownlee in his October 1973 report to the annual meeting, the details vary from one account to the next. One could say the same of other accounts. What follows is as accurate a rendering of the society's founding story as is possible, given the fact that participants in the events of 1897 and 1898 recorded only a small part of what occurred.

It seems that the major impetus for the press association's sponsorship of a state historical society came from Columbia. Three Columbians in particular would play central roles: E. W. Stephens and Walter Williams of the *Herald* and Isidor Loeb of the university's history and political science faculty. Although both Stephens and Williams were past presidents of the press association, the older Stephens carried greater influence within the organization. A newspaperman since the late 1860s and the president of a large job printing plant associated with the *Herald,* Stephens represented a pioneer Boone County family. His grandfather began farming there in 1819, and his father founded a Columbia mercantile business in 1843 and endowed Stephens College in 1870. Along with his protégé Williams, E. W. Stephens displayed a deep interest in his community's past that found expression in years of service as an officer of the Boone County Historical Society. It was in 1897 that Stephens, in conversations with Williams, Loeb, and others, launched the plan for press association sponsorship of a state historical society.

On the second of its two-day Fifth Winter Meeting, January 21, 1898, the press association acted on Stephens's recommendation. No one can know what preparations the leadership had made prior to the morning meeting that day in the New Coates House hotel in Kansas City. But, according to the published proceedings, after Stephens had read a speech for the absent University of Missouri President Richard H. Jesse, W. O. L. Jewett, a past president of the press association, offered a resolution. The association's members believed that Missouri should have a historical society "embracing the whole state," the proposal asserted. The editors should, therefore, authorize their president to appoint a committee of five members to write a constitution and bylaws for such a society by the time of the press association's summer meeting.

E. W. Stephens, the highly regarded publisher of the *Columbia Herald* and an amateur historian, headed the movement for the Missouri Press Association to found a state historical society. A member of the committee directed to draft a constitution and bylaws for the organization, Stephens was also elected as its first president. He served in that position from 1898 to 1903.

The editors approved an amended resolution that named Stephens as the committee's chair and Columbia as the society's location.

Between the January meeting and the press association's thirty-second annual meeting held in the resort city of Eureka Springs, Arkansas, on May 25 and 26, 1898, the Stephens committee accomplished its assignment. Serving with the Columbia publisher were Jewett of the *Shelbina Democrat*, A. A. Lesueur of the *Lexington Intelligencer*, H. E. Robinson of the *Maryville Republican*, and Perry S. Rader of the *Brunswick Brunswicker*. As they wrote the proposed society's constitution and bylaws, committee members consulted the framing documents of other state societies. The State Historical Society of Wisconsin, with a half-century's experience by 1898, seems to have been an especially influential model. On February 22, the committee met with the university's board of curators, the faculty, and President Jesse. Stephens, a former chairman of the curators, and Williams, who would begin an influential term on the board in 1899, easily gained the enthusiastic support of the university's governing body. Tangible evidence of that support was the assignment of space to the society in what would be called Jesse Hall. (In 1898 the building carried the name Academic Hall, the same as that of the structure destroyed by fire six years earlier.) University officials also promised to petition the legislature for funds to pay a society librarian. Even before the press association had launched the society, therefore, its one hundred years of close cooperation with the University of Missouri had begun.

Members at the Eureka Springs meeting on May 26 quickly endorsed the work of Stephens's group. A special committee of three, which included Walter Williams, after examining the proposed constitution and bylaws, recommended their approval. The editors concurred. The press association then selected Stephens as president of the State Historical Society of Missouri and Loeb as its secretary or administrator.

The Missouri editors created an organization with laudable and ambitious goals but provided no funding. No one in 1898 imagined that the historical society could or should draw its financial lifeblood from the university for long. As other states had demonstrated, the State Historical Society of Missouri could not exist without regular legislative appropriations independent of other state agencies. In 1899, the society's leadership began the process leading to state financing of its activities. On February 14, Stephens, Perry Rader, and Loeb petitioned the Circuit Court of Boone County for a proforma decree of incorporation "for the purpose of promoting education especially in the fields of historical study." The court granted the decree on February 21, and on March 9 the secretary of state certified the society's articles of association, or constitution.

On May 4, 1899, Governor Lon Stephens signed a bill passed by the Fortieth General Assembly "creating the State Historical Society [as] a trustee for the State, prescribing its duties and defining its powers." The act made the society eligible for state funding. In making the society a trustee of the state, Missouri followed a precedent set by Wisconsin and adopted by other states. It meant that the society would not own its collections and be free to dispose of them, for example, for its officers' personal gain. Rather, the society held and administered the properties entrusted to it for the state, and thus for the people of Missouri. Not until the spring of 1901 did the Forty-first General Assembly approve

The Missouri Press Association held its thirty-second annual meeting at the Crescent Hotel in Eureka Springs, Arkansas, on May 25–27, 1898. At this meeting, the members unanimously adopted a constitution and bylaws for the State Historical Society of Missouri and elected E. W. Stephens and Isidor Loeb as president and secretary, respectively, of the newly created organization.

the society's first appropriation: $4,500 for the 1901–1902 biennium. Thus did a privately established organization evolve into a public agency in three years' time.

Both the society's constitution and the May 1899 legislation established goals for the new agency that coincided with Jameson's and Thwaites's advice. Together they projected a program of service that, although later modified in some respects, has guided the society through its first century. While the two charges agreed on most matters, they contained differences worth noting. The constitution channeled the society's efforts by employing four verbs: to *collect, preserve, exhibit,* and *publish* historical materials. The society's framing document then specified functions that would achieve these broad objectives. One was to explore the archaeology of the state, that is, the remains of cultures active prior to European settlement. While some state historical societies have assumed archaeological and anthropological functions—Ohio's is one example—Missouri's has not. Years later the society removed this goal, which the General Assembly's bill had mentioned only in a brief reference to "antiquities," from its constitution. The state's journalists also anticipated that the society would maintain "an ethnological and historical museum." The 1899 law omitted mention of this function. Through the years many Missourians have expressed regret over the absence of a state historical museum under the society's direction. As later chapters of this study will explain, the society has had sufficient reasons to decline acceptance of the museum function.

The editors and the legislators agreed on other charges to the society that it has performed from its earliest days. The heart of the State Historical Society of Missouri's mission is and always has been to build collections of historical materials; to preserve and maintain them; to make them available to readers of printed resources and viewers of visual documents such as paintings; and to diffuse historical information through publications and other means. The press association envisioned the society "acquiring documents and manuscripts, obtaining narratives and records of pioneers." In more detailed language, the state established essentially the same goal. The society's constitution and legislative grant of power both required the operation of "a library of historical reference," which the 1899 act specified should be "open at all reasonable hours on business days for the reception of the citizens of this state, without fee."

The society's constitution anticipated "a gallery of historical portraiture"; the legislature directed the society to "procure portraits." The Stephens committee of the press association, in surveying the activities of existing state societies, may have borrowed this idea from the Wisconsin society, which in turn may have adopted it from private societies in eastern states, where portrait artists had created a rich visual record of America's colonial elite. Reuben G. Thwaites often spoke of the Wisconsin society's art collection as an assemblage of portraiture, not of other types of painting or other art genres. The Missouri society's leaders, beginning in earnest during the 1940s, interpreted the "gallery of . . . portraiture" charge liberally, as they began to build a significant art collection.

The society's initial collection was of newspapers, and the ongoing relationship that the historical society has maintained with Missouri editors deserves emphasis. The society's constitution gave the privileges of membership to editors who regularly contributed issues of their papers to the collection and life memberships to those who did so "continuously for ten years." Hundreds of editors have supported the society in this manner, and one result is the most comprehensive collection of one state's dailies and weeklies in existence. In the months that followed the society's founding, Acting Secretary Isidor Loeb solicited the editors' support. In a letter, after outlining the new society's goals, he asked: "Will you not cooperate in this movement and contribute to the permanent archives of the state by sending your paper and thereby becoming a member?" In a letter dated January 30, 1899, President E. W. Stephens reported to cooperating editors that "203 papers representing 91 counties" regularly came to the society's quarters. A few publishers also had contributed "valuable back numbers" for binding, and Stephens promised that the society would request money from the legislature to bind the newspapers and carry out its other functions.

The early records of the State Historical Society of Missouri include stacks of three-by-five-inch index cards that reflect the society's ongoing awareness of its origins. Until 1948—and therefore throughout the first half-century of the organization's life—staff members kept track of the "descendants of members of the Missouri Press Association in 1898 who are still engaged in journalistic work." The widows, sons and a few daughters, and grandchildren of those present at the founding represented a valuable, living resource for the society.

The constitution established other membership categories and set two dollars as the annual membership fee. In 1901, the society's officers reduced that figure by one-half, and it remained at one dollar into the 1960s, perhaps the best, longest-running bargain in the state of Missouri. The constitution also allowed local societies to become auxiliary members of the state society, provided for an annual meeting, and created leadership positions, both citizen and professional.

The professional manager, who would bear the title "secretary" into the 1960s, was responsible for conducting the society's day-to-day business with the assistance of a staff. The secretary would work closely with a finance committee, which "shall exercise supervisory control" of the society's affairs. Named annually by the president from a larger group of trustees, but in practice through repeated appointment, finance committee members served as long as they were willing and able. Key finance committee members such as Loeb, Williams, L. M. White, George Rozier, Francis M. Barnes, William Aull, Virginia Young, and

Avis G. Tucker have been nearly as significant to the society's success as have been the salaried secretaries/directors.

Standing behind these active overseers of the society's immediate business and long-range plans was a group of trustees. Holding positions that were largely honorary, the trustees represented the state's congressional districts or were state officials. Together with the society's president and secretary, the trustees constituted an executive committee, according to the original constitution. Finally, the officers of the society included a president, six vice presidents, and a treasurer, all chosen by the executive committee from the roster of trustees.

The society's location in Columbia, although that community enjoyed a central location, might have seemed remote to many Missourians at the turn of the twentieth century. That was a common complaint, in fact, about the state university's location there. A perception of inaccessibility could have harmed the society politically once state tax dollars subsidized it. But the support of editors from across Missouri and the presence of trustees from each congressional district assured a statewide representation in the society's operations that has proved significant to its success.

The press association, the Boone County Circuit Court, and the state legislature all recognized the State Historical Society of Missouri as the new agency's name. The Missouri Historical Society in St. Louis had long since appropriated the other obvious possibility. The existence of two organizations including the words "historical society" and "Missouri" in their titles has, of course, created a degree of confusion. Most of it has been of minor importance, such as one society receiving the other's mail. The chair of the AHA's meeting of historical society directors in 1910 introduced Francis Sampson's employer as the "Missouri State Historical Society." Sampson did not complain. At other times and to other people, however, the misnomers have loomed more significant. In 1954, L. M. White of the *Mexico Ledger* publishing family complained about recent newspaper stories that had erroneously identified the state's publicly funded society. He asked Floyd Shoemaker: "Don't you think that in the [press] releases that you send out in the future, for at least a time, you could have an editor's note drawing attention to the fact that the proper name of the society is *The State Historical Society of Missouri*? We may as well get the credit for the things we are doing." Through the decades, notwithstanding some confusion, the public and historians have recognized the historical societies named "Missouri" for their distinct achievements.

III

The society's first seventeen years—1898 to 1915—divide naturally into three distinct phases. Until the appropriation of state funds in the spring of 1901, the society could make little progress. E. W. Stephens, the president, and Isidor Loeb, acting secretary and later secretary, borrowed what time they could from their full-time jobs to encourage editors to contribute newspapers. But Loeb's eighteen-month leave from teaching to study in Europe from June 1899 to September of the next year rendered the society virtually inactive. With several significant occurrences in 1901, however, it came to life. Among the events of that year was the hiring of Francis A. Sampson as the society's first paid, full-time secretary. Although Sampson filled that office until 1915, the hiring of Floyd C. Shoemaker as assistant secretary and librarian in May 1910 opened a third phase of the society's earliest history.

Secretary Isidor Loeb's accomplishments, while necessarily limited, were genuine. In an appeal to Missourians dated 1901, he solicited a comprehensive list of "objects particularly desired by the society." His list began with what an organization establishing a reference library most needed: books, pamphlets, reports, and other documents reflecting Missouri public life as well as the record of its private groups; newspapers and periodicals; and original manuscripts. Loeb assured potential donors of rare papers that "the society has the use of a fire proof vault in which valuable manuscripts will be preserved." The secretary also solicited nonprint sources of historical knowledge, including maps, engravings, paintings, photographs, autographs of famous citizens, medals, coins, and "war relics, old arms, weapons, etc." Assuming that all the society's stated goals would materialize, Loeb also asked for "Indian relics." To encourage such donations, the society promised to pay freight charges to transport items to Columbia.

Also in 1901, Loeb and the university librarian negotiated an agreement of cooperation and division of labor. In charge of libraries located in a large new building completed in 1895 that was rapidly filling with varied university offices and functions, the two men had a strong incentive for using their assigned space efficiently. They agreed that the society's library would specialize in state and local history and state law—the latter one of Loeb's specialized fields—even though the university's law department collected legal titles as well. While the society would build strength in the history of the Mississippi valley, the university would collect works in general U.S. history. While the university library would catalog other states' documents, the society would restrict its collection to Missouri government documents. The society's staff would prepare "slips" listing its titles for inclusion in the university's main card catalog. The cooperative efforts begun by Loeb would continue as the two collections grew and eventually moved together to a separate library building.

A "meeting of the society" held on April 29, 1901, took several important actions. Those present proposed four amendments to the society's constitution. The changes included a reduction of the annual membership fee from two dollars to one and the elimination of the requirement that society officers come from the group of trustees. The society's members would consider these changes at the first annual meeting, which the finance committee later scheduled for December 5–6, 1901. An outside speaker of note, the Wisconsin society's Reuben G. Thwaites, would deliver the "annual address" then. The late April meeting also filled the society's leadership positions, many for the first time. It reelected Stephens as president, while Walter Williams became the society's treasurer, a trustee, and a member of the key finance committee. With the exception of Francis Sampson of Sedalia, a lawyer by training, the other trustees who were not elected public officials were editors. In addition to Williams, the finance committee consisted of Robert M. White of Mexico and Perry S. Rader of Brunswick. Finally, at its April 29 meeting, the newly staffed finance committee hired Minnie K. Organ as assistant librarian, to begin her duties on September 1.

Preceding the first salaried secretary by several months, Organ was the society's initial employee. Born in Dent County on December 29, 1870, her family's business tied her to the press association and the historical society. Organ's father, John E., published the *Salem Monitor* and became one of the society's first trustees on the same day the society hired his daughter. Following her graduation from the Salem public schools, Minnie Organ first taught there and then left for college. After receiving a

Minnie Organ, the society's first paid staff member, was a native of Dent County. Hired as assistant librarian in 1901, Organ remained with the society until 1910.

B.S. degree at the Warrensburg Normal School, she returned for a second round of classroom teaching in Salem and then departed for Columbia, where she earned both bachelor's and master's degrees. Organ, one of Isidor Loeb's students, had charge of the political science library during part of her stay at the university. She also completed summer school course work in library science at the University of Wisconsin, in preparation for her position with the society. Minnie Organ remained with the society through July 31, 1910. In three *Review* articles in 1909–1910, Organ, then the assistant to the secretary, published the results of her research on the county press in Missouri. After leaving Columbia, Organ pursued graduate studies at the University of Chicago, served as the principal of Salem High School, and taught at the state teachers' college in Springfield. She died on December 8, 1931.

The finance committee members who hired Minnie Organ included men who fundamentally shaped the State Historical Society of Missouri during its first three decades and beyond. When one of the original members, Perry S. Rader, left the committee later in 1901, Isidor Loeb replaced him. Loeb was a rock of stability and fount of wisdom until resigning from the finance committee in the fall of 1942. His colleagues on the three-member committee served extraordinarily long terms, as well. Robert M. White was a member until 1932 and also society president from 1914 to 1916. Walter Williams, who like White departed in ill health, remained a member until 1934. No other person served on the finance committee, except Rader, until 1933. As a team, Williams, Loeb, and White directed the society's affairs during Sampson's years as secretary and nearly twenty years into Shoemaker's lengthy secretaryship.

The finance committee's membership during the society's first fifty years, or until 1948, totaled only eight, all of them men. Meeting periodically with, listening to recommendations from, and issuing instructions to the secretary, the finance committee's members, within the limits set by the society's constitution and state legislation, largely determined what the society became. The biographies of the committee's first triumvirate indicate the sources and quality of leadership upon which the society drew.

Isidor Loeb, born on November 5, 1868, in Roanoke, a village in Howard County, was the son of German nationals Bernhard and Bertha (Myer) Loeb, who had immigrated three years earlier. Bernhard was one of the Jewish merchants common in small-town America in the nineteenth and early twentieth centuries. His son's long association with the University of Missouri began when he entered the preparatory department at the age of thirteen in 1881. By 1893, Loeb had earned two bachelor's and a master's degree from the university. While he oversaw the early activities of the state historical society and taught classes, Loeb also completed his Ph.D., which Columbia University awarded in 1901.

When he left for Washington University in St. Louis in 1925, Loeb had taught history and political science at Missouri since 1892, had served as dean of the faculty and of the School of Business and Public Administration, and, for a few months in 1923, had been acting university president. At Washington University between 1925 and 1940, Dr. Loeb taught political science and administered that institution's School of Business and Public Administration. In 1933, he served as president of the American Political Science Association.

A faculty member at the University of Missouri, 1892–1925, and at Washington University, 1925–1940, Isidor Loeb served as the society's first secretary, 1898–1901. He maintained an interest in the society throughout his life, serving on the finance committee for over forty years and as president, 1944–1947.

An authority on constitutional and tax law, Loeb helped E. W. Stephens and Walter Williams to write the historical society's constitution and bylaws in 1898, and he drafted the bill that made the society the state's trustee in 1899. His influence on the society was indirect as well as direct. Floyd Shoemaker, like Minnie Organ, was his student. As they worked together on the society's business into the 1940s, Shoemaker never ceased to think of Loeb as his mentor. Reporting to Walter B. Stevens in 1926 that his former professor was happily settled in St. Louis, Shoemaker added: "I am sorry, so very sorry, that old MU lost this man, who is really a great man in every way."

While Isidor Loeb matured in Howard County, Walter Williams learned the newspaper business from the ground up in neighboring Cooper County. Born in Boonville on July 2, 1864, this commanding, self-educated man became owner and editor of the *Advertiser* in his hometown before the age of twenty. He was only twenty-three when he served as president of the Missouri Press Association in 1887. From 1890 to 1908, Williams and Edwin Stephens worked together on the *Herald* in Columbia, a newspaper with a national reputation as a "model country weekly." From their base at the *Herald,* Stephens and Williams worked through the press association and the university's curators to establish a chair of journalism. When, in 1908, the University of Missouri founded the world's first professional school of journalism, Walter Williams became its dean.

The author or editor of a shelf full of books, including several on Missouri history, a dynamic public speaker, and a tireless world traveler, Williams received most of the honors available to a journalist. They included the presidency of the National Editorial Association in 1895 and the presidency of the Press Conference of the World from 1915 to 1925. Recalling Walter Williams's career in 1958, University of Missouri President Elmer Ellis asserted that this man "had a tremendous influence upon all phases of journalism, not alone in the United States but in all other free nations." Although in frail health, Williams, who had never attended college, accepted the presidency of his university in 1930. During the worst years of the Great Depression he provided it with the same capable leadership that he gave to the State Historical Society of Missouri for thirty-three years.

The third important early member of the society's finance committee was its chair from 1901 to 1932, Robert Morgan White. Like Williams and Stephens, R. M. White, as he signed his name, gained a national reputation as a small-town editor and publisher. Later termed "the best known country newspaper editor in the United States," White bought the *Mexico Ledger* in 1876, the year of his graduation from Westminster College in Fulton. In 1888, he began publishing a daily, the *Evening Ledger.* Born in Southampton, Long Island, in 1855, White's interest in history came by way of his family's deep roots in America. Both parents' ancestors had immigrated to the colonies, and R. M. belonged to the tenth generation of Whites in America. At the age of eleven, in 1866, White moved to Audrain County with his parents, where father Albert both farmed and taught school. Choosing journalism over a professional baseball career, White was president of the Missouri Press Association in 1885. In 1918, R. M. White gave the editorial responsibilities of the *Ledger* to his son L. M. (Leander Mitchell), who later would assume as active and significant a role in the society's leadership as had his father.

At its meeting of October 11, 1901, the finance committee hired the society's first professional secretary and obtained the foundation of its reference library. The library and the man arrived as a package.

Francis Asbury Sampson was a Missouri-variety Renaissance man from the rough-and-tumble railroad town of Sedalia. In the same years that its African American subculture nurtured Scott Joplin's ragtime music, that city's genteel white subculture harbored Sampson. According to the agreement signed that day, Sampson donated his large library of Missouriana to the society. For its part, the committee hired Sampson for not less than four years "to devote his time to the work of collecting books, pamphlets, etc." for the society, "and in general to do that which will promote . . . [its] interests." Sampson's annual salary, which would increase to $2,500 by 1905–1906, began at $1,000.

Although Sampson's training was in the law, the terms *bibliophile, bibliographer, conchologist, paleontologist, journalist,* and *banker* name his avocations. Like R. M. White, Francis Sampson migrated to Missouri from the East. His parents, Francis and Margaret (Evans) Sampson, immigrants from Ireland and Wales, respectively, welcomed their son into the world on February 6, 1842, in Harrison County, Ohio. Although his age suited Sampson for service in the Civil War, available biographical sources are silent on the matter. Instead, he pursued a college education, graduating with an A.B. in 1865 from the College of the City of New York. In 1868, he received both a master's degree from that institution and a law degree from the University of New York, also in New York City. In the autumn of that year, Sampson moved to Sedalia to join an older brother in the practice of law. In his new home, Sampson's diverse talents soon found outlets. For many years, he was an officer of a bank and active in its management; for a short time, he was the associate editor of the *Sedalia Times;* he also volunteered his services as a member of the school board, public library board, natural history society, and the Missouri Chautauqua organization.

In addition to collecting printed sources on Missouri life in the nineteenth century, Sampson searched likely sites for fossil and shell specimens. An 1895 biographical sketch observed of this skilled amateur naturalist: "Many shells and fossils have been named in his honor. . . . Probably no man in this portion of the Mississippi Valley is more thoroughly acquainted with its mineral and geographical formations." Sampson's publications included scientific as well as historical articles and bibliographies. After his hiring in 1901, the new secretary arranged for the donation to the society of 1,343 books, 3,678 pamphlets, and 125 maps and charts owned by the Sedalia Natural History Society.

Sampson's larger collection of historical materials consisted of 1,886 books and 14,280 pamphlets. It was the first of several significant collections acquired during the society's first century. If Francis A. Sampson had done nothing more for the State Historical Society of Missouri than give it his library, he would have done much to insure its future.

But, of course, he accomplished considerably more than that. Fifty-nine years of age when he became secretary, Sampson continued in that position until his seventy-third year in 1915 and remained in the society's employ until his death in 1918. Shortly after his appointment, R. M. White wrote Sampson to thank him for the "grand donation" of his collection. "I feel sure that our relations will be most pleasant," White added. "You are just the man that we needed. The rest of us have not the time or the talent to accomplish results." In Columbia, Loeb was equally enthusiastic. "I feel that we are all to be congratulated upon the determination that has been made as I feel that it will be productive of great good to us and to the state." The outgoing secretary reported that many Missourians had responded to the announcement of Sampson's appointment with offers of books and other materials. Between mid-October and late November 1901, Loeb arranged for the arrival of the scores of boxes containing Sampson's collection and the natural history library. The university's cooperative bookstore vacated a room in Academic Hall in which carpenters began building bookshelves on November 22. E. W. Stephens helped Sampson obtain a favorable shipping rate from the Missouri-Kansas-Texas Railroad, and the new secretary sent the books on November 26. Sometime in December, Sampson assumed his duties in the society's quarters.

Under Sampson's direction, the society began to move toward the goals that the press association and the state government had envisioned a few years earlier. Some of its activities reached out visibly to statewide and even national constituencies. Other functions, essential but routine, fell into the category of administration, such as managing and enhancing the newspaper and reference collections. While Secretary Sampson excelled in the performance of some responsibilities, his record in other areas proved less successful.

The finance committee sent Sampson to the annual Conference of Historical Societies sponsored by the American Historical Association each December. At these meetings, he publicized the work of the society

Shown here in the society's quarters in Academic Hall, Francis A. Sampson, the first full-time, paid secretary of the state historical society, was a native of Ohio. In 1868, he settled in Sedalia, where he practiced law and pursued diverse avocations. His rich and extensive collection of Missouriana served as the foundation for the society's reference library. Elected secretary in 1901, Sampson held that position until 1915.

among his coprofessionals, obtained ideas from the representatives of other societies, and occasionally contributed papers. At the 1910 meeting in Washington, D.C., for example, Sampson spoke to his colleagues on "Publicity as a Means of Adding to Collections." The Missourian also helped to form what in time became the leading organization of historians of the United States: the Mississippi Valley Historical Association. Originally composed of officers of midwestern historical societies, the group selected Sampson as its first president at the charter meeting, held in Lincoln, Nebraska, in 1907. From its earliest days, the State Historical Society of Missouri has actively fostered cooperative efforts among state and local historical societies.

Enlisting new members, welcoming them to the society's annual meetings, and publishing a quarterly journal—all were ways to involve growing numbers of Missourians in the society's work and in Missouri's history. As he traveled extensively about the state seeking materials for the collections, Sampson promoted his fledgling institution at every stop. While the number of dues-paying members grew slowly, 556 persons had joined by the end of 1910. Ninety-one of these resided outside of Missouri in thirty-six states and Canada. Paying members totaled 538 four years later. Nonpaying editorial members outnumbered those who paid for society membership during the years to 1915. They, of course, contributed their newspapers, which were much more valuable to the society than the membership fee. It received more than 700 current newspapers in 1914, up to 200 issues arriving in a single day's mail delivery. At the end of 1914, total society membership in all categories was 1,365.

During the years 1901–1915, the State Historical Society of Missouri's annual meetings were intimate gatherings largely attended by journalists and those actively engaged in the researching and writing of history. The finance committee occasionally attempted to obtain politicians as keynote speakers: former Senator John B. Henderson in 1903, for example, and Governor Joseph W. Folk in 1905. It failed in both attempts. By 1915 and perhaps earlier, the society's leadership scheduled a dinner following afternoon meetings of society members and the executive committee. The annual meeting often occurred on a Thursday and Friday, perhaps a concession to weekday train schedules that made Columbia more accessible to visitors than the more restricted weekend service.

University history professor Jonas Viles served as program chair for the annual meetings in 1904 and 1907. The materials he saved allow some insight into those occasions. The printed program for the 1904 meeting reveals that both men and women, as well as professionally trained and avocational historians, took part in meetings held both on Friday afternoon and Saturday morning, December 9 and 10. Viles had encouraged several potential speakers to prepare papers, with mixed results. Agreeing to appear, William F. Switzler drew from personal experience as he spoke about "Pioneers in Missouri." But Charles K. Harvey of the *St. Louis Globe-Democrat* lacked the time to participate. Society President H. E. Robinson spoke on "The Lincoln, Hanks, and Boone Families," while Isidor Loeb analyzed Missouri legislation. Another paper dealt with Jesuit-Indian relations along the Missouri River. Two women, the society's employee Minnie Organ and member Mary A. Owen, prepared remarks on public school administration in the state and "Missouri's Roll of Honor," respectively. Visitors to the 1904 meeting took advantage of the opportunity "to inspect the library and collections" in Academic Hall.

Including Viles himself, academics dominated the presentations at the 1907 annual meeting. Viles spoke on his continuing concern with records preservation in the state capitol. Other speakers included William G. Bek, a university history instructor, and James Madison Wood, a graduate student who spoke on "The Nativity of the Early Settlers of Columbia, Mo." Five years later, Wood became president of Stephens College. Two visitors from Illinois also appeared on the 1907 program. The remarks of Clarence W. Alvord, who taught in the University of Illinois's history department and was archivist for his state's historical society, concerned the Spanish and the American Revolution. Dr. J. E. Snyder, former president of the Illinois Historical Society, read a paper on Democratic Party state conventions in 1860. The 1904 and 1907 gatherings were typical of annual meetings during the early period of the society's history.

If annual meetings involved few Missourians in the work of the society, a special exhibit mounted at the 1904 St. Louis World's Fair touched many more. In the summer of 1903, the Missouri World's Fair Commission accepted the society's proposal to prepare a display of the state's newspapers and Missouri authors' books. A total of 928 bound volumes of 1903 newspapers and 1,855 publications written by Missouri authors composed the exhibit, and the society's staff prepared a printed catalog to accompany the large display. The two thousand dollars that the commission committed to the project came at an opportune time, for in April the finance committee had reduced Minnie Organ's salary by one-third as part of an attempt to balance its budget. For the eight months in 1903 and 1904 that Organ worked on the St. Louis exhibit, the state's exposition committee agreed to pay fifty dollars of her sixty-dollar monthly salary.

In time, the *Missouri Historical Review* became the society's primary means of reaching its growing membership and educating an even larger readership. Like the annual meeting, the *Review* had modest beginnings. The question of "a quarterly historical magazine" first appeared in the finance committee's minutes of December 1905. A subcommittee consisting of professors Loeb and Viles, in addition to Walter Williams and Secretary Sampson, determined the journal's format and sought printers' bids. Anticipating that the *Review* would be suitable for school use, Loeb discussed publishing plans with a meeting of the state's history teachers before the end of the year. A Sedalia publishing company printed early volumes of the magazine at costs typical for the day. The society paid $136.40 for both the January and April issues of 1911, for example. The printer's charge for the 1912 issues of the *Review* was $1.30 per page for one thousand copies.

Francis Sampson, who served as editor of the first eight volumes, brought out his initial issue in October 1906. In addition to publishing papers that their authors had read at annual meetings, the *Review* offered other features through which a variety of readers could encounter Missouri's history. These included edited original documents, bibliographies, genealogical studies of important early families, reports on historical landmarks, reprinted newspaper articles of historical value, and lists of cemetery inscriptions. The first article on Senator Thomas Hart Benton appeared in volume 1, number 1, while the first on George Caleb Bingham came two issues later, in April 1907. Their names have appeared as often as any in the *Review*'s pages over the years. Sampson solicited reminiscences from participants in historic events. Judge Thomas Shackelford, for example, wrote about the amendment that he had introduced in the state convention of 1861. Women's history made an early debut in the journal with Susan A. Arnold McCausland's "The Battle of Lexington as Seen by a Woman," in the April 1912 issue. Diverse in its offerings and carefully edited by the meticulous Sampson, the journal's physical format also appealed to readers. "I received the last number of the *Review*," an Iowa attorney wrote to Sampson in August 1914, "and must compliment you upon the improved appearance of the journal." Since 1906, the *Missouri Historical Review* has been the most visible and widely available evidence of the society's efforts to fulfill its goals.

Not much evidence survives to reveal who used the society's reading room during this era. A reasonable guess is that university students, university faculty members, and Columbia residents were the most frequent visitors to the reference and newspaper libraries and that editors from around the state dropped by when in the city. Two researchers left a trace of their visits. Harrison Anthony Trexler searched the society's collections for information on slavery in Missouri for his Ph.D. dissertation, published in 1914 by the Johns Hopkins University Press. According to Sampson, Trexler discovered enough "original source material to keep him at work for weeks." After his visit to the society's library, Professor Albert Bushnell Hart of Harvard praised its "rare collection."

The society's location on the University of Missouri's campus helps to explain how it met its staffing needs. Beginning in October 1909, two freshmen students put in several hours per day at fifteen cents an hour—one in the periodical room, the other in storage areas. Even before Sampson assumed his duties, the society employed a part-time stenographer at twenty dollars per month, and, in the fall of 1902, a "periodical clerk and helper" at the same salary. These and other part-time employees supplemented the work of Sampson and Organ, the society's only full-time staff members prior to Floyd Shoemaker's hiring in 1910.

The staff worked in a growing number of rooms in Academic Hall. By 1902, the society enjoyed the use of a basement storage and workroom directly below its first-floor library, which occupied two rooms next to the university's library. In December 1912, the society's quarters totaled fourteen rooms, eleven in the basement and three on the first floor. Much of the collection resided in the damp basement of Academic Hall, and the building (like its predecessor) was in no way fireproof. As grateful as society leaders were for the free space and utilities, their annual appeal for a new building to house their own and the university's library stressed the fire danger. That concern naturally became more acute after the state capitol fire of February 1911.

As early as December 1902, the committee authorized President Stephens and Secretary Sampson to approach the legislature about a new building for the society. In the following year, the finance committee passed a resolution requesting a building from Andrew Carnegie, who in his retirement was funding libraries in communities across the nation. The society "has already outgrown the space that the curators of the university have given it," the appeal for a joint library building with the university asserted. Although neither of these early efforts proved successful, a new building was near. In a 1913 article appealing for a "fire-proof home which will make its collections safe for the future," Sampson cited a recent resolution passed by the Missouri Press Association. The group had urged, "without delay," that the General Assembly fund a new facility. The legislature responded to these and other appeals later in 1913. With a building under construction, the society's 1914 annual meeting expressed "its sincere appreciation of the university's liberal treatment of the society in the past, and its generous provision for the needs of the society in the new library building." The dedication of what today is the central portion of the Elmer Ellis Library facing Lowry Mall occurred on January 6, 1916. Since 1915, the society has made its home in various locations in the general library building of the University of Missouri in Columbia.

As the press association's and the university's support of the society continued, so also did the legislature's financial commitment grow. But it grew slowly, requiring what Floyd Shoemaker later described as "the practice of rigid economy" in the society's operations. The state appropriation for each year from 1901 through 1914 averaged less than $3,700. The most generous grant of funds was $5,800 annually for the 1913–1914 biennium. Limited financial resources forced the society's early leaders to adopt a policy that has characterized the agency's entire history, one of "planned, restricted activity," as Shoemaker phrased it. The leaders of the society were well aware that they could not afford to open a museum or send touring exhibits around the state.

The society's relationship with the legislature during this period established a pattern of high expectations and disappointing results. For the 1903–1904 biennium, for example, it requested $15,335, approximately the funding enjoyed by the Iowa and Minnesota state societies. The actual appropriation was $5,000. For 1913–1914, the society requested $19,084; the legislature and the governor granted $11,600. Beside salaries, major categories of expense included book purchases, cataloging, and the binding of newspapers. While the move to the new library building in 1915 created increased expenses for furnishings, it also permitted at least one saving. The finance committee allowed the society's fire insurance to lapse in October 1915, both for lack of funds and because the new library was "a fire-proof structure."

Probably the most effective way the society conveyed its needs to the General Assembly during this period was through the press association.

The society's first-floor reading room as it appeared in the newly constructed university library building in 1915. In addition to the reading room, the society occupied an office on the first floor and four rooms in the basement plus the basement book stacks.

Officers and trustees overwhelmingly were editors, and some of them, especially the society's presidents, traveled to Jefferson City to present the society's budget requests. In the 1930s, Floyd Shoemaker recalled his appearance in 1913 before the House Appropriations Committee with R. M. White. When a legislator challenged Shoemaker to justify his salary, the Mexico editor jumped to his feet to lecture the committee on the society's contributions to the state. White's remarks prompted a significant increase in the society's appropriation over the previous year, Shoemaker remembered, and won over key legislators to the society's cause.

In one area, increasing the collections, the society proceeded aggressively, in part because Francis Sampson's passion for acquiring historical materials continued undiminished. Perhaps his enthusiasm increased, now that he had state funds to spend and a public agency's goals to fulfill. Henry O. Severance, the secretary of the American Bibliographical Society, once wrote of Sampson's dedication to collecting: "I have never seen him happier than when he had secured a rare railroad report which was not in the possession of any other library, or when he was able to pick up an old report of a Missouri religious or fraternal organization." The library that Sampson assembled, before and after he moved to Columbia in 1901, was of inestimable value to the society's long-term ability to serve the people of Missouri.

The secretary knew that historical societies possessed three methods for building their libraries: "by purchase, by donation, and by exchange." Exchange meant trading duplicate copies of publications for other societies' duplicates. "We have 50,000 duplicate publications that we want to give to other states," he said in 1910. The titles available for barter included "60 copies of everything published by the state." His society was able to purchase relatively few titles, Sampson told colleagues at an AHA meeting. "For Dr. Thwaites, with his $60,000 and 40 employees, the situation is different from that in which one finds himself who has but $7,500 and 2 employees." Gifts of materials—the third method—therefore became very important to the society during its Sampson years, and later as well. The society received one gift of note in 1902. Samuel L. Clemens, in Columbia to receive an honorary degree from the university in June, came into the library to donate a new twenty-two-volume edition of his collected works.

Secretary Sampson used the state's railroads to visit numerous Missouri communities in search of books and pamphlets. In each town, his first destination was the printing office, usually a newspaper, and then the county courthouse. Sampson traveled so frequently on public business that the finance committee, in May 1905, instructed him to apply for free railroad passes, a privilege that the era's reformers denounced as unethical when granted to politicians. In December of that year, the secretary detailed recent collecting expeditions for the committee. They included visits to Fulton and Mexico, during which Sampson obtained 4 bound books, 305 unbound books and pamphlets, 199 "serial numbers," and 4 maps. A trip to the communities of Marshall, Lexington, Higginsville, and Sedalia yielded 22 books, 262 unbound books and pamphlets, 34 serials, and "an exceedingly valuable" collection of the papers of Thomas A. Smith. A gift of Smith's grandchildren who lived in

Saline County, the collection included letters dating to the War of 1812. Traveling to towns northeast of Columbia, Sampson's catch included twenty-five years of bound newspapers from Edina. The society paid the secretary's expenses on these trips and the freight charges for his acquisitions. In addition to the tangible benefit of library acquisitions, the expended funds brought returns more difficult to measure. Secretary Sampson functioned as a historical evangelist, spreading the society's gospel from county to county.

Surviving in the papers of the State Historical Society of Missouri is a handwritten journal, the daily record of a book-seeking trip that Sampson made to southwest Missouri in 1914. In Galena, Cassville, Mount Vernon, and other towns, newspaper editors and courthouse officials suggested persons who might be interested in society membership. On July 7 in Mount Vernon, Sampson visited the printing office of Euphrates Boucher. Although he had recently sold his newspaper, Boucher had retained back issues, including duplicate files from 1877 to 1914. Sampson cut a deal with the publisher: for the gift of one of the files of Boucher's paper, the society would bind his own copy for him. Boucher refused, however, to part with some Civil War documents, and across town a former state legislator wanted to retain copies of bills that he owned.

Two days later in Forsyth, Sampson visited the offices of the *Taney County Republican* and the courthouse. To his dismay, he found a supposedly complete file of the newspaper "thrown indiscriminately in a pile in the office." "In the court house there are no old books," he recorded in his journal, "no old [property tax] assessment books, and the clerk had never seen any oaths of loyalty" from the post–Civil War years. Sampson asked about such records in every county that he visited.

Sampson's trips for the society blazed a trail that others would follow. In preparation for writing his book on pioneer merchants, historian Lewis Atherton visited Missouri communities during the 1930s in search of business records. When he directed the Western Historical Manuscript Collection in the 1950s, Atherton budgeted funds for a "road man" who would travel the state and beyond seeing potential donors about research materials. Floyd Shoemaker, too, would reprise Sampson's role as an itinerant acquisitions librarian.

With Sampson frequently on the road pursuing one of his primary assignments, increasing the society's collections, Minnie Organ remained in the office with numerous functions to perform. In October 1907, the finance committee defined the duties of the assistant librarian. Although that was her title, Organ's assigned tasks drew more on general clerical and administrative skills than professional librarianship. She was to maintain accounts of all funds received and paid out, to update the membership rosters, to mail copies of the *Review* to members, to maintain the newspaper collection and prepare newspapers for binding, to record library acquisitions, and to answer incoming correspondence.

At its May 30, 1910, meeting, the finance committee hired Floyd C. Shoemaker as assistant secretary and librarian. He assumed his duties on August 1, as Minnie Organ left. At first working less than full-time for the society, Shoemaker also drew a university salary as a five-hour-per-week "assistant" in the political science department. Available sources do not disclose how well Sampson and Minnie Organ worked together, but they do reveal that the Sampson-Shoemaker relationship soon became strained. As an administrator, Francis Sampson suffered shortcomings. He struggled to work within budgetary constraints and had difficulty delegating authority and respecting his top assistant's job responsibilities.

By early 1911, members of the finance committee and Jonas Viles from the history department intervened in the Sampson-Shoemaker relationship to clearly define each man's duties. After conversations with Loeb and Shoemaker, Viles suggested a "division of activities" in a letter to Loeb dated March 16. In his most revealing remarks, Viles stated: "Mr. Shoemaker must be left free to work out his systems in detail without constant interference and suggestion. . . . efficient and cheerful service is impossible in the face of constant interruptions and trivial criticism, however well meant." That Sampson and Shoemaker did not work well together was for Viles "the most serious obstacle just now to progress" in the society's affairs.

Twice in the following months, the finance committee tried to draw a clear jurisdictional line for the society's two professionals. In April 1911, with Shoemaker's position about to become full-time, committee members defined as his duties those it had listed for Minnie Organ in 1907, plus responsibility for exchanges with other societies. The April clarification apparently failed, for in September the committee commissioned Loeb, Williams, and Viles "to make rules for the division of work between Mr. Secretary and the assistant."

The group reported on November 1, 1911, announcing first a change in Shoemaker's title to assistant secretary. Hoping for "greater efficiency and harmony" in the activities of the society, the ad hoc committee did not propose any substantial redistribution of duties or powers between the two men. Instead, it wished to help Sampson more clearly understand the April instructions. The committee also made clear that Francis Sampson's duties "of especial importance" were "the soliciting of members . . . the editing of the *Missouri Historical Review,* and above all the collecting of new material for the society." Shoemaker would be the administrator, the attender to the details of membership, correspondence, printing, cataloging, and similar tasks. Both men would have the continued assistance of part-time staff members. The absence of additional evidence of conflict between Shoemaker and Sampson suggests that the settlement of late 1911 succeeded. That agreement, while it retained Sampson in his position as secretary, placed an unusually large share of the society's administrative responsibilities and power in Shoemaker's hands. The society hired Mary E. Edwards as a cataloger in 1913; she became the third full-time staff member.

The final stage of Francis Sampson's contribution to the society began with his resignation as secretary in 1915. In a letter of April 27, he made the resignation contingent upon his appointment to a new position, with no reduction in salary, as collector of materials and compiler of bibliographies on Missouri history. The finance committee appointed Sampson "bibliographer of the society" on May 5, and Shoemaker its secretary and librarian. For the following two years and nine months, Sampson pursued the activities at which he excelled. Small towns throughout the state continued to receive the society's emissary, who located interesting printed materials and an occasional packet of letters or an old ledger book, persuaded their owners to part with them, and arranged for railroad freight clerks to ship packages to the society in Columbia.

Sampson's enthusiasm for the hunt and unconcern about detail soon encroached on the society's budget. In December 1915, the finance committee told him that he must itemize all expenses for which he expected reimbursement. And it required "that in the future you plan your trips in advance" and report "the general purpose and extent of each trip. . . . one week's notice . . . will be adequate." Sampson's accountability continued to vex the committee into 1916. It instructed Shoemaker to place this directive in a letter to Sampson: "The committee has never made an agreement to pay you any amount over and above your salary and actual traveling expenses." In April 1917, Sampson's status with the society changed again. His "advanced age" prompted the finance committee to reduce the bibliographer's obligation to the society to "not less than half-time."

Until his death from pneumonia in Columbia on February 4, 1918, Francis Sampson continued to devote his efforts to promoting the society's interests. First hospitalized in December 1917, he returned to work in January, and during his last days on the job turned up a bound volume of a church organization's minutes that had eluded him for years. "Now we've got them," Sampson exalted over his find, "and they will never be lost to the people of Missouri."

Many years later, as he retired from the society's top administrative position, Floyd Shoemaker made a meaningful comparison. Francis Sampson, he said, "was Missouri's Draper"; Shoemaker called himself "Missouri's Thwaites." He was referring to the two men so important to the State Historical Society of Wisconsin: Lyman C. Draper, who between 1853 and 1886 built its unequaled collections, and Thwaites, who by contrast was the administrator, the careful shepherd of the society's interests beginning in 1887. Thus far, in our history of the State Historical Society of Missouri, we have observed Sampson, the collector, at work. In 1915, the era of Shoemaker, the administrator, began in earnest.

2

The Floyd C. Shoemaker Years, 1915–1940

he construction of a new library building, the *Seventh Biennial Report* concluded in 1914, "is beyond question the most important event in the society's history since the date of its founding." Other observers could make a case for the acquisition of Francis Sampson's library as the key event in the society's earliest years. No single event, however, dominated the second period in the development of the State Historical Society of Missouri. That era began in 1915, when the society moved into its new quarters in the university library and appointed Floyd Shoemaker its secretary. It ended with the opening of the 1940s.

The society's special projects during the 1920s and 1930s included a very successful membership campaign, deep involvement in two centennial commemorations, and an early experiment in placing historical markers along a Missouri highway. Such activities brought the organization to the attention of Missourians in all sections of the state and gave it roles beyond its central mission of building and maintaining collections of research materials. A mature agency by 1940, the agency had demonstrated its usefulness within the state and gained national standing among state historical societies.

I

Although Floyd Calvin Shoemaker was born in Kissimmee, Florida, on May 7, 1886, he was not a true Southerner. Both parents, Frank Calvin and Emma (Dreyer) Shoemaker, were Pennsylvanians born during the Civil War decade. While Frank grew up in that state, Emma spent her childhood and received her public school education in Macon County, Missouri. The Shoemaker family settled in Bucklin, Linn County, in November 1893, when Floyd was seven. There Frank operated a store for the next forty-six years and became a justice of the peace and the town mayor. Both he and Emma were deeply involved in the organizational life of their community, religious and secular, until their deaths in 1946.

While Minnie Organ had taught in rural schools before she attended college, Floyd Shoemaker had only a slight collegiate preparation for his first teaching job. Having earned thirty-two hours of college credit at the Kirksville State Normal School, he graduated in 1906 with a B.P. degree—a Bachelor of Pedagogy. In Shoemaker's personal papers are documents tracing the brief public school career he later omitted from many autobiographical sketches. The state of Missouri issued a teaching certificate to Shoemaker in August 1906. The Amity, Colorado, public schools signed him to a contract on September 8, 1906, stipulating that he serve as school principal for $75 per month. In a letter dated April 19, 1907, the Amity school board certified that the twenty-year-old principal's service had been "eminently satisfactory." Floyd Shoemaker came to Columbia in September 1907 to enroll as a sophomore in the University of Missouri. In three semesters and a summer session, by February 1909, he not only had completed the requirements for a bachelor of arts degree but also had earned membership in Phi Beta Kappa.

Needing money, Shoemaker completed the 1908–1909 school year —from February to May—teaching history and Latin at the Gallatin, Missouri, high school. He fully intended to return to Gallatin in the fall as principal at a salary of $1,500 when he came to Columbia in May for his university graduation. It was then, as Shoemaker told James Cash Penney years later, that "Dr. Isidor Loeb persuaded me to resign my Gallatin position and become assistant professor of political science and public law . . . at $500—a poor business man I was as you can readily see." From 1909 to 1911, Shoemaker held that teaching position at the university, while earning his master's degree in political science and, in August 1910, becoming Sampson's assistant in the historical society. Shoemaker did not explain why he abandoned public school teaching and administration in favor of different methods of educating

Missourians through the society's work. He admitted that he did not apply for the job as Francis Sampson's assistant, thus implying the powerful persuasiveness of Loeb and the finance committee. In June 1911, Shoemaker and his first wife, Caroline Tull of Ridgeway, Missouri, married. That spring, he also completed his M.A. with the thesis, "Missouri's First Constitution, 1820." A revised and expanded version of that study became his first book, *Missouri's Struggle for Statehood, 1804–1821* (published in 1916).

Both as the society's secretary and as an individual author, Shoemaker wrote many books, articles, and speeches on the history of Missouri. In addition, his name appeared as editor below other book titles and on volumes 9 through 54 of the *Missouri Historical Review.* His books published prior to 1940 included *A History of Missouri and Missourians* (1922) and volume 2 of *Missouri, Mother of the West* (1930). In the latter's broad coverage of the state's history since 1860, Shoemaker discussed economic development, politics and government, education, "military affairs during the Civil, Spanish-American and [First] World War periods, social development of the people, and . . . literature and journalism." Richard Brownlee, after he became the society's director in 1960, discovered that the responsibilities of the job derailed his own plans for further research and writing. Shoemaker's use of the society's staff and his own paid research assistants only partially explain his prodigious output as author and editor.

Floyd Shoemaker seems to have been a natural writer. He greatly enjoyed communicating through the written word, and he did so with ease and effectiveness in a voluminous correspondence as well as in his publications. As a young man, Shoemaker had suffered a serious hearing impairment, which he largely overcame in 1936 with the purchase of a "Sonotone hearing instrument." Worn over the head like earphones, the device was quite effective, amazing the secretary when he attended a dinner party the week of its purchase. He reported: "For the first time in several decades I was able to hear a considerable portion of the conversation at the table." In his professional and personal life, Shoemaker now emerged from "a world of silence into a new world of most unimaginable noises." Although one can only speculate, Shoemaker's reliance on the written word, especially in his very extensive correspondence, might partially have compensated for his difficulties in understanding and conducting oral communication.

Floyd C. Shoemaker was a staff member of the society for almost fifty years; for forty-five of those years, 1915–1960, he served as director, secretary, and librarian. Under Shoemaker's leadership, the society strengthened its reference and newspaper collections, carried on an active publications program, and engaged in special projects such as the statehood centennial celebration and the erection of historic markers along Missouri's highways.

Or, his large correspondence may simply have been the product of a keen mind with much to communicate to many friends, acquaintances, and professional colleagues. Shoemaker's writing reveals one who recognized the complexity of the subject matter at hand, and he seemed compelled to explain each nuance of meaning to his readers, whether finance committee members or students of Missouri history. During his lifetime, Floyd Shoemaker's accomplishments attracted numerous tributes. None of the praise, however, recognized his letter-writing skills. Shoemaker, admittedly, could be wordy, and his letters do not constitute important literature or philosophy. But his observations were interesting and informative, his stories captivating, his wit engaging. And his surviving correspondence constitutes the best single source for understanding the functioning of the State Historical Society of Missouri from about 1920 to about 1960.

With what activities did Secretary Shoemaker fill his days? Some of the answers to that question simultaneously reveal the society's outreach to its constituencies—disclose how it served Missourians during the 1920s and 1930s. As have all of the society's chief administrators, Shoemaker traveled extensively, around Missouri and beyond it, in the society's interests. "I am making more public addresses and hope I am making some impression," he wrote to former president Walter B. Stevens in October 1930. "I am trying to interest the people to put Missouri history into the public schools." To promote that goal, he attended the state teachers' association meeting in St. Louis in November 1929 and then crossed the state to mingle with editors at the press association's gathering in Kansas City. In December 1928, Shoemaker visited Topeka, Kansas, to "close the deal" for back issues of Missouri newspapers no longer needed by the Kansas State Historical Society. The "deal" was favorable, requiring only the payment of freight charges by the Missouri society. Late that month, the secretary renewed other professional contacts while attending the American Historical Association's annual meeting in Indianapolis.

Speaking engagements and other appearances around Missouri were "profitable to the society in material, members and influence," Shoemaker believed. On a trip to several cities in southwestern counties in September 1934, he stopped in Bolivar for the Ozark Press Association meeting. "I met a number of editors, lawyers, legislators and other members of the society," he reported to Isidor Loeb, "and had tentative promise of a fine newspaper file going back into the sixties." On a June 1936 tour of south Missouri, Shoemaker spoke to county historical societies in Salem and Springfield, attended a dinner in Carthage organized by the society's local members, and spoke during the Ozark Folk Festival in Rolla. A trip in October 1936 brought Secretary Shoemaker to fourteen south Missouri communities, where he visited with seventeen newspaper editors about promoting the society among their readers and about donating materials to the collections. "I am planning to do more of this kind of work," he resolved that year, "in order that our people may become more familiar with what our society is doing and what it has to offer our citizens."

Back in the office, Shoemaker performed a remarkable variety of duties. In 1928, the secretary wrote the Federal Radio Commission in Washington, D.C., on behalf of Stephens College's noncommercial station. To escape the interference of other stations' signals, the college desired a different wavelength for its broadcasts. The society's interest in this problem grew from its assistance to the college in producing a program series entitled the *Radio School of Missouri History.* Missouri's exhibit at Chicago's Century of Progress Exposition in 1933 presented visitors with a fifty-page illustrated booklet demonstrating the state's advances. Shoemaker and his staff assisted in its preparation. In the summer of 1940, the society's director proofread the chapter on agriculture in *Missouri: A Guide to the "Show-Me" State* for Charles van Ravenswaay, director of the Missouri Writers Project, Works Progress Administration (WPA). As an author himself, Shoemaker closely followed the advance subscription sales of *Missouri, Mother of the West.* In parts of the state, he had reported in September 1927, sales were good, but in northeastern counties "the sales are poor—bankrupt in fact." For that condition he blamed the farm depression of the 1920s, which ravaged parts of Missouri.

An interesting assortment of researchers visited or inquired about visiting the society's collections during the interwar years. Although the new university library building now housed the historical society, the agency soon outgrew its assigned space. Until 1936 it used two rooms on the first floor, one of them Shoemaker's office; four rooms in the basement; and the basement level of book stacks. Researchers worked in the reference library reading room on the first floor, to which staff members brought books and newspapers, both current and bound back files, from the lower level.

Professor Frederic A. Culmer of Central College in Fayette could attest to the usefulness of the society's collections to a variety of researchers. In 1933, he received letters from authors in five states, including Maine and California. "All requested information upon the material in the archives of the society." Culmer could answer their questions because he used the book and newspaper collections frequently, and he recognized their resources as among "the richest of mines of information for our own Missouri [college] students." Reference librarian Sarah Guitar completed the processing of the recently accessioned James S. Rollins manuscript collection just prior to the university's 1936 summer session. She expected that soon "we will . . . begin having requests from thesis students to use this collection." Attorney Rush H. Limbaugh of Cape Girardeau was one member who used the society's resources when he visited Columbia. As a student assistant in 1915, he had helped the society move into its new quarters. Limbaugh wrote to Shoemaker in 1934: "I have designs on a number of things . . . which are not available elsewhere." Artist Albert Christ-Janer did much of the research for his

1940 study of George Caleb Bingham in the society's quarters. And Fletcher M. Green, of Emory University and the Southern Historical Association, consulted materials relevant to his research on nineteenth-century editor-politician Duff Green at the society in 1931. "And if I may repeat what I then said," he wrote to Shoemaker five years later, "no one was kinder and more helpful to me anywhere than you were."

Experimenting with Saturday afternoon hours, the society's staff recorded patrons' use of the collections during that half-day from March to June, 1937. Their tabulations may be the only surviving records, not of who, but of how many people, used the society's materials. A total of 164 patrons entered the first-floor reading room on seventeen Saturday afternoons, an average of over nine per day. On one Saturday the two staff members on duty served twenty clients; on three days they found materials for only five readers. The visitors' interests ranged from genealogy to current newspapers, from reference works on the state's history to manuscripts and rare books from the Mark Twain Collection. While Saturday afternoon hours may not have been cost-effective, they did draw people to the collections on the one day each week when most Columbians, including many students, headed for Broadway and other downtown commercial streets to do their shopping. No doubt the society would have experienced a slimmer turnout on autumn Saturday afternoons when thousands of spectators flocked to the university's football stadium.

Even in this early period, the society's collections supported scholarship in African American and women's history. When sociologist Charles S. Johnson of Fisk University in Nashville inquired in 1936 about "the manuscript documents in your collection dealing with slavery and the Negro," Shoemaker responded, perhaps too hastily, that the society had none. Yet a few days later the secretary supplied a writer in Kansas City with a brief list of published sources on slavery in Missouri. In the autumn of 1936, Sarah Guitar mailed to Sarah Williams a packet of citations and data on Missouri's women leaders that she had culled from volumes on the reference shelves. The widow of Walter Williams, Sarah Williams intended to prepare a series of talks on this subject for a St. Louis radio station.

Most of the Missourians who drew on the wealth of information in the society's collections did so by mail. "The correspondence alone is 10,000 letters a year," Shoemaker reported early in 1933. And by the end of that year he had discovered that "the calls made upon the society for information have increased, instead of decreased, during the depression." Many correspondents requested information on their families' histories, and staff members routinely recommended local genealogists who did such work for a fee. Teachers wrote for information or bibliographies of reliable sources for use in their classrooms. Owners of allegedly rare and valuable old books asked for appraisals of their treasures, and by return mail they received the names of book dealers who might help them. Authors sought publishers, auto tourists desired information about historic sites, and clubs needed speakers. Some queries were easy to answer, others more difficult. Where was a fort located? "What can you tell me about French Christmas customs?" "Was a woman once hanged as a witch in Ripley County?" The folklorist Vance Randolph asked the last question; the society could not verify the oral tale he had discovered. "What Indians camped on Grand River near the [Iowa] state line that Robert and Howard Moore used to run horse races with?" "Did the Indians grow the Indian Peach?" The questions flowed in a seemingly endless stream onto Shoemaker's and the reference librarians' desks. Rarely losing their composure, staff members answered as best they could.

Contemporaries were unaware of the essential contributions made by Floyd Shoemaker's key staff members because the secretary did little to make their work known. Sarah Guitar was one of the underpaid assistants who did much of the behind-the-scenes labor for which the secretary received the credit—or blame, when the society could not satisfy a researcher's needs. Guitar was born on January 20, 1892, in Columbia to businessman and sometime local officeholder James H. Guitar and Sallie (Young) Guitar. A descendant of four of Columbia and Boone County's oldest and most prominent families, Sarah Guitar was herself a walking summary of local history. Her heritage, indeed, was a bit overwhelming. Guitar's obituaries in Columbia newspapers spoke more of her ancestors' accomplishments than of her own life. Her maternal great-grandfather David H. Hickman, for example, had sponsored the Missouri school law of 1853, which originated the use of state revenues to support public schools. The extent of Sarah Guitar's education is not known. At the age of twenty-six, in February 1918, she joined the society's staff and soon earned the title of reference librarian. Guitar became a highly skilled professional, one who pursued her own scholarship as she facilitated the projects of others. She published several articles in the *Review,* including one on the Arrow Rock Tavern in July 1926.

In January 1936, editor George A. Naeter of the *Cape Girardeau Southeast Missourian* sent Shoemaker a sheaf of pages containing historical dates and events culled from his newspaper. The secretary handed the notes to Sarah Guitar, who, in thirty hours of reading, could verify or disprove only some of the items in Naeter's chronology. Having no firsthand knowledge of the matter, Shoemaker placed whole sentences from Guitar's report to him in his letter to the editor, claiming, for example: "I have not attempted to check every date, but have checked only those dates of general historical significance and statewide interest." In 1937, Dean Frank L. Martin of the university's School of Journalism requested information on the history of county-level editorial associations. After looking into the matter, Sarah Guitar wrote a memo to her boss expressing some frustration with scholars like Martin who seemed to believe "that all they have to do is to write us for data and we will send them material and notes from which they can sit down at their desks and in a few evenings write . . . [their] histories." Shoemaker asked that Guitar draft a letter to Martin explaining the limits of the society's ability to assist him. The secretary's communication to the dean duplicated hers almost exactly.

W. Francis English, a history teacher in Carrollton's high school in 1938, furnishes another example of an author's request for assistance that created unrealistic demands on the time of reference librarian Sarah Guitar. He asked that a staff member check for accuracy two articles on Missouri topics that he had written for the *Dictionary of American History.* Guitar spent ten hours on one of the essays but could spare no time from other responsibilities for the second. Shoemaker's report to English noted that the society's limited staff prevented any additional work on his articles and invited the teacher to utilize the society's library in person. But Shoemaker did not credit Guitar for the investment of labor already made. Offering skilled and helpful service to thousands of the society's patrons, Sarah Guitar spent thirty-nine years with the State Historical Society of Missouri. She retired in 1957 and died in Columbia on November 5, 1963.

II

Much of the voluminous correspondence that left the society's offices concerned membership. A central preoccupation of Floyd Shoemaker during the 1915–1940 period was his campaign to make the society first in membership in the entire United States. A 1954 tribute to the secretary in the *Missouri Alumnus* magazine reported that, of all his accomplishments, he was most proud of his membership-building success. And the article attributed that success—probably correctly—to Shoemaker's personal efforts to attract and retain members. In this endeavor, he required little staff assistance beyond a stenographer's skills. The society's elected leadership—officers and trustees—and other friends from around the state also were instrumental in the campaign to increase the membership.

Table 2.1 offers information on the State Historical Society of Missouri's changing membership numbers. Of all the membership categories that the society maintained during this era—honorary, exchange, corresponding, life, annual, and editorial—Table 2.1 focuses on the most numerous and important. What the society called "pay members" were those who annually remitted their one-dollar dues. Each biennium the society reported separate counts of annual pay members who resided in Missouri and those who lived anywhere else. At the end of 1924, for example, the two numbers were 1,980 and 265. In December 1936, 291 annual members lived elsewhere, 2,121 in Missouri. That distinction, although interesting, seems of little significance to this discussion.

The proportion of editorial members in the society's total membership declined dramatically over the years shown in Table 2.1. Their absolute numbers also fell, a reflection, presumably, of the agricultural depression of the 1920s and 1930s, the consequent decline of the rural and small-town population, and the resulting disappearance of newspapers. Although their numbers declined, Missouri editors continued to exercise a disproportionate, and welcome, influence in the life of the society. As recorded in Shoemaker's biennial reports of the historical society's activities, 1920 was the first year in which annual pay members surpassed the number of editorial members. Their growing numbers, of course, produced revenue for the society independent of the state appropriation. The large increase of pay members in 1920 over 1918 boosted the society to first place in total membership among historical societies located west of the Mississippi River.

The Great Depression had surprisingly little effect on the society's membership numbers. The net loss of members in the 1931–1932 and 1935–1936 periods was temporary in each case. Reflecting on a net loss of members in 1933, society president George A. Mahan

Table 2.1 The Society's Membership, 1916–1938

	Total Members All Categories	Annual "Pay Members"	Editorial Members: Number and as Percentage of Total Membership
1916	1,285	486	644 (50.1%)
1918	1,368	596	628 (45.9%)
1920	1,685	1,057	484 (28.7%)
1922	2,485	1,959	387 (15.6%)
1924	2,847	2,245	457 (16%)
1926	2,894	2,327	428 (14.8%)
1928	2,916	2,359	415 (14.2%)
1930	3,048	2,509	391 (13.6%)
1932	2,872	2,336	391 (16.7%)
1934	2,975	2,440	389 (13%)
1936	2,954	2,412	385 (13%)
1938	3,356	2,850	379 (11.3%)

Source: Biennial reports to the governor (totals as of December 31 each year).

commented early in 1934: "Our society has not been as hard hit by the depression as other enterprises throughout the state." Membership revenues for 1932 fell $407.74, or 21 percent, below 1931 receipts. When Secretary Shoemaker discovered late in 1933 that the year's income from membership dues was down only $71.72 from the 1932 figure, he predicted a rebound in 1934. At the end of May 1934, he could, indeed, report an upsurge in membership. The 153 new members enrolled during the first five months of 1934 "is a larger number than we have obtained during a similar period since 1926."

The society's membership growth during a decade usually associated with decline was no accident. It happened by design and through persistent effort. In thousands of letters to individuals, Secretary Shoemaker solicited members. A typical "pitch" was this: "There is no initiation fee and the annual fee due is $1.00. The *Missouri Historical Review* is sent free to members. I am enclosing application for your convenience." When members did not respond to renewal notices, Shoemaker wrote personal letters to urge another year's membership. If his first letter brought no response, he sent a second. The society made extraordinary efforts to meet the financial circumstances of hard-pressed members in times when even one dollar loomed large. In 1936, it suspended its rule that annual dues be paid in advance of a given year's membership, allowing members to pay after they had received four issues of the *Review*. When William G. Bek, a Ph.D. graduate of the University of Missouri who taught history at the University of North Dakota, had his salary "cut all to pieces" in 1933, Shoemaker refused to drop the professor as a member. Pay when you can, was his offer. He made another deal with an El Dorado Springs farmer who wanted to trade contributions on Cedar County history to the *Review* for a society membership. Shoemaker countered with another plan: a free trial membership for a year, then join the society if you can.

Several campaigns to win new members who could pay the annual fee were more important to the society's growth than the secretary's individualizing of membership terms. In September 1933, Shoemaker attended the Missouri Bar Association's meeting in Kansas City, accompanying President George A. Mahan, an attorney. The secretary counted 250 lawyers among the society's members but believed that number would double "if they were approached personally and if the work of this society were explained to them." After the Kansas City meeting, Shoemaker mailed the latest issue of the *Review* and membership forms to 140 lawyers. Two-thirds of the way through October his plan "didn't work out so well so far," he commented to a friend. "I haven't found the right key to unlock this problem." But a number approaching 10 percent of the lawyers contacted did join the society.

In December 1934, Shoemaker reported the success of another membership initiative to Isidor Loeb. The superintendent of Carroll County's 128 rural schools and officials of Carrollton's school system, after meeting with the society's secretary, agreed to place a copy of the *Review* in each school. More distant prospects lived in the state of Oregon. In mid-1938, Shoemaker asked the president of the Missouri State Society of Portland for the group's membership list. He wished to send an issue of the *Review* and a membership application to these Missouri expatriots and the descendants of former state residents living near the western terminus of the old Oregon Trail. The society assigned one of its federally funded Civil Works Administration (CWA) temporary employees to membership retention and expansion efforts in 1934. Without explaining the details of this assignment, Shoemaker claimed that it had paid dividends. The secretary and his staff targeted Missouri counties in which there were few members. The society's greatest concentrations of members during the 1930s were in Jackson, Boone, and St. Louis Counties and the city of St. Louis. At the other extreme of interest in the society's work, only one person in Bollinger County, a newspaper editor in Marble Hill, belonged to the society in 1939. Shoemaker obtained the names of likely members from that journalist and directed his appeal to them.

Beginning in 1936, and intensifying in 1937 and 1938, officers, trustees, and other friends of the society took on the role of salesman in the interest of expanding membership. A judge in St. Louis and a professor in St. Charles were among those who, with membership application forms in hand, approached their friends and acquaintances about joining the society. Trustee Justus R. Moll of Springfield gave this tactic a boost at the society's executive committee meeting held on April 24, 1937. Moll observed, to use Shoemaker's words, "that the time seemed opportune for making especial effort to raise the society's membership to first place in the United States, since only one state, New York, was now in the lead by a relatively small margin." The committee, by consensus, agreed that each trustee and officer should enroll ten members in 1937. Shoemaker also enlisted some veteran members in this recruitment campaign, including William T. Kemper of Kansas City and Thomas K. Smith of St. Louis. Charles L. Woods of Rolla, L. M. White of Mexico, and George A. Rozier of Perryville were among the trustees who paid for dinner parties attended by prospective members.

The focused campaign to increase membership succeeded. In late October 1937, Shoemaker reported to Loeb: "Our membership is increasing very nicely." He hoped for a net gain of twenty to thirty for the month of October, a number that would have been higher except that nonrenewals offset some new members. As the society's recruiters labored around the state, Shoemaker traveled to northeastern counties in October to enroll sixteen new members and attended a luncheon in Kansas City in early November to promote the society among a group of community leaders. "I believe we are getting between fifty and one hundred new members as a result of the luncheon," he reported to society president Allen McReynolds. On December 15, 1937, Shoemaker predicted that within sixty days the society would surpass New York's membership figure. It took a few more days than sixty, but on April 16, 1938, Floyd Shoemaker announced to George Rozier: "Our society has passed the state society of New York and is now the largest in membership among all state historical societies in America."

Shoemaker realized the costs of growth as he celebrated success. More members required a larger staff to serve their needs, higher printing costs to produce additional copies of the *Review*, and a greater postage expenditure to mail membership renewal cards, annual meeting announcements, and the society's quarterly. Still, for Floyd Shoemaker the achievement far overshadowed the costs. For more than three decades, the State Historical Society of Missouri would continue to lead all state societies in membership.

III

Helping Missourians to celebrate the anniversaries of notable events is a natural and proper activity for their state historical society. During the period from 1915 to 1940, four such commemorations—one of interest to the entire state and three primarily of local or regional significance— drew upon the resources of the State Historical Society of Missouri. The events were the centennial of Missouri statehood in 1918–1921; the Ste. Genevieve bicentennial and Mark Twain birthday centennial, both in 1935; and the Platte Purchase centennial of 1938.

While the society gave meaningful, tangible support to all four commemorations, the method and level of its involvement differed from case to case. In the most important of the four, the celebration of Missouri's difficult and nationally momentous struggle for statehood from 1818 to 1821, the society took the initiative. It energetically formulated plans for the state's birthday party, only to discover that the state government refused to follow its lead with financial and other support. Lacking a well-planned central focus, Missouri's centennial commemoration became a complex of uncoordinated local events plus a last-minute but well-funded celebration at the 1921 state fair in which the society played a relatively minor role.

In the three local and regional commemorations, by contrast, the initiative came from Jefferson City when the General Assembly appropriated $10,000 for each occasion. The Platte Purchase grant of funds, made directly to the society in 1937, had an important effect on its future. The "unsolicited and unexpected" appropriation, as Floyd Shoemaker termed it in his 1948 history of the society, when combined with other demands on the agency's limited resources, taught the organization's leadership to beware of obligations imposed from without. The need to control its own destiny was the lesson the society learned from the Platte Purchase celebration and other events of the 1930s.

The centennial observance of Missouri statehood offers a fascinating case study in public history: how people view, value, and use their collective past in present time. The State Historical Society of Missouri played an important role in the planning of a statewide commemoration and in carrying out a set of activities much altered from the original plan.

With commendable foresight, the society began to plan the celebration of the centennial of statehood at its annual meeting in 1915. Since the process of becoming a state had extended from 1817, when citizens of Missouri Territory circulated petitions to Congress requesting statehood, to 1821, when Missouri gained admission to the Union, the society anticipated centennial events that would occur over the same number of years. Among the reasons for the society's early and abiding interest in Missouri's centennial, one surely was Floyd Shoemaker's scholarship. His master's thesis of 1911 was an analysis of the state's 1820 constitution, and his first book, published in 1916, was a study of Missouri's "struggle for statehood." Steeped in the original sources that reflected the events and issues that the centennial would celebrate, this was Shoemaker's genuine field of expertise. Involved in research that was relevant to the celebration and still in his first year as secretary, Floyd Shoemaker enthusiastically helped to launch a centennial project that could demonstrate to the entire state his and the society's ability to lead.

The society's December 10, 1915, annual meeting directed President Robert M. White to appoint a nominating committee of five, which in turn would create a much larger body "representative of the vocations, industries and institutions of the people of the state." The records of the time variously referred to this large planning group as the Centennial Committee of the State Historical Society of Missouri or the State Centennial Committee of 1,000. The Committee of 1,000 would endorse a plan for the centennial celebration and create an executive committee to implement and oversee its decisions. Early in 1916, White named the nominating committee of five with himself as chair, plus

Floyd Shoemaker as its secretary. Its other members were Jay L. Torrey of Fruitville, Walter B. Stevens of St. Louis, who became the society's president in 1916, Purd B. Wright of Kansas City, and Walter Williams. At their initial meeting on March 11 in St. Louis, committee members divided the labor of nominating five persons from each Missouri county, five from St. Louis city, and at-large delegates for membership on the Committee of 1,000. In addition to participating in statewide planning, these county members were to promote centennial observances in their localities.

The society's nominating committee, White explained in a 1916 press release, applied the "broadest principles of democracy" in appointing a large centennial committee "truly representative" of Missourians. That claim was true only within the framework of prevailing values, as very few women and no blue-collar workers or members of racial minorities belonged to it. It is unlikely that one thousand persons agreed to serve on the planning committee, and it is certain that far fewer than that number ever took part in its activities. The first and, it turned out, only meeting of the State Centennial Committee of 1,000 occurred at Kansas City's Hotel Muehlebach on November 24 and 25, 1916. Present at the meeting were 145 delegates representing 48 of the state's 114 counties and the city of St. Louis. Floyd Shoemaker was justified, though, in praising the slim turnout, given that delegates traveled to Kansas City at their own expense and that the city was not easily accessible from every part of the state. The convention named Lieutenant Governor William R. Painter of Carrollton as chair of the executive committee. He would present the centennial celebration movement's appropriation request to the General Assembly.

The Kansas City meeting also approved a general plan for the celebration. Dates worthy of special celebration were January 8, 1818, when Congress first received petitions from Missouri settlers; July 19, 1820, when Missouri became a state; and August 10, 1821, when the state entered the United States. The centennial committee also encouraged all local celebrations of town or county foundings and "firsts" of other sorts that fell within the 1917–1921 time span as acceptable parts of the statewide commemoration. If Missourians gained knowledge of the era of their state's founding and a patriotic appreciation of the events leading to statehood, Shoemaker and others believed, the movement begun by the society would achieve positive results. To give the celebration some focus and yet retain its decentralized, something-for-everyone aspect, the centennial committee suggested six larger events: in 1920 in St. Louis, Kansas City, Jefferson City, and Sedalia; and in 1921 in Columbia and St. Charles. Dependent on funding that did not materialize, however, these events never occurred.

To this point, the society had laid plans and formed a corps of volunteers without a specific grant of authority or funds from the legislature. The justification of its actions lay solely in its constitution's injunction to disseminate knowledge of the past among Missourians. In 1917, Lieutenant Governor Painter went before the Forty-ninth General Assembly's Joint Appropriations Committee to request a $10,000 appropriation to implement the centennial committee's plans. The appropriations committee recommended $2,000, and both houses sanctioned that amount. But Governor Frederick D. Gardner vetoed it in April as a "new project" that the state could not fund in a time of financial distress. In 1919, the society's centennial leadership again requested funding from the Fiftieth General Assembly but withdrew the attempt by late March. The legislature faced a welter of centennial proposals by this time, introduced by its members and groups from around the state. The only one to gain passage was a joint resolution creating a centennial planning committee consisting of top state officials. Governor Gardner, because of stringent state finances, vetoed the legislature's $20,000 appropriation to this committee.

The society "has financed this movement to date out of its own meager resources," Shoemaker wrote after the legislative disappointment of 1917. "It is a financial impossibility for the society to continue doing so." At the conclusion of his comments on the centennial in the society's ninth biennial report, dated December 31, 1918, the secretary commented: "It lies with the General Assembly . . . to make possible the success of Missouri's centennial." While the state government eventually did fund a statewide celebration, the commemoration's success, in fact, did not depend wholly upon the political process in Jefferson City. The State Historical Society of Missouri had already done much, and would do more, to make the occasion meaningful.

In 1916, the Missouri Press Association had endorsed the society's centennial planning, and its members gave the Committee of 1,000 and its local affiliates considerable publicity. Given all of the newspaper discussion of what had happened a century ago that justified a celebration now, many Missourians must have taken some interest in and learned something about their state's past. Put simply, that was a major reason taxpayers supported a historical society. In more specific efforts, Shoemaker and his staff advised many schools and communities on appropriate ways to commemorate the events of 1817–1821. These methods included community festivals, civic parades and pageants, and the writing of town and county histories. The October 1916 issue of the *Review* presented a model constitution and bylaws for readers interested in forming county historical societies. Few Missouri counties had historical societies during the World War I era, but several acquired them during the statehood centennial years. As the Committee of 1,000 met in Kansas City in November 1916, the society placed on public display some interesting documents in the Hotel Muehlebach's lobby, including original petitions for statehood and a first edition of the 1820 constitution.

The society also marked Missouri's statehood through special publications and in two annual meetings. Volume 15, issues 1 and 2, of the *Missouri Historical Review* (October 1920 and January 1921) were special "Missouri Centennial Numbers." Double the length of a normal issue, these special editions contained centennial-related articles and news of events. For Missouri's *Official Manual* of 1921–1922, the society's staff prepared a forty-four-page chronology of events from the state's beginnings down to 1921. And in 1920, the society published its first books. Isidor Loeb and Floyd Shoemaker, teacher and former student, coedited a two-volume *Journal of the Missouri Constitutional Convention of 1875*. The title page read: "A Missouri Centennial Publication by the State Historical Society of Missouri."

The society canceled its annual meeting scheduled for December 13, 1918, because of the influenza epidemic that ravaged the nation at the end of World War I. But it used the meetings of January 1918 and March 1920 to highlight centennial events. On January 8, 1818, Congress had accepted the first petitions requesting statehood for Missouri. The society's centennial committee designated that day as "Missouri's first centennial," and at its meeting in Columbia the society modeled a day of celebration for the rest of the state. Following the business meeting in the morning, members and guests "adjourned to the Daniel Boone Tavern," Columbia's best hotel and banquet facility. The one hundred people in attendance at the afternoon session and the nearly two hundred present for a banquet and the evening session heard enough toasts to "old Missouri," proclamations, speeches, and semischolarly papers to do honor to any historic occasion. The annual meeting of March 25, 1920, observed the signing of the Missouri statehood enabling act by President James Monroe on March 6 a century before. A business meeting, a round of addresses, and a pageant entertained members on that occasion.

On February 28, 1921, Missouri's new governor, Arthur M. Hyde, signed a centennial appropriation bill of $150,000. The state seemingly compensated for its tardy acceptance of responsibility to celebrate Missouri's centennial by the amount of the grant. It paid for a grand celebration of Missouri's anniversary at the state fair in Sedalia, August 8–20, 1921. August 10, the date of Missouri's admission to the union of states, fell within the fair's thirteen-day run. The State Historical Society of Missouri, which had dropped its own plans for a statewide commemoration because of political inaction, was eager to participate in the event at Sedalia. The society prepared one of the many exhibits available at the fair, and to prepare it and to act as consultant to others, Floyd Shoemaker took a three-month leave of absence in the summer of 1921, with his salary paid by the centennial authority. Shoemaker also wrote a *Book of the Pageant* to provide an accurate historical context for viewers of "The Missouri Pageant and Masque." This depiction of the state's history in poetry, dance, and music involved three hundred performers and attracted twenty thousand spectators for each presentation at the fair. The pageant, written by a group affiliated with the University of Missouri's English department, also appeared in other cities during 1920 and 1921.

Missouri's centennial celebration, like its application for statehood a century earlier, encountered a hostile environment. A different setting would have permitted a different celebration. Just as sectional conflict had delayed statehood, epidemics of war and disease between 1916 and 1920 limited Missourians' opportunity to honor their past. But to the extent that the state achieved a positive centennial experience, the State Historical Society of Missouri played a key role.

The three commemorations of the 1930s offered different challenges and opportunities to the society. In each case, the legislature responded to local requests for an appropriation to fund historical observances, political negotiations in which the society played no part. A Mark Twain Centennial Celebration Commission appointed by the governor, and an organization for Ste. Genevieve's bicentennial, administered the money for their two events. Floyd Shoemaker and the historical society played advisory roles in both celebrations. Because George A. Mahan of Hannibal was the historical society's president in 1935, and because important Twain materials were part of its collections, the society's involvement in the Twain centennial was the greater of the two. The finance committee sent an exhibit of books and newspapers and Mark Twain's orchestrelle to Hannibal during the centennial year. The orchestrelle, a mechanical musical instrument that simulated the sound of an orchestra, had been a gift to the society in 1930. The society's annual meeting also honored Twain. On the morning of May 9, the organization held its business meeting in Columbia. Then officers, trustees, and members traveled to Hannibal for the annual dinner that evening. Never before had a portion of the annual meeting met outside of Columbia. Secretary Shoemaker did make one important acquisition for the society at the Ste. Genevieve festivities in August 1935: he first met George A. Rozier, who would become one of the society's most important leaders.

That the society's 1937–1938 appropriation request, following several years of austerity budgets, was sailing through the Fifty-ninth General Assembly was surprise enough. But the legislators handed Floyd Shoemaker and the finance committee a second surprise in June 1937. Senator Emmett J. Crouse of St. Joseph persuaded the senate to approve a $15,000 expenditure to fund a Platte Purchase centennial celebration later that year. Crouse successfully defended the item in conference committee before Governor Lloyd C. Stark's veto reduced the appropriation to $10,000. The law gave the State Historical Society of Missouri responsibility for administering the grant.

Floyd Shoemaker, who would do most of the administering, believed the observance of the Platte Purchase was "highly meritorious." The "Platte Country" consists of the triangular, far northwestern portion of Missouri that Congress and President Martin Van Buren had made part of the state in March 1837. Between that year and 1845, six counties emerged from the region, including Buchanan, with its bustling county seat and jumping-off place for far-western travel, St. Joseph. Agreeing that a celebration was in order, Shoemaker had counseled Crouse to create a special commission to oversee centennial events. "I . . . did not suggest that our society have anything to do with the celebration or the appropriation," he wrote to the society's president in 1937, state senator Allen McReynolds, "since we have our hands full, and since we have never undertaken such work." The secretary asked McReynolds to assure Governor Stark that the centennial appropriation "is not our baby" and that his approval of it should not be an excuse to reduce the society's regular appropriation. If given the Platte Purchase assignment, Shoemaker conceded, "we will do the best we can."

Too little time remained in 1937 for a well-planned event, thus the Platte centennial observance occurred after the 101st anniversary of the purchase, in August 1938. From the summer of 1937 until the successful celebration a year later, the society's goal was twofold: to prod the local organizers in northwest Missouri to create specific commemoration plans accompanied by a budget and to responsibly disburse the funds entrusted to it by the state. Both absorbed considerable time and effort. Notwithstanding the society's best efforts to convey its own role and expectations of organizers in the six counties, poor communication and delay characterized the months of planning.

On July 24, 1937, President McReynolds, Isidor Loeb, and Shoe-maker met in St. Joseph with a group that included Senator Crouse and W. H. Fitzpatrick, the manager of the local chamber of commerce. At that meeting and in subsequent letters, the society made its policy known. It would only review plans originated locally, not design the celebration itself. Leaders in the Platte Purchase counties should form a broadly representative committee to generate ideas for the commemoration and a smaller executive committee to formulate and implement a detailed plan and to work with the state historical society. The society's finance committee requested $500 of the appropriation to fund a dinner meeting for its members and friends in St. Joseph during the celebration. Through the remainder of the summer and fall of 1937, nothing happened. Fitzpatrick of the chamber of commerce wrote to McReynolds on November 5: "We have not as yet been able to formulate a satisfactory program. . . . Frankly, all of the ideas that we have had up to the present would cost the people of St. Joseph several times the $9,500 allotted for this celebration." In mid-April 1938, Floyd Shoemaker had to explain to Fred Karr, newly elected chair of the centennial's executive committee, the society's policies as deter-mined nine months earlier. And as promotional literature issued from St. Joseph, the society insisted that it state accurately the relationship of the society to the celebration: it "approved" of but did not "sponsor" the event.

Given the problems of planning, Floyd Shoemaker might have expected a lackluster result when northwest Missourians finally celebrated the Platte Purchase centennial on August 18–20, 1938. Instead, every event pleased him and the historical society's elected leadership, particularly the society's own dinner held in the Robidoux Hotel on the 18th. Ever the public relations man, Shoemaker took special note of the "unusually fine and complete publicity" that local newspapers gave that event. The celebration also featured a pageant presented outdoors to a crowd of thirty thousand people, a parade through the streets of St. Joseph seen by sixty to eighty thousand spectators, and a historical costume ball. "In short, there was nothing to mar the three days' celebration," the secretary reported to Loeb in St. Louis. "I am delighted with the society's part in the occasion." At the end of 1938, with all bills paid, Shoemaker reported to Governor Stark that $138.77 remained in the centennial account, "which, of course, will revert to the state." The secretary had a second point to impress upon the governor: although the society had managed this event flawlessly, "it frankly has no wish for a repetition." Shoemaker had stated the same conclusion to finance committee member E. E. Swain in September: "I think the society was greatly benefitted, yet I hope we never get mixed up again in such an occasion since it involves too much work on top of the society's regular duties."

The State Historical Society of Missouri had a similar experience with New Deal programs during the 1930s. While certain employment and history-related programs of the federal government offered the society clear benefits, they also tended to divert staff attention from other work and reduced the agency's freedom of action. Its independence had become an important issue by the late 1930s.

The society obtained temporary workers through several federal programs designed to counter the nation's massive unemployment. A financial aid program for college students that required that they hold campus jobs sent several University of Missouri students to the society's quarters. In February 1934, at Professor Jonas Viles's suggestion, Shoemaker planned to use five of them "to arrange, collate, and index the old Jefferson City archives which were brought over after the fire" in 1911, twenty-three years earlier. With additional space in a new library wing to fill, Shoemaker used six young men for up to a month early in 1937. Provided by the National Youth Administration (NYA), these workers moved books and bound newspapers. In 1933 and 1934, the society profitably used the talents of sixteen CWA workers, all women, whom the Civil Works Administration selected on a needs basis and paid thirty cents an hour for a thirty-hour week. Under the supervision of full-time staff members, these temporary assistants added information to the Who's Who in Missouri file (today called the Surname Index in the reference library), indexed selected newspapers, and arranged manuscript collections. George A. Mahan, the wealthy corporation lawyer who, in 1934, was the society's president and a Democrat, praised the CWA program. "It is . . . highly beneficial and entirely proper to secure these good women, give them something to do and let them earn a living." Shoemaker concurred. As he put it to Loeb in December 1933: "I do not believe that superficial critics of the C.W.A. program would be so happy in their criticisms if they had the experience I am having with just this little group." The society's regular staff, the secretary added, agreed with him.

Other New Deal programs, rather than facilitate ongoing work, made new demands on the society that it could not meet. A good example was the Historical Records Survey of the Works Progress Administration (WPA), which began in 1936 and extended to 1942. The society clearly approved of the program's intent, which was to locate the records of city and county governments and of private organizations such as churches and to disseminate information about these collections. The WPA eventually deposited the data that it had assembled with the historical society for use by its patrons. What the society's leadership objected to was the apparent assumption by state WPA administrators that the society possessed unused resources with which it could assist the records survey. Given the agency's small staff, Shoemaker wrote to finance committee member Roy Williams in June 1937, "the amount of work involved in the sponsorship of such a survey would be prohibitive." But even if staff time existed, "it would be impossible for the society to exercise adequate control over any work directed and financed by a different organization."

Other WPA programs of the late 1930s posed the same problems. In March 1936, for example, those in the Federal Writers' Project responsible for compiling the Missouri guidebook requested the society's help in checking and updating bibliographies. Part of a multivolume national series, the Missouri guidebook presented a comprehensive portrait of the state as of the late 1930s, including eighteen detailed automobile tours. Sarah Guitar in the reference library feared that "we will have a continual stream of bibliographies to check—a volume of work which we could only accomplish if we abandoned our own activities." When a state-level WPA administrator in 1936 tried to elicit the society's endorsement of the Watkins Mill property as a state park, Shoemaker replied: "The society confines its activities to its own immediate functions, leaving other matters in the hands of the regularly delegated authorities."

The pressure to commit to new projects came from private citizens as well as government functionaries. In the spring of 1939, Mrs. J. T. Talbert, on behalf of the Daughters of the American Colonists, asked the society's aid in obtaining WPA funds for a genealogical project. Before the tombstones in small private cemeteries became unreadable, the group desired, under a public subsidy, to copy inscriptions. The Talbert request was not unique, as other appeals for aid had come from the United Daughters of the Confederacy, the Daughters of the American Revolution, and similar patriotic groups. But Talbert's proposal precipitated an important decision by the society's trustees in 1939, one that revised existing policy.

On January 20, 1931, the finance committee had broadened its jurisdiction to include all state-funded programs related to history. The General Assembly should consider the society, the minutes read, as "the proper historical agency for exercising general state supervision over historical matters." Eight years later, a new policy statement reflected the impact of state and federal governmental, as well as private, demands that the society assume new roles and perform new functions. On April 25, 1939, both the finance and the executive committees approved a resolution that limited the scope of the society's mission. A first clause asserted that the society would oppose state appropriations "for other purposes" than "its necessary work." In voting for this principle, some, no doubt, recalled the recent Platte Purchase centennial. A second assertion affirmed that "the society will not sponsor any project which is not under the full control of the society." In a final statement, the resolution established that only after a vote of the finance committee, the executive committee, or the membership would the society endorse any state or federal "project or proposal."

Two fears prompted approval of this resolution. One was the added burden of work that new projects entailed, with no guarantee of additions to staff. A second concern was that the Missouri legislature might reduce the society's regular appropriation by the amount of any special project's appropriation and, in the process, shift the society's priorities from those of its own choosing to others selected by members of the General Assembly. Trustee Jonas Viles expressed this danger. Special history-related projects assigned to the society, he worried, "could be an entering wedge which might eventually lead to the legislature dictating policies of the society." The care with which the organization's leadership asserted its independence in the spring of 1939 reflected the experience of the 1930s. The issue of control would re-emerge after 1940.

IV

During the 1930s, the society's top leadership did not view gifts as threats to its autonomy, although they can be that. The receipt of a historic site obligates a society to maintain it, for example, or of an art collection to storage and gallery space, and such commitments could crowd out other activities. Nevertheless, the society heartily welcomed most of the donations that came to it in increasing volume during the 1930s. An excellent example of a generous benefactor was the society's president from 1925 until his death in 1936, George A. Mahan.

Mahan was the seventh president of the society, and the first to represent a profession other than journalism. His eleven-year presidency remains the longest in the society's history. Mahan may have possessed greater statewide prestige and influence—that is, power without the advantage of public office—than any other of the society's leaders. Born August 6, 1851, on a Marion County farm, Mahan spent his postcollegiate life in Hannibal. In an age when most budding lawyers "read law" in a practicing attorney's office, Mahan chose an academic preparation for his profession. After undergraduate training at Bethel College in Palmyra and Washington and Lee College in Virginia, he graduated from Indiana University's law school in 1872. Mahan began his law practice in Hannibal in 1873 and a decade later married Ida Dulany of Paris, Missouri. The couple had one child, Daniel Dulany, who later joined his father's practice. George Mahan served three terms as prosecuting attorney in Marion County and one term in the lower house of Missouri's legislature in the 1870s and 1880s. A successful corporate attorney, Mahan had clients that included the Atlas Portland Cement Company of Hannibal and a number of railroads, among them the Wabash and Burlington lines. He died on December 16, 1936.

With part of their fortune, George and Ida Mahan became patrons of history. They exerted their greatest influence in their adopted town, where they helped to make Hannibal a shrine to Mark Twain and his characters Tom Sawyer and Huckleberry Finn. In 1912, two years after Twain's death in Connecticut, the Mahans purchased the writer's boyhood home and deeded it to the city as a museum. In 1926, the Mahan family gave a statue of Tom and Huck to Hannibal. Other philanthropies included an orphanage for boys and prize money to several colleges, including $10,000 to the University of Missouri "for original literary productions and oratory."

George Mahan's association with the State Historical Society of Missouri began in 1910 when he became a member. He served as a trustee from 1914 to 1925, as first vice president from 1916 to 1925, and as president. Mahan was a generous and an enlightened lay leader of the society. Open to new ideas and supportive of its undertakings, he advocated increased appropriations even during the early depression years when others called for economy in government. After his death, the society used a small bequest from Mahan's estate to purchase books for its Twain collection and, in his honor, named it the Mahan Memorial Mark Twain Collection.

It was George Mahan's earlier gift to the society that attracted the greatest public notice, however. In 1931–1932, he paid for twenty-nine roadside historic markers, four each in Hannibal and St. Joseph and twenty-one others strung along U.S. 36 between those cities. That experience was the society's introduction to marking historic sites, an enterprise that, with state funds, would grow much larger in the 1950s and 1960s.

The impulse to mark historic sites grew during the early automobile era, as inexpensive individual transportation transformed travelers into tourists. Historian Richard Johnson has calculated that "the major part of the money expended in Missouri during the 1920s for purposes of a historical nature" underwrote statues and plaques. The society joined that movement when its finance committee approved Mahan's highway marker proposal on July 20, 1931. The society's staff researched each subject and wrote inscriptions. The state highway department selected the sites, erected the markers, and landscaped the surrounding ground. Markers recognized a variety of nineteenth-century events: at Monroe City, the Civil War battle of Monroe; at Laclede, the birthplace of General John J. Pershing. The Livingston County marker noted the last spike driven on Missouri's Hannibal and St. Joseph Railroad. The DeKalb County marker stood at the point on U.S. 36 nearest the home of former Senator David R. Atchison, who had served as president for a day on March 4, 1849. Although eastern states like Ohio and Connecticut had already launched major highway marker programs, Mahan's gift made Missouri the first state in the Middle West to place markers along the entire length of a highway. In 1937, the Nebraska State Historical Society used Missouri's project as the model for its own program.

Early in the 1937 legislative session, the same one that approved the Platte Purchase appropriation, Floyd Shoemaker learned that the General Assembly might create a statewide highway marker program. Eventually, Shoemaker was correct in conceding that "nothing may come of the matter," but he and Isidor Loeb were alarmed by the prospect. The secretary revealed that George Mahan's gift of the north Missouri markers in 1932 had not been entirely "free." "I think it cost the society in labor at least fifty dollars a marker for compiling the inscriptions." Should the state now create a marker program, they believed, it ought to do so through a separate appropriation, which would not reduce the society's funds available for other work and would allow the hiring of a new staff member. Shoemaker affirmed that a seemingly simple highway marker, to "successfully meet the challenge of a million pair of eyes," required much research, writing, and rewriting.

Mahan's willingness to spend his own funds on a society function in 1934 illustrates that gifts could come without strings attached. In April of that year, the Mississippi Valley Historical Association held its annual meeting in Columbia. It did so because university history professor Jonas Viles was the group's president and the University of Missouri had invited the association to use its facilities. The state historical society

George Mahan, of Hannibal, served the longest tenure as president of the society, 1925–1936. Particularly interested in the history of northern Missouri, Mahan helped preserve the boyhood home of Mark Twain and financed historic markers erected by the society along U.S. Highway 36 between Hannibal and St. Joseph.

rescheduled its annual meeting to coincide with the visit of historians "who are coming from every state from the Alleghenies to the Rockies and Canada to the Gulf," as Floyd Shoemaker described them. The guests and the members of the society shared several social and scholarly sessions during the three days of meetings, including a dinner at the Tiger Hotel on April 26. Following custom, the local hosts offered this meal gratis to the visitors. President Mahan paid one-third of the cost of the banquet for between 150 and 175 persons. The menu did justice to Missouri's reputation for gracious hospitality. Shoemaker quipped: "Well, that's enough food for a Missourian and is a much better meal than those fanatic Kansans and Nebraskans ever get."

As keynote speaker for the 1934 meeting, the society brought Governor Guy B. Park to campus. A wide variety of speakers graced the programs of other annual meetings following 1915. They included Warrensburg professor Clarence H. McClure in 1928 and bank cashier B. M. Little of Lexington in 1929. At the 1936 meeting, Roland G. Usher of Washington University spoke on "The Present International Crisis." A year later, President Allen McReynolds, a state senator, used the occasion of the society's annual meeting to make history, not simply report it, by proposing the reorganization of Missouri's government. Considering guests who would create widespread publicity for the society's 1938 meeting, Secretary Shoemaker toyed with the idea of inviting the Roosevelts, Franklin and Eleanor, or either one, to speak.

That plan failed to develop, but it illustrated the flexibility of scheduling annual meetings during the period. Isidor Loeb explained that welcoming President Roosevelt "would involve making the date of the annual meeting correspond with his itinerary, but there should be no difficulty in regard to this." Annual meetings normally convened in winter and spring months: in December in 1916 and 1922, for example; in January in 1930; in March in 1920 and 1935; and in April in 1928 and 1934. While the society's annual business meetings were held in its own reference library, the dinners occurred off campus. Beginning in 1929, Columbia offered two large banquet rooms, in the Daniel Boone Tavern and the Tiger Hotel. But as Shoemaker noted in January 1940, each facility had drawbacks. The Boone Tavern's dining room had "two or three large posts in the center" that obstructed vision while the Tiger's had a loud fan. But "seeing people almost faint and get sick if the fan doesn't run" was less desirable than the noise.

Later generations should imagine the annual meetings and dinners as congenial social affairs that left spaces for humor and enjoyment among the reports on the society's condition and the papers on historical topics. During the April 1937 dinner, for example, member Justus R. Moll of Springfield wrote a poem about what he observed, which included verses like this: "The Dan Boone Inn was free from sin / The lobby full of smoke / The big shots from the capitol / were drinking cherry-coke!" Even the historically minded knew how to have fun during the depression years.

One of several functions that annual meetings performed was to put the state society into meaningful contact with the several local historical societies active in Missouri. There were far fewer of these organizations during the interwar years than there are at the time of this writing, and most of them were of relatively recent origin. Local societies could affiliate with the state society and send delegates to its annual meetings, and in 1938 and 1939 Shoemaker and President McReynolds arranged sessions at which these delegates could become acquainted and share ideas. Given the positive reception accorded these two meetings, it was unfortunate that the practice did not become institutionalized.

Ethel Withers from Liberty spoke as president of the Clay County Historical Society in 1938. Organized in 1934, its original purpose was to save the nineteenth-century courthouse that the county planned to raze, and when that effort failed, to secure a room in the new courthouse for a museum and society meetings. Recent activities had included an essay contest in the schools. B. H. Jolly represented the St. Charles County Historical Society, which was a year old in 1938. Reflecting Jolly's interests as the county school superintendent, that society focused its efforts on teaching Missouri history in the schools. It placed the *Missouri Historical Review* in each county school library. Charles van Ravenswaay and Lilburn Kingsbury reported for the combined Cooper-Howard County Historical Society. The preservation of Thespian Hall in Boonville, a mid-nineteenth-century theater building, was high on the list of the group's goals. Its 390 members also had begun a manuscript collecting program. The two representatives gave examples of recently discovered collections, "and if the record is more than local, we immediately deposit it with the state historical society, where we feel that it is safer and more accessible to research workers." Representatives of only a handful of local societies attended the 1938 and 1939 sessions, but those present seemed to profit from the interaction. Professor Kate Gregg of Lindenwood College was one satisfied participant. Writing to Shoemaker in 1939, she commented: "That exchange of ideas last year in the county part of the state meeting was one of the best features of last year's meeting."

V

In 1949, former president Allen McReynolds referred to the finance committee as "a board of three in whose hands rests the direction and destiny of" the State Historical Society of Missouri. The committee experienced its first change in personnel in thirty-two years when E. E. Swain replaced R. M. White in 1933. When Walter Williams retired in 1934, his nephew Roy D. Williams joined the committee. Including its chair, continuing member Isidor Loeb, the reconstituted finance committee guided the society to a fiscal recovery in the second half of the 1930s, following drastic reductions in income during the early depression years. In this achievement the committee enjoyed crucial assistance from two members of the state senate, Democrat McReynolds and Republican George A. Rozier.

While Rozier, McReynolds, and Roy Williams were lawyers, Edward Everett Swain was one more editor who volunteered years of service to the society. He was born on February 2, 1883, in Ewing, Illinois. Following his college graduation in 1905, Swain learned journalism while working for several big-city dailies, including St. Louis's *Republic* and *Post-Dispatch*. Swain's life work as a small-town editor began in 1909, when he and a partner purchased the *Kirksville Daily Express*. Becoming sole owner two years later, Swain eventually bought the *Daily News* and merged the two papers. Advancing to the historical society's presidency in 1950, the Kirksville editor also headed the Missouri Press Association in 1930 and served as a longtime member of the board of regents of Northeast Missouri State College. The recipient of the society's third Distinguished Service Award in 1970, Edward Swain died in Kirksville on February 12, 1972.

Two months after Swain's death, Roy D. Williams passed away in Boonville, the town he had called home his entire life. Williams was the son of William Muir Williams, a lawyer, justice of the Missouri Supreme Court, and brother of Walter Williams. Born on New Year's Day, 1881, Roy attended Kemper Military School in Boonville and the University of Missouri. During his senior college year, Williams taught himself shorthand and typing and, with these skills, became secretary to Congressman Dorsey W. Shackelford of Missouri's eighth district. After two years in Washington, Williams began the study of law in his father's Boonville office and served as the firm's stenographer. The Missouri bar admitted him in 1906. Williams's record of public service included the chairmanship of the state tax commission from 1919 to 1922 and a two-year term as commissioner of the Kansas City Court of Appeals beginning in 1929. Thirty years after he became a trustee of the historical society in 1932, Williams launched his term as its president.

Allen McReynolds, who became acting president upon the death of George Mahan in 1936 and then held the office in his own right, was one of four presidents to serve during the period 1915–1940. Robert M. White had served as president from 1914 to 1916. Walter B. Stevens of

St. Louis succeeded White and preceded Mahan in a presidential term that extended from 1916 to 1925.

Stevens brought a unique background to the society. An urban journalist, he was a reporter rather than an editor-publisher. He served as Washington correspondent for the *St. Louis Globe-Democrat* from 1884 to 1902 and was a prolific writer of historical works, including a two-volume study, *Missouri, The Center State, 1821–1915* (1915), and a three-volume history, *St. Louis, The Fourth City, 1764–1909* (1909). As one who helped plan and operate the 1904 Louisiana Purchase Exposition in St. Louis, Stevens gained useful experience for his term as the society's president during Missouri's centennial celebration of 1918–1921. Educated at the University of Michigan, where he earned a B.A. degree in 1870 and an M.A. two years later, Stevens was a native of Meriden, Connecticut. He died at the age of ninety-one in Georgetown, South Carolina, on August 28, 1939.

Allen McReynolds lived his entire life and practiced law in Carthage. Born there on November 7, 1877, he was a third-generation Missourian whose parents' families had roots in Virginia and Tennessee. The recipient of a bachelor's degree from the University of Missouri in 1901, McReynolds was admitted to the Missouri bar two years later after study in his father's law office. McReynolds served two terms as state senator, representing the twenty-eighth district, from 1935 to 1943. He established a reputation as an expert on the new Social Security system while helping to bring Missouri law into conformity with that set of federal programs, and as an opponent of Kansas City's Pendergast organization. Although McReynolds carried the outstate counties in his failed bid for the 1940 Democratic gubernatorial nomination, he lost both Pendergast's town and St. Louis. The state senator was a principal organizer of the movement to replace Missouri's 1875 constitution, which his maternal grandfather, Westley Halliburton, had helped to write. As a delegate-at-large to the Constitutional Convention of 1943–1944, McReynolds played a key role, serving as chairman of the Committee on Rules and Order of Business and as a member of six other committees. Between 1945 and 1956, he was a curator of the university and of Stephens College. Elected to honorary membership in the historical society in 1957, Allen McReynolds died on September 29, 1960.

Senator McReynolds and his wife, Maude (Clarke) McReynolds, had two children, one of whom was Helen Elizabeth. In 1941, Elizabeth married Senator George A. Rozier, one of her father's young legislative colleagues. Rozier represented another old Missouri family. His paternal great-grandfather, Ferdinand, left France for the United States in 1806 and settled in Ste. Genevieve in 1811. George, born on August 13, 1902, in St. Mary, Ste. Genevieve County, was the descendant of three generations of merchants in southeast Missouri. His father, Pratte, founded the Rozier Mercantile Company in Perryville in 1903. George Rozier received his undergraduate and law degrees from St. Louis University—the latter in 1924—and was admitted to the bar in the same year. Active in local and state bar associations and in Republican politics, Rozier won election to the twenty-sixth district senate seat in a decidedly Democratic year, 1934, and returned for a second term following reelection in 1938. Of importance to the historical society, Rozier served on the Senate Appropriations Committee. He resigned his seat in October 1941 to become chief counsel for the state Unemployment Compensation Commission—the same year that he began his term as president of the State Historical Society of Missouri. Rozier practiced law for more than fifty years, most of them in Jefferson City. In April 1937, still at an early stage of their friendship, Floyd Shoemaker found Rozier to be an able man who easily gained the respect of those with whom he worked. "Eventually, we should tie him to our society." The society's history from the late 1930s into the mid-1980s reveals Shoemaker's success at doing just that.

Table 2.2 reveals some dimensions of the State Historical Society of Missouri's financial circumstances during the quarter-century that this chapter reviews. During this period, legislative and executive branches considered and approved the expenditure of state funds for two years at a time. Therefore, one-half of the society's request, and one-half of the General Assembly's and governor's appropriation, applied to a single year in a given biennium. Perhaps the most important generalization supported by the data is that throughout the period, and not only during the depression years of the 1930s, the society struggled with inadequate funding—inadequate, that is, in relation to the society's realistic requests for funds to support the functions that the state had given to it in 1899. It was also inadequate when weighed against the support that comparable states gave to their historical agencies.

In only one of the thirteen biennial periods beginning with 1915–1916 and ending with 1939–1940—that is, in 1937–1938—did the

Table 2.2 Biennial State Appropriations, 1915–1916 to 1939–1940

Biennial Appropriation Requested by Finance Committee		State Funds Available to the Society
1915–1916	$22,160	$13,600 appropriated by General Assembly – 1,000 withheld by governor $12,600 net appropriation
1917–1918	$32,455	$20,840 appropriated – 4,000 vetoed by governor – 2,815 withheld by governor $14,025 net appropriation
1919–1920	$35,685	$35,650 appropriated – 3,500 withheld $32,150 net appropriation
1921–1922	$46,670	$46,670 appropriated – 6,900 vetoed $39,770 net appropriation
1923–1924	$50,870	$50,870 appropriated – 4,400 vetoed – 300 withheld $46,170 net appropriation
1925–1926	$55,080	$47,720 appropriated – 4,200 vetoed $43,520 net appropriation
1927–1928	$54,170	$49,570 appropriated – 6,850 withheld $42,720 net appropriation
1929–1930	$53,890	$45,690 appropriated and approved by governor
1931–1932	$57,260	$49,285 appropriated –12,579 withheld $36,706 net appropriation
1933–1934	$36,705	$24,045 appropriated and approved by governor
1935–1936	$42,300	$36,520 appropriated and approved by governor
1937–1938	$47,540	$47,540 appropriated and approved by governor
1939–1940	$59,820	$59,040 appropriated and approved by governor

Source: Biennial reports to the governor.

state appropriation satisfy the society's request for funds. In the following biennium it received 99 percent of its request. For six consecutive budgeting periods beginning in 1919–1920, the agency that Floyd Shoemaker administered won at least 79 percent of its funding proposals. But in 1915–1916, it received 57 percent of its submitted budget, and in the war years 1917–1918, only 43 percent. In 1921–1922, when the State Historical Society of Missouri enjoyed a nearly $40,000 appropriation, the Nebraska and Kansas societies, in states with much smaller population totals than Missouri, received $31,000 and $34,000, respectively. Minnesota spent $50,000, Illinois $61,740, and Wisconsin $126,000 on their state historical societies in 1921–1922.

If the supposedly prosperous 1920s witnessed less than enthusiastic fiscal support in Jefferson City of the society's work, the early and mid-1930s saw an erosion of its programs. Or, at the very least, the budgets of those years forced a holding pattern in which the staff postponed important tasks while moving slowly ahead on others. Beginning in 1933–1934, following the dark depression winter of 1932–1933, the society significantly reduced its requests for funding. It won only 66 percent of its austerity budget for that biennium and 86 percent of a relatively small 1935–1936 request. The society's proposed budget for 1933–1934 dropped to within $1,000 of its proposal for 1919–1920, fourteen years earlier. The last net appropriation smaller than that of 1933–1934 was the one received for the 1917–1918 biennium, sixteen years before. The 1935–1936 net appropriation fell below the level of funding in 1921–1922.

During the 1920s and especially the 1930s, the effects of financial stringency forced the society's leadership to cope with budgets that never matched legitimate needs. One response to the problem was to use the society's second source of income, mainly derived from the dues paid by a growing membership and from sales, to cushion the impact of reduced state support. Despite the pressing financial concerns, those responsible for the state historical society's well-being never despaired and rarely revealed discouragement. Shoemaker, Isidor Loeb, and others recognized the society's strengths, including growing collections and a large and increasing number of members, and they seemed to agree that state government did as well as it could for the society, given political and economic realities in Missouri.

Floyd Shoemaker's mail during the 1930s dramatically revealed that some other state historical societies suffered considerably more than Missouri's did. Wisconsin was not the only meaningful standard of measurement. In March 1933, Paul M. Angle, director of the Illinois State Historical Library, asked about Floyd Shoemaker's salary. The Illinois legislature was poised to cut $500 from Angle's $3,000 annual salary. "I think this is going a little too far. The information you can give me may be helpful." If Shoemaker had answered, he would have told Angle that his salary also was reduced. While the *Missouri Historical Review* continued to be printed, J. Cecil Alter, editor of the *Utah Historical Quarterly*, informed Shoemaker in early January 1934 that his journal's next issue would be the last, at least for awhile. "The legislature did not appropriate money for the publication during the next two years." An even more dismal tale came from Lawrence K. Fox, secretary of the South Dakota State Historical Society, where both political partisanship and reduced state revenues encouraged legislators to weaken the society. Fox wrote: "When I severed connections with Uncle Sam's forces in 1919, I fondly hoped that my fighting days were over. The World War was a picnic [compared] to what I have been through since January 1933."

Detailed examples will illustrate the occasional financial distress that inadequate state appropriations caused the State Historical Society of Missouri, before as well as during the Great Depression. When, in 1917, Governor Gardner vetoed or withheld 33 percent of the society's appropriation as approved by the General Assembly, the finance committee borrowed $300 from a Columbia bank to pay salaries for February and March. Two years later, the society borrowed for the same purpose. Funds withheld by Governor Sam A. Baker in the 1927–1928 biennium forced several changes in the society's operations. Secretary Shoemaker delayed the photostating of nineteenth-century newspapers, reduced the schedule for binding newspapers and books, and restricted book purchases "to items badly needed and offered at bargain prices." The society terminated the employment of two staff members it could no longer afford on September 1, 1927, leaving only five people to do its work. One later returned, but the personnel reductions caused the temporary suspension of two significant functions—cataloging the book collection and indexing newspapers.

Governor Baker struggled with an expanding state budget and static revenues. His successors in the 1930s faced drastically reduced tax revenues. Retrenchment was the society's experience in each case. On June 1, 1930, it released several hourly employees who had been indexing important nineteenth-century newspapers. At its December 11, 1931, meeting, the finance committee adopted several austerity measures. While it assured the staff "that no reduction in salaries would be made during the next six months," recent layoffs had already reduced the staff to its smallest size in years. At the start of 1932, the society employed six persons full-time and one on an hourly basis. Three weeks after Franklin Roosevelt's inauguration in 1933, Isidor Loeb instructed Secretary Shoemaker to "notify all regular employees that it is extremely probable that the finance committee" would lower their salaries on April 1. Ever mindful of comparative data, Shoemaker knew that the state's funding of the historical society in the 1930s fell short not only of the expenditures of earlier years, but also of the support given other societies by their states. His biennial report for 1935–1936 showed that Missouri's appropriation of $36,520 compared with an average appropriation of $96,825 for the states of Illinois, Iowa, Minnesota, and Wisconsin for the same period. In 1937–1938, Shoemaker's agency received $47,540, while the other four societies enjoyed an average state appropriation of $120,837.

The society's programs did not suffer the damage they might have during the depression years. Sources of income that supplemented the state appropriation placed its financial condition somewhere in the middle on a scale at whose extremes were Utah and South Dakota, and Illinois and Wisconsin. Supplementary income, often called "private" funds by society leaders, derived from membership dues, gifts, and the sale of the society's publications and of duplicate items from the collection, most often newspaper files. It is unclear when these revenues became significant, although their increase paralleled the growth of membership. On several occasions in 1915, the finance committee approved book purchases made with funds in a membership dues account. Throughout World War I, the committee bought Liberty Bonds with the cash in a membership fund. By 1924, when all ten of the society's wartime government securities matured, their value was $8,000. When, in early 1918, the society launched a drive for life members, the receipts appeared in an endowment fund. In 1921, anticipating the sale of the *Journal of the Missouri Constitutional Convention of 1875,* the finance committee established a publishing fund.

A consolidation of these accounts occurred on January 21, 1927, when the annual meeting approved a constitutional amendment creating the Membership Fund (Trust) and the Membership Interest Fund. The society's income went to the first account, and all interest generated by it flowed into the second. These monies were a significant supplement to the state appropriation even before the depression hit. The annual meeting of April 3, 1928, for example, approved the expenditure of membership interest account funds to cover deficits in the salary and other budget categories.

Beginning in 1931, as state support fell, private funds allowed the society to narrow the gap between available appropriations and continuing program needs. In that year, membership dues helped pay bills for binding materials and printing a volume of the debates of the 1875 Constitutional Convention. In 1932, the society could photostat the 1817–1818 issues of the *Missouri Gazette* only because supplementary funds existed. In 1934, the sale of the society's duplicate file of the *St. Louis Globe-Democrat* increased the Membership Fund (Trust) by $1,000. Table 2.3 indicates, for three biennial periods, how membership and other forms of income supported the society's budgets.

Senate Bill 124, which became law in the 1933 legislative session, seemed to threaten the society's reliance on its private funds. The law brought under the General Assembly's control all sources of income enjoyed by state agencies. These departments feared, with reason, that their appropriations would decline by the amount of income received from fees, sales, and other legitimate sources. The legislature, for its part, had strong motivation to reduce state spending in years of disastrous revenue shortfalls. Encouraged by Isidor Loeb's expertise in legislative matters, Secretary Shoemaker wrote in March 1933: "I still do not think that bill is going to get our money and securities, but it might." The leadership believed the law did not apply to the state historical society, which operated under its 1898 constitution and a set of elected officers, and the 1899 law making it a trustee of the state.

The finance committee, in the fall of 1933, instructed Shoemaker not to make the "voluntary quarterly reports to the governor on the society's private Membership Fund (Trust)" that the new legislation required. On April 10 of that year the finance committee had merged

Table 2.3 The Membership Fund (Trust)'s Support of the Society's
Budget in Three Biennial Periods

	Amount Spent from State Appropriations	Amount Spent from Membership Fund (Trust)
1933–1934		
Salaries	$19,500.00	$2,679.75
New Equipment and Additions	693.00	617.27
Operations	3,660.00	3,386.37
Repairs/Replacements	192.00	—
	$24,045.00	$6,683.39
1935–1936		
Salaries	$25,020.00	$3,229.73
New Equipment and Additions	2,200.00	690.52
Operations	8,900.00	1,313.45
Repair/Replacements	400.00	—
	$36,520.00	$5,233.70
1937–1938		
Salaries	$30,000.00	$4,885.16
New Equipment and Additions	5,000.00	—
Operations	11,840.00	2,036.15
Repairs/Replacements	700.00	—
	$47,540.00	$6,921.31

Source: Finance Committee minutes.

the two membership funds created in 1927 into the Membership Fund
(Trust), and in a letter written a few days earlier, Shoemaker explained
why. "I thought that if we were questioned in regard to our private
funds, it might be a little easier to say we had only one fund." When,
in the spring of 1934, the state budget office required a report on
funds expended during 1933, Shoemaker did not mention the society's
use of its supplementary income. As he wrote to Loeb on May 4: "I
am becoming more and more convinced that the present and future
welfare of the society depends upon our keeping complete control of
our investments and our private income." If the membership account

were in Jefferson City, even if state officials promised the society access to it, Shoemaker feared that the funds would simply disappear into Missouri's growing budget deficit. "It is simply horrible to contemplate our difficulties if we lost these sources of income." The society did not lose them. The Membership Fund (Trust) has assisted it, during good times and bad, in serving the interests of Missouri history up to the present day.

VI

The state historical society used its appropriated and supplementary funds for a variety of ongoing programs in addition to those already discussed. Among the most important were the growth and management of the collections and the expansion of the society's publications to include volumes of primary documents as well as the *Missouri Historical Review.*

As Francis Sampson had done, Floyd Shoemaker wrote to thousands of potential donors in his quest for research materials. Ignoring his already crowded shelves of uncataloged titles, the secretary grandly proclaimed "that this society endeavors to maintain a complete file of all important publications in the state." To that end he solicited such items as the *Scottish Rite Magazine,* the catalogs of the Academy of St. Teresa, and the "Ad Club News"—all from Kansas City institutions in the early 1920s. Valuing the campaign literature generated by a pluralistic political system, Shoemaker sought the Missouri addresses of the Communist, Socialist-Labor, and Single-Tax parties in 1924. The secretary of state in Jefferson City supplied two of the three. The society encouraged the donations of newspapers, of autographed copies of books for the Missouri Author Collection, and of the journal of the state constitutional convention in 1922 and 1923. The library disposed of as well as acquired materials. It offered to sell some Illinois telephone directories to that state's historical library in 1925 and in 1935 transferred to the University of Missouri library some federal and non-Missouri state documents of marginal value to its patrons.

Gifts were a significant means of increasing book, newspaper, and art holdings during the 1930s. While most donations were of materials, cash gifts occasionally appeared. Beginning in 1937, the society used

George Mahan's bequest to purchase items for the Mahan Memorial Mark Twain Collection. Among the Mahan acquisitions was a first edition, first issue (1867) of Twain's story "The Celebrated Jumping Frog," purchased for $100, and a recent edition of *Tom Sawyer* illustrated by Missouri artist Thomas Hart Benton. Floyd Shoemaker explained in 1936 that the historical society's Mark Twain collection "was built up by two men whose hobby was collecting various Mark Twain editions," Francis Sampson and Purd B. Wright of the Kansas City Public Library. The society had purchased Wright's collection for $650 in 1923, an early expression of its policy on acquiring Twainiana: "We have not attempted to become specialists in this highly technical field and have merely tried to fill in a few gaps in our Mark Twain Collection, where we could do so without spending much money." The Mahan bequest promoted that objective.

In 1930, Walter Williams, at that time the president of the university, arranged for the society to receive Twain's Aeolian Orchestrelle, an instrument that played music rolls much as a player piano does. The author's friend and biographer, Albert Bigelow Paine, had offered the piece to Twain's home state university, which had awarded him an honorary degree in 1902. Williams suggested the historical society as a more appropriate recipient. Lacking a museum, in fact it was no more able to accommodate the gift than was the university. President George Mahan paid for the restoration of Twain's favorite musical instrument in 1930, funding a visit to the society's reading room by an expert technician from the Aeolian Company in New York. The society loaned the orchestrelle to the museum in Hannibal for the 1935 Twain centennial and later extended the loan.

In each biennial report, Floyd Shoemaker summarized and cited important examples of donated materials, and the finance committee's minutes as well as the "Historical Notes and Comments" section of the *Missouri Historical Review* contained additional information on gifts. Together these sources constitute an index to the generosity of the society's friends. In 1921–1922, donations of books totaled 1,467 and of pamphlets 564. Ten years later, donors bestowed on the society 1,207 books, 964 pamphlets, 1 painting, 86 photographs and negatives, 28 manuscript collections, 3 ledger books, 1 medal, 49 clippings, 4 sheets of music, and 4 poems—in addition to donations of newspapers, both current issues and back files. An important manuscript collection received in 1932 was the papers of Judge Abiel Leonard, covering the years 1819–1862. Dr. Frederic Culmer of Central College in Fayette was instrumental in arranging this gift from Leonard's descendants.

Extended conversations with the heirs of James S. Rollins brought Missouri's most famous painting, George Caleb Bingham's *Order No. 11*, to the society's reading room in 1939. Rollins and Bingham had been close personal friends and mid-nineteenth-century political associates. In 1934, C. B. Rollins of Columbia, on behalf of his family, offered to "deposit" the work "for several years" with the society, a proposal that the finance committee quickly accepted. But when Rollins withdrew the offer while negotiations for purchase proceeded in 1935 with the Nelson Gallery in Kansas City, the society sought an option to buy. Offered the painting in the autumn of 1935 at the Nelson Gallery's price— $10,000—the committee had to decline. The money was not available, and "since the society has no art gallery a more proper depository would be . . . the Nelson Art Gallery." Yet, the temporary disposition of the matter was the Rollinses' original offer: a deposit of Bingham's work with the society for display in the reading room. There it would hang for the next several years.

Other donors made outright gifts of portraits. The daughters of Judge Robert B. Todd presented his likeness in 1935, for example. The society found the funds to purchase some historical portraits. In 1932, it acquired the only portrait painted from life of Benjamin Howard, the first governor of the Territory of Missouri, from a descendant in West Virginia. By purchase, gift, and loan, the society began to build its art collection before 1940, although significant growth would come after that date.

The most important acquisitions through donation between 1915 and 1940 were back files of newspapers. In 1929, for example, former Missouri Attorney General Jesse W. Barrett gave the files of his family's Canton newspaper, which dated from 1862, to the society. Roy King, the staff member who oversaw the newspaper collection, traveled to northeast Missouri to pack and ship the valuable acquisition. "As soon as the files reach us," Shoemaker assured Barrett, "we shall begin going over them, repairing them, getting them in shape preparatory for immediate binding." The most important newspaper acquisition of 1931–1932 came to the society's collection not on newsprint, but rather as photostatic copies of the actual newspaper. In that biennium,

Secretary Shoemaker purchased duplicate pages of the *Missouri Gazette* from 1808 to 1818. The Missouri Historical Society in St. Louis owned the original of this first newspaper published west of the Mississippi River. As early as 1916, the State Historical Society of Missouri had purchased a photostat machine, and in the proposed budget for 1927–1928 it allocated $2,650 for the reproduction of newspapers by the photostatic process.

Before the 1930s ended, a new technology appeared that made photostating obsolete as well as eliminated the problem of repairing and preserving brittle, yellowed newsprint. As early as 1935, Secretary Shoemaker investigated the process commonly known as microfilming, recently developed by the Kodak Company. In 1937, Shoemaker's correspondence carried references to the purchase of "a microphoto-graphic filming machine." Society personnel could, Shoemaker hoped, visit collections of newspapers around the state, placing tiny images of their pages on rolls of machine-readable cellulose acetate film. Rather than purchase the expensive microfilming camera, the society apparently rented the equipment in late 1937 or early 1938 and began purchasing newspapers filmed by commercial firms. By March of the latter year, the secretary wrote to Allen McReynolds about "the remarkable economy which has been affected [*sic*] in the reproduction of newspapers . . . by using the new photo film process. We are now reproducing scores of volumes of old Missouri newspapers that are in editors' offices and which can be obtained only on loan as the editor does not wish to part with the ownership." In the 1937–1938 biennium, the newspaper library purchased over 140,000 pages of newspapers and manuscripts on microfilm. This total included the manuscript census records from 1830 through 1860.

Microfilming proved to be an almost miraculous way of preserving both newspapers and space. It would be quite impossible today for the State Historical Society of Missouri to house, preserve, and make easily available to patrons in their original format all of the newspapers acquired through a century of collecting. Instead of having a newspaper library of national significance—on film—the society would own many rooms full of crumbling, unusable newsprint.

The state historical society purchased materials when acquisition through donation was impossible. In 1915, the finance committee approved an expensive purchase: the seventy-three volumes of Reuben G.

Thwaites's *Jesuit Relations* for $150. Three years later the committee spent $25 for the books and pamphlets in the library of the late Odon Guitar, a Boone County notable who had been a Union general during the Civil War. In 1931, for a fee, Dr. A. P. Nasatir, a professor of history at the State Teachers' College in San Diego, California, copied the correspondence of the Spanish lieutenant governors of Upper Louisiana (which included Missouri) in the archives at Seville, Spain. The society had tentative plans, never realized because of the depression, to publish these records.

The most significant purchase made during this era was of a large part of the William Clark Breckenridge library of Missouriana. Assembled over a period of forty years, the collection was second in size and quality only to Francis Sampson's, which had formed the core of the society's holdings since 1901. Floyd Shoemaker spent nine days in St. Louis from late January to early February 1928, checking Breckenridge's titles against lists of the society's collection and assessing their physical condition. Before leaving Columbia, Shoemaker had told President Mahan: "An opportunity like this comes very seldom in a lifetime," and he believed that the society should grasp it, even if by doing so it overspent its book purchase budget for the entire biennium. The Breckenridge estate and the finance committee signed a contract early in February 1928: $1,250 for the 1,031 books, pamphlets, and engravings that the society most wanted, with an option to buy all or part of the remainder. "Dean Williams and Dr. Loeb are elated," Shoemaker wrote, "and frankly, I never felt happier in my life." Although it would take thirteen years, events would prove Shoemaker's prediction about the long-term significance of the purchase to be incorrect: "I doubt if we ever again have such an opportunity to add such a valuable collection to the society's library."

VII

During the quarter century from 1915 to 1940, the state historical society's publication program moved in two new directions. While its quarterly, the *Missouri Historical Review*, continued to be the society's most significant and versatile publication, a series of brief, popular articles gained a broader readership. Inaugurated on February 1, 1925, as a free service to newspapers, "This Week in Missouri History" appeared in at least one paper in 97 of the state's 114 counties, plus the city of St. Louis, at the end of 1939. In that year the staff mailed the articles to 375 Missouri newspapers. Various assistants joined Shoemaker in writing these essays, which focused on interesting personalities and notable events associated with a particular week in the year. The articles' journalistic style and brevity held reader interest. This long-running series may have brought the society's work before a larger audience than anything else it did, with the possible exception of the roadside markers erected during the 1950s and 1960s.

The second initiative was the publication of original source materials. By 1939, the society had published twenty volumes of documents in three different series. As part of Missouri's centennial celebration, the society issued the first of these in 1920. *The Journal of the Missouri Constitutional Convention of 1875* was not intended as a centennial observance. The finance committee first asked for funds to support the work in 1913 and continued to do so at two-year intervals until the Fiftieth General Assembly approved the $4,000 request in 1919. Since the manuscript journal was in longhand and some members of the 1875 convention had left little trace of their lives, the editorial challenge was considerable. But staff members like Sarah Guitar gained valuable experience on the journal project that they applied to later documentary series. When issued in 1920, the two-volume work, under the general editorship of Floyd Shoemaker and Isidor Loeb, sold for $2.50, postpaid.

The society's second series of published source materials eventually became a forty-three-year project totaling twenty volumes. *The Messages and Proclamations of the Governors of the State of Missouri* (1922–1965) seems to have been initiated by the legislature. In its fifty-first session, 1921–1922, that body first appropriated funds for the publication. Volumes 1–12, issued between 1922 and 1930, included all gubernatorial administrations from 1820 to 1929. Publication of the series did not resume until 1947. While several staff members helped to prepare the volumes for press, Sarah Guitar was the most involved assistant during this era. Her name joined Secretary Shoemaker's on the title pages of volumes 7 (1926) through 12 (1930). Each volume included biographical sketches of the governors covered. In volume 1, journalists and early leaders of the society were the authors, including presidents Edwin Stephens, William N. Southern, and Walter Stevens. In 1922, the finance committee authorized the printing of five hundred copies each of the first three volumes of the *Messages* series and anticipated that the staff would send copies gratis to state officials. Purchasers paid $1.25 per volume, postage included.

At its meeting of October 8, 1929, the finance committee authorized the publication of *The Debates of the Missouri Constitutional Convention of 1875.* Aware that this would be a much larger project than the *Journals,* the committee determined to "continue . . . [it] until completed." Coeditors Shoemaker and Loeb, who issued volume 1 in 1930, published volume 6 in 1940. They completed the series in twelve volumes in 1944. Again, staff members did most of the actual preparation of copy for the editors and printers. In a 1939 letter, Secretary Shoemaker revealed that cataloger Pearle McCown and reference librarian Guitar "have handled the manuscripts of all the volumes." Volume 6 gave the women particular problems. The 1875 convention's proceedings for June 21 were missing from the handwritten record. Shoemaker sent a letter to many librarians and newspaper editors requesting a search of papers in their possession for a transcript of the June 21 debate, after a search of the society's own collection did not yield it. In addition, the convention stenographer did not transcribe his notes until sometime in 1876, months after he took them. That delay resulted in ambiguities and confusion that McCown and Guitar had to resolve.

Simultaneously directing several society publications, Floyd Shoemaker undertook personal publishing projects as well. The most important was *Missouri, Mother of the West,* which he and Walter Williams wrote in 1926 and 1927 and published in 1930. The authors divided the state's history at 1860, with Williams covering the early years and Shoemaker the Civil War and after in volume 2. Contract writers employed by the Lewis Publishing Company of Chicago composed the biographical sketches that filled volumes 3–5. The information in these sketches still proves useful to researchers.

The centerpiece of the society's publication program remained the *Missouri Historical Review.* In 1939, Floyd Shoemaker described the "magazine . . . as one of the four outstanding state historical publications in the country from the standpoint of scholarship and close editorial supervision." Although the cost of printing the quarterly seems quite low today, it was a major budget item: $4,500 for the eight issues of the 1939–1940 biennium, for example. The journal was a major preoccupation of its editor, Shoemaker, and several staff members. The *Review* reached a milestone in 1932–1933 with the publication of the twenty-fifth volume. The finance committee then authorized the 1934 printing of a cumulative index, prepared by the Columbia Literary Club, for those volumes.

The *Review,* although dedicated to the past, could respond to current events. That was true of the two special centennial issues of 1920–1921. It also applied to a lengthy "History of the Woman Suffrage Movement in Missouri" edited by Mary Semple Scott that appeared in a double issue for April–July 1920. It was in August 1920 that the Nineteenth Amendment granted women the right to vote in all states. The authors of the report's several sections were participants in the suffrage campaign, qualifying their contribution as important primary source material.

A third example of the *Review*'s treatment of contemporary history was its coverage of World War I. From American intervention in April 1917 into 1920, the journal carried fifteen reports on the state's involvement. Some focused on key Missourians like General Enoch Crowder. In the most comprehensive series of articles, "Missouri and the War," Shoemaker compiled data by which he intended to demonstrate the loyal commitment of the state to the nation's mission. The articles remain, decades later, useful sources of facts and ideas for historians of Missouri and the Great War.

The society also made itself a repository for materials that represented the war experience. It collected "war literature and posters" and kept records on the casualties suffered by Missourians and honors won by them. In the summer of 1918, the society accepted a proposal of the Missouri State Council of Defense. Already collecting materials on its own initiative, the historical society agreed to serve as the Missouri War History Commission. Rather than attempt to recover the state's war experience after the fact, it would assemble that record while the fighting still raged. At the conflict's end, the Missouri Council of Defense and the state's branch of the Food Administration deposited their records with the society.

Staff members experienced the war in a personal way when former colleague Ivan H. Epperson died while serving in the Navy. Twenty-nine years old when he volunteered for service in 1917, Epperson need not have left his job as head of the newspaper department. He volunteered out of "a sense of duty to his country," Shoemaker recalled.

A graduate of the School of Journalism who had editorial experience on a La Plata newspaper, Shoemaker's contemporary had developed a deep interest in history. That and his friendship with the secretary who, but for his hearing problem, might also have gone to war, could have caused him to stay with the society for a lengthy career. Epperson contributed biographical articles on Missourians at war to the *Review,* including one of General John J. Pershing. Ivan Epperson died of pneumonia on the transport ship *George Washington* while ferrying troops to France in October 1918. His family buried him in his native Macon County.

Floyd Shoemaker did not work with an editorial board to evaluate manuscripts submitted for publication in the *Review.* He passed judgment himself or relied on the advice of staff members. To a greater extent than would be true of later editors, Shoemaker solicited the articles that he published, which meant that their authors tended to be members of his network of friends. And what he asked of them was more often a personal memoir than a documented scholarly monograph. In the 1920s, the editor repeatedly urged Walter Stevens to write two articles for the journal. One, which Stevens wrote, was on the career of Joseph B. McCullagh, noted editor of the *St. Louis Globe-Democrat* and once Stevens's boss. The article that he did not write would have attempted an explanation of why Missouri had evolved from a predominantly Democratic state after the Civil War to one characterized by a close party balance beginning about 1904. Also more frequently than in later years, authors during this period were lawyers and journalists rather than academics with university degrees in history or a related discipline. In 1928, the *Review* published George Mahan's essay on the Salt River as a setting for events in northeast Missouri. Ten years later, Shoemaker accepted North Todd Gentry's recollection, "Some Judges I Have Known."

Dr. Kate L. Gregg, professor of English at Lindenwood College in St. Charles, represented the scholarly contributors to the *Review* during the 1920s and 1930s. A native of Chehalis, Washington, and a descendant of Forty-Niner gold seekers, she was born in 1883. The University of Washington awarded her a Ph.D. in 1916, and Lindenwood hired her in 1924, where she taught until 1946. Her family background created her research specialties: western trails, particularly the Boon's Lick and Santa Fe, and Fort Osage. Among her publications was *The Road to*

Santa Fe (1952), in which she edited three diaries of travelers, including that of one of the surveyors, George C. Sibley. Gregg submitted several manuscript articles for publication consideration in the *Review*. In 1933 she sent one on the Boon's Lick Road in St. Charles County, which the editorial staff decided was too lengthy. "Since we have been forced to decrease the size of the *Review*," Shoemaker wrote in the spring of that depression year, the several articles in each issue must be briefer. He pointed to a natural break in Gregg's narrative that would allow it to become a two-part article appearing in successive issues of the magazine, which it did. Gregg, an active member of the St. Charles County Historical Society, became a warm friend of the society and often attended annual meetings with colleagues from St. Charles.

As important as the contributed articles were to the *Review*, Shoemaker's own regular departments may have been more instructive to readers. In the back of each issue they found book reviews, often written by the secretary, obituaries of late members of the society, and such features as episodes of Missouri history "not found in textbooks." In his "historical notes and comments" section, the editor offered, in an almost conversational style, a survey of historical news and opinion. In a given column, Shoemaker might comment on the articles found in that issue or their authors, the activities of a county society, a historical preservation effort somewhere in the state, or one of the society's recent acquisitions. The editor's quarterly feature was a clearinghouse of useful and interesting information.

The library building, which had seemed so spacious in 1915, quickly filled with university and historical society materials and their users. By 1931 at the latest, Shoemaker and the finance committee actively investigated ways to expand the work areas and storage space available to the society. Most acute was the need for newspaper storage space. In October 1931 and June 1932, the committee considered requesting of the General Assembly a special appropriation for construction of a separate newspaper storage building. The society did not make the request, since the depression was drying up funds for its regular appropriations. In 1933, Isidor Loeb, aware that for the first time the federal government was granting funds for job-creating construction projects, suggested that Washington could provide either a newspaper storage facility or a new wing for the library building. The Public Works Administration (PWA) seemed the most likely supplier of funds.

By the mid-1930s, the society was once again experiencing severe space problems. The lack of adequate storage space necessitated stacking bound volumes of newspapers in a corridor.

In February 1934, the society applied for a $1,200 PWA grant, to be supplemented by $2,800 of the society's funds, for new storage space. Uncomfortable with what he felt were government red tape and inefficiencies in the expenditure of funds, however, Shoemaker continued to explore ways that the society alone could fund a storage building on campus land belonging to the College of Agriculture. By enforcing additional economies of operation, he calculated, increasing membership and therefore income, and soliciting contributions from the state's newspaper editors, the society could generate $2,500, enough to construct an economical structure for storage only. But Loeb resisted any solicitation of editors or "any drastic economy in our present budget" to pay for a building. By June 1934, the discussion had turned from creating new space to using present space more effectively. That spring Loeb stated the consensus: "The most pressing need for the society . . .

is the addition of two wings to the library . . . part of which would be available for the needs of the society."

The prevailing assumption, in 1913–1915 when the university library was planned and constructed and ever since, was that east and west wings would eventually join the original central portion. In 1936, the state constructed the west wing. That action quieted talk of a separate historical society storage facility for several decades. But it created a new debate that occupied the society's leadership during the fall months of 1936. As the *Eighteenth Biennial Report* of December 31, 1936, posed the question: "Since the new wing was constructed for, and will be used by the university library," what space would the university give to the society in the old portion of the building?

One of the society's best friends and most effective advocates over a span of five decades, Elmer Ellis, helped to answer that question. University President Frederick A. Middlebush placed Ellis, then a professor of history, on the university's library committee to "watch out for the needs of our society," as Shoemaker put it. To shorten the tale of a long and somewhat petty dispute over small but coveted spaces, Ellis obtained for the society nearly all that it had requested when university librarian Henry O. Severance resisted some details of its proposal. In the final agreement, the State Historical Society of Missouri gained a first-floor room for its cataloging department, the entire first-floor book stacks, expanded use of the basement stacks, and a basement newspaper reading room.

If Floyd Shoemaker imagined that the society's own quarters in the promised east wing of the library building would materialize during the second half of his long career, he was doomed to disappointment. From its initial promise in 1915 to its realization in 1960, the wait for that addition consumed the entirety of Shoemaker's secretaryship. While he was able to plan the new space, its dedication coincided with his retirement in 1960. By that year, the historical society would display some traits that an observer in 1940 would find quite familiar, but others that would measure departures from the normality of 1915–1940.

3

The Floyd C. Shoemaker Years, 1940–1960

The beginning of a new decade in 1941 was also the start of a new era for the State Historical Society of Missouri. A rush of events in the years 1941–1945 inaugurated a period of significant achievement, which slowed some but moved steadily forward through the late 1940s and the following decade. The most significant work of the society included the acquisition and publication of historical materials and the evaluation and marking of historic sites.

Increased funding by the General Assembly and a reduced use of their veto power by governors encouraged the society's leaders to commit to a policy of significant growth. The state appropriations that appear in Table 3.1 permitted Floyd Shoemaker and the members of the finance committee to believe that the society, for the first time in its history, was adequately funded. Large increases immediately following World War II were especially welcome as a sign of approval in Jefferson City of the society's recent initiatives. The biennial appropriation nearly tripled from 1941–1942 to 1959–1960, as did state support calculated on a monthly basis.

Because membership increased by the numbers that Table 3.2 reports, so also did the discretionary funds filling the Membership Fund (Trust). Secretary Shoemaker continued his policy of actively promoting the society's membership. He also periodically measured his organization's membership against that of comparable state societies. At the end of 1942, he compiled a list showing that the membership of the second

Table 3.1 State Appropriations for the State Historical Society of Missouri, 1941–1942 to 1959–1961

	Total Appropriation	Appropriation Prorated on a Monthly Basis
Jan. 1941 to Dec. 1942	$67,660 (24 months)	$2,919
Jan. 1943 to Dec. 1944	$67,000* $66,420† (24 months)	$2,767 (2% decrease)
Jan. 1945 to June 1947	$95,840‡ (30 months) In three parts: $16,800 Ja–Je '45 $39,520 Jl '45–Je '46 $39,520 Jl '46–Je '47	$3,194 (14% increase)
July 1947 to June 1949	$118,200 (24 months) In two parts: $47,100 Jl '47–Je '48 $71,100 Jl '48–Je '49	$4,925 (36% increase)
July 1949 to June 1951	$137,200 (24 months)	$5,716 (14% increase)
July 1951 to June 1953	$148,600 (24 months)	$6,191 (8% increase)
July 1953 to June 1955	$159,060 (24 months)	$6,627 (7% increase)
July 1955 to June 1957	$171,520 (24 months)	$7,146 (7% increase)
July 1957 to June 1959	$187,556 (24 months) In two parts: $91,540 Jl '57–Je '58 $96,016 Jl '58–Je '59	$7,814 (9% increase)
July 1959 to June 1961	$196,675 (24 months)	$8,194 (5% increase)

Source: Biennial reports to the governor.
* General Assembly approved. † Governor approved. ‡ Start of annual appropriation under new constitution; fiscal year began in July.

largest society, New York's, amounted to only 36 percent of Missouri's membership total. The societies that occupied positions four through nine in Shoemaker's ranking of the largest memberships represented Middle Western states. The largest, Minnesota, claimed 1,535 members; the smallest of these, Ohio, had only 649. A citizen of Ohio, of course, did not have to belong to that state's historical society to tour its museum in Columbus or to partake of other sponsored activities. In that and perhaps other ways, membership figures do not automatically translate into contact or influence. But they are not irrelevant to estimates of outreach. The growing number of Missourians enrolled in the society may have helped to persuade legislators to expend more of the people's tax dollars on this agency.

Throughout the 1940s and 1950s, membership dues remained at one dollar. With a swelling membership increasing the society's non-appropriated income, few cries arose for an increase in dues. The arguments for and against a doubling of the dues, which the society's leaders debated in 1946 and again in 1958–1959, were complex and, on both sides, persuasive. On the one hand, increased revenue from higher dues might persuade the legislature to reduce the appropriation. And a higher membership fee might drive away current and potential members, making the society an exclusive club, unaffordable to many, especially in the 1940s, when two dollars was still a meaningful sum. On the other hand, dues revenue did not cover the cost of editing, printing, and mailing the *Review* to all members. Should not those who used the society's services, rather than all taxpayers, pay for them? This interesting discussion would re-emerge in the 1960s.

Floyd Shoemaker continued to administer the society's operations. One of Shoemaker's tasks was to consult with and make recommendations to the members of the finance committee, "who shall exercise supervisory control" of the society's business, according to the constitution. While "all their actions . . . [are] subject to ratification by the executive committee," the finance committee directed the society's expansion.

Until 1942, the committee's membership remained unchanged: Dr. Isidor Loeb of St. Louis, Roy D. Williams of Boonville, and Ed Swain of Kirksville. In 1942, the first two retired, Loeb having served continuously since 1901. He left the committee not to enjoy inactivity, but rather to free time for his wartime assignment with the Missouri Office

Table 3.2 Membership of the State Historical Society of Missouri, 1941–1961

	Life Members	Annual Members	Editorial Members	Total
1941–1942 (as of 12-31-42)	4	4,258	390	4,796
1943–1944 (as of 12-31-44)	9	4,409	377	4,938
1945–1947 (as of 6-30-47)*	16	5,218	358	5,746
1947–1949 (as of 6-30-49)	18	4,962	339	5,470
1949–1951 (as of 6-30-51)	—†	5,471	340	6,303
1951–1953 (as of 6-30-53)	77	6,248	337	6,695
1953–1955 (as of 6-30-55)	123	7,456	332	8,068
1955–1957 (as of 6-30-57)	196	10,014	318	10,688‡
1957–1959 (as of 6-30-59)	314	10,956	320	11,630
1959–1961 (as of 6-30-61)	—	—	—	13,140§

Source: Biennial reports to the governor.
* Counting period changed to match new fiscal year dates.
† Life and annual not reported separately.
‡ Membership surpassed 10,000 on May 14, 1957.
§ Richard Brownlee's first biennial report did not break total membership into categories.

of Price Administration. The annual meeting of 1941, months prior to Loeb's resignation, passed a resolution ordering that a gift be awarded "to the present member of the finance committee of forty years seniority" and to all future members with equal length of service. The society presented its gift, a portrait of Dr. Loeb by artist J. Scott McNutt, at the annual dinner in April 1942. Continuing as a member of the finance committee was Swain, who was its chair from 1942 to 1959.

In 1943, the first new member in nearly a decade, L. M. White of Mexico, joined the committee. The son of R. M. White, a charter member of the group, Mitch White served on the finance committee well beyond 1960. So did George A. Rozier; as president of the society from 1941 to 1944, the senator met regularly with the committee, inaugurating a practice continued by other chief elected officers. When he left the presidency, Rozier became an appointed member of the finance committee.

The expansion of the committee's membership in 1955 brought three others into top leadership roles. On October 7 of that year the executive committee amended the 1898 bylaws to permit the president to appoint five rather than three trustees to the finance committee. The change also eliminated the requirement, established during the pre-automobile era, that committee members live within a convenient distance of Columbia. In 1955, President L. M. White added Elmer Ellis of Columbia and T. Ballard Watters of Marshfield to the committee. When Swain retired in 1959, W. C. Hewitt of Shelbyville joined the group.

Of the four new committee members during this era, Ellis was the only academic, the successor to Loeb in that respect. Perhaps because of the prominent roles played by journalists in the origin and continuing evolution of the State Historical Society of Missouri, teachers and professionally trained historians have not been numerous in the society's elected leadership. But in the person of key individuals like Elmer Ellis, they have exerted a creative and lasting influence.

Of New England heritage, Ellis was born on his parents' homestead near Anamoose, North Dakota, on July 27, 1901. He grew up in the village of Towner, whose public schools he attended. Bright but poor— Elmer was one of eleven children—the future university president struggled to obtain an education. Like many others, he taught in and was principal of a rural school prior to completion of his bachelor's degree, which he earned partly through correspondence courses. Graduating from the University of North Dakota and elected to Phi Beta Kappa in 1924, Ellis taught high school while earning his M.A. from the same institution in 1925. After three years on the faculty of North Dakota State Teachers College at Mayville, and two more completing the requirements for the Ph.D. at the University of Iowa, Elmer Ellis came to the University of Missouri in 1930.

Like his junior colleagues W. Francis English and Lewis E. Atherton, Ellis cared as much about the art of teaching as the content of courses. He taught aspiring social studies teachers in the School of Education as well as history students in his own department. While serving as Dean of the Faculty of the College of Arts and Sciences in 1949, Ellis was instrumental in gaining a large grant from the Carnegie Foundation for the Advancement of Teaching. It made possible a five-year study intended to improve instruction throughout Missouri's post-secondary system. In 1951–1952, Professor Ellis was a Fulbright Scholar in the Netherlands. Actively involved in historical research, Ellis's major publications focused on dissenters and critics: free-silver Republican Senator Henry M. Teller of Colorado, an important political figure during the economically distressed 1890s, and newspaper humorist Finley Peter Dunne of Chicago, creator of "Mr. Dooley." After serving for a year as acting president of the University of Missouri upon Frederick Middlebush's resignation in 1954, Ellis became president in 1955. As a professor of history, an administrator, and in retirement, Ellis was strategically positioned to aid the society at several critical junctures. His dedication to its role as public educator was as firm as his commitment to classroom instruction.

Of the three journalists who joined the finance committee after 1943, L. M. White gave the longest and most significant service. Leander Mitchell White inherited both a newspaper and an interest in the State Historical Society of Missouri from his father. The only surviving child of R. M. and Isabella (Dinsmore) White, L. M. was born on May 21, 1883, in Mexico, Missouri. His mother grew up in Illinois; both parents could trace their ancestry to the American colonial era. As a high school student, White attended Westminster Academy in Fulton in 1899 and then remained at Westminster College from 1900 to 1904, where he was captain of the football team all four years. Between 1905 and 1917—when he succeeded his father as editor and publisher of the *Evening Ledger*—White held several positions with the *Denver Post* and

In his roles as a university faculty member and administrator, and as a society trustee and officer, Elmer Ellis proved to be a lasting influence on the society. A native of North Dakota, Ellis came to Columbia to teach at the University of Missouri in 1930.

was the central Missouri correspondent for Kansas City and St. Louis papers. His marriage to Maude See produced a daughter and a son. The latter, Robert M. White II, succeeded his father as head of the family publication. In 1921, White became the first president of the Missouri Press Association whose father also had held the office. During World War II, White's numerous war-related services included action as an accredited war correspondent in Alaska and on the Alaskan Military Highway. L. M. White served as the society's president from 1954 to 1957 and was also a long-term member of the finance committee.

Like White, T. (Theron) Ballard Watters and W. C. (William Cresap) Hewitt were small-town newspaper editors. Watters published the *Marshfield Mail* in that southwestern Missouri community, while Hewitt's paper was the *Shelby County Herald,* published in Shelbyville in the north-central part of the state. Each was a lifelong resident of his community. Watters was born in Marshfield on August 25, 1897; Hewitt in Shelbyville on June 23, 1893. Hewitt's family heritage was southern; one set of grandparents from Kentucky had farmed in Shelby County as early as 1835. Watters's father and mother were natives of Illinois and Ohio, respectively. Both future editors attended the university in

Columbia, but neither graduated. Before Hewitt purchased the *Herald* in 1917, he worked for a Shelby County railroad and was principal of a rural school. Watters interrupted his college training in 1917 to join the aviation branch of the army's Signal Corps. He learned the journalist's craft while working for the family business and assumed direction of the *Mail* in 1922, when his father became the town's postmaster. T. Ballard Watters was president of the Missouri Press Association in 1946. From 1968 to 1971, he served as the society's president, and in 1973 the society gave him its Distinguished Service Award. Watters died on March 13, 1976. Hewitt's death came on June 25, 1967, while he still served on the finance committee.

Seven presidents led the society between 1941 and 1960. Four also served on the finance committee and for that reason have frequented this account: Rozier, Loeb, Swain, and White. The three remaining chief elected officers were G. L. Zwick, Rush H. Limbaugh Sr., and E. L. Dale. Six of these seven presidents fulfilled one of the strongest of the society's traditions: they were either lawyers or journalists by profession. As of 1960, in fact, only Isidor Loeb of all the society's fifteen presidents had not followed one of those lines of work, and his academic specialty was state law and lawmaking.

Attorneys Limbaugh of Cape Girardeau and Zwick of St. Joseph represented the extreme southeast and northwest sections of the state. While the society's constitution assured that trustees would originate in all parts of Missouri—one from each congressional district—no legal requirement guaranteed an equitable representation of the state's diverse sections in the presidency over time. But Secretary Shoemaker and incumbent officers and finance committee members included a fair geographic distribution among their criteria when nominating vice presidents and presidents. Other desired goals included a balance of political party affiliation among elected officers and trustees and a demonstrated commitment to the society. The first fifteen presidents of the society represented the communities indicated in Table 3.3. Their incumbencies spanned the years 1898 to 1962, or the first sixty-four years of the society's history.

G. L. (Galius Lawton) Zwick and Rush H. Limbaugh Sr. shared several experiences. Both graduated from the University of Missouri School of Law—Zwick in 1899, Limbaugh in 1918. Active in public life, Limbaugh served one term in the lower house of the legislature following

Table 3.3 Presidents of the State Historical Society of Missouri, 1898–1962

E. W. Stephens, Columbia	1898–1903
H. E. Robinson, Maryville	1903–1907
W. O. L. Jewett, Shelbina	1907–1910
William Southern Jr., Independence	1910–1914
R. M. White, Mexico	1914–1916
Walter B. Stevens, St. Louis	1916–1925
George A. Mahan, Hannibal	1925–1936
Allen McReynolds, Carthage	1936–1941
George A. Rozier, Perryville/Jefferson City	1941–1944
Isidor Loeb, St. Louis	1944–1947
G. L. Zwick, St. Joseph	1947–1950
E. E. Swain, Kirksville	1950–1953
L. M. White, Mexico	1953–1956
Rush H. Limbaugh Sr., Cape Girardeau	1956–1959
E. L. Dale, Carthage	1959–1962

his election in 1930, while Zwick was a member of the Constitutional Convention of 1922–1923. Both served their communities as elected city attorneys and were active in voluntary service organizations. Both the state and the nation recognized contributions such as these. Zwick was a member of the state university's board of curators from 1911 to 1917, and Limbaugh conducted seminars in India about the American legal system in 1959–1960, under a State Department appointment. A legal scholar as well as a practicing attorney, Limbaugh wrote *Pleading, Practice, Procedure, and Forms in Missouri,* a two-volume reference work, and articles for legal journals. He was president of the Missouri Bar Association in 1955–1956.

Born in Macon on the hundredth birthday of the United States, July 4, 1876, G. L. Zwick was another representative of the non-southern segment of Missouri's population. His father was Canadian, his mother from Iowa. Limbaugh's family, by contrast, left North Carolina for Missouri. His grandparents began farming in Bollinger County in 1811, where Rush was born on September 27, 1891. While Zwick exceeded the life expectancy of men in his generation, passing away on September 22, 1961, at the age of eighty-five, Rush Limbaugh confounded actuarial science. He died on April 8, 1996, at the age of 104, leaving behind a famous radio talk-show host in his grandson and namesake, as well as a productive legal career of seventy-eight years.

Journalist E. L. Dale, publisher of the *Carthage Evening Press,* had already begun his career when the university established its journalism school in 1908. He was, in fact, a rarity among those occupying the society's active leadership positions in never having attended college. Born August 14, 1890, in Kendall, Wisconsin, Dale worked as a printer's devil both in Iola, Kansas, and Carthage to help support his fatherless family. He was only twelve years old when he took his job with the *Carthage Democrat* in 1903. Later he served as reporter, city editor, and, beginning in 1944, publisher of the *Press* (later called the *Evening Press*). President of the Missouri Press Association and the Missouri Associated Press, Dale in 1953 earned the University of Missouri's award for exemplary service to journalism. He died on December 22, 1969.

I

The finance committee's actions at its December 9, 1944, meeting suggest much about the society's rush of acquisitions during the World War II years. The committee convened in Kansas City, following a dinner with the artist Thomas Hart Benton. The State Historical Society of Missouri now owned nine of Benton's well-known war propaganda paintings, and its leadership wished to meet the artist before inviting him to Columbia for a formal unveiling of his work. Committee members considered two other additions to the society's collections at their December 9 meeting. They authorized the purchase of Vance Randolph's "Ozark Folksongs" manuscript and gave first consideration to the donation of Daniel Fitzpatrick's *St. Louis Post-Dispatch* editorial cartoons. The society's most significant acquisition of the 1940s, and the most important since the Francis Sampson collection had arrived in 1901, was not on the agenda in late 1944, except when questions of managing it arose: The J. Christian Bay Collection already occupied its own room on the second floor of the university library building.

Dr. J. Christian Bay immigrated to the United States from his native Denmark in 1892. Born in 1871, he received a science education at the University of Copenhagen that led to several careers in his adopted country. Bay's first American home was St. Louis, where he was an assistant at the Missouri Botanical Garden until 1894. His résumé included such varied positions as bacteriologist for the Iowa State Board of Health in the mid-1890s and head of the medical reference section of the John Crerar Library in Chicago from 1909 to 1927. Bay came to the Crerar in 1905 and spent the remainder of his working life there, serving as its head librarian from 1927 to 1947. From his father, who had spent nearly two decades on the American frontier as a young man, Bay acquired an interest in the broad region defined by the Ohio, Mississippi, and Missouri River valleys. By 1941, he had for forty years collected original print sources—books, maps, manuscripts—"on western travel, exploration and activity," as Dr. Bay himself described their content. We today would substitute the term "Midwest" for what he called the "West." As the head of a richly endowed private library, Bay found many opportunities to purchase materials on the region. He was free to add such items to his personal collection because the Crerar was a science library uninterested in Americana.

Floyd Shoemaker learned of Bay's collection in October 1940. The Chicagoan was a member of the State Historical Society of Missouri, and Shoemaker claimed that he "is a friend of mine although I have never met him." When University of Missouri librarian Ben E. Powell purchased a private book collection in Chicago for the university, Shoemaker recommended that he consult with Bay about the collection's value. Upon his return to Columbia, Powell told the secretary about the hundreds of volumes that lined the walls of Bay's Crerar Library office. "I could not get the matter out of my head," Shoemaker admitted, and on February 26, 1941, he wrote to Bay, suggesting that if the librarian had "reached that stage in life when you have begun planning disposal of" his private collection, the society would be interested in learning its price.

Bay's answer, dated March 3, was promising. He was nearly seventy years old, Bay wrote, and knew that his children were uninterested in maintaining his personal library. Several book dealers and university libraries had inquired about purchasing it, but Bay had put them off, fearing that his books would be "scattered by auction or bookseller's sale. It also would be contrary to my principles to fish for offers and accept the highest bid." Whether, as Shoemaker believed, Bay decided to deal with the society because it resided in the state that was his first

American home cannot be known. But, clearly, the librarian appreciated Shoemaker's candor in asking for a cash price and his promise that the society would not sell any part of the collection. Bay's response was as direct as Shoemaker's question: "I would accept $17,500 for all my holdings, nothing reserved, if the material could be kept together. . . . I feel satisfied that this price would be fair to both of us."

Floyd Shoemaker knew full well that for his agency, a single expenditure of $17,500 was not only large, but positively enormous. During the several months of deliberation over the purchase of Bay's library, the secretary calculated that the historical society had spent, between 1901 and 1940, a total of $17,544.85 of state funds for books and an additional $2,091.13 from the Membership Fund (Trust). That was a total of $19,635.98 for all the books it had ever purchased, as against $17,500 for a collection comprising more than 2,500 items. It was incumbent on the society to prove what Shoemaker, and soon members of the finance committee, wanted to believe. That is, that Bay's collection of mint-condition rare books and other printed materials would achieve for the society's library a reputation that, good as it was, it still lacked. As the secretary phrased it to Isidor Loeb in early March: "The acquisition of such a collection would attract and maintain national attention. It would give our society . . . national rank in the great field of Middle West and Western Americana." Loeb, still chair of the finance committee, caught Shoemaker's enthusiasm. "I feel that you should examine the collection as soon as possible and if it turns out to be as good as represented we should make every effort to secure it."

The secretary spent a week with Bay's collection in March 1941, and returned home with the cards on which the Crerar's librarian had recorded information about his purchases. Over the next several months, head cataloger Pearle McCown categorized Bay's holdings, checked for duplications among the society's existing titles, and tried to assess the value of what Bay owned by consulting booksellers' catalogues and auction lists. Completed in early June, McCown's evaluation went to the finance committee members and President Rozier. This careful analysis counted 2,817 items in the collection: 2,039 books, with the remainder including pamphlets, manuscripts, maps, and other materials. McCown placed "an approximate total value of $35,919.12" on the library. Since the society did not already own 83 percent of the sources in the Bay collection, that share of his library was worth $31,991.94, by her calculations. McCown and Shoemaker agreed that the superb quality of many of Bay's rarest titles and the care that the collector had given his library made its actual value close to $50,000. All that for $17,500! Having demonstrated to his satisfaction the value of Dr. Bay's library and the acceptability of his asking price, the secretary recommended purchase.

The finance committee quickly agreed. At their meeting of June 13, 1941, committee members "felt impelled," as their minutes worded it, "to close the deal as soon as possible." On June 16, Bay accepted the society's offer to purchase his library at his price. Lawyers George Rozier and Roy Williams drew up a contract, which both parties signed while meeting at the Hotel Jefferson in St. Louis on June 27.

From early March through the summer of 1941, the society's leaders struggled with an even more complex question than that of making the purchase: how best to pay for it. The question of whether to buy Bay's collection offered only two choices, yes or no. How to finance the transaction required examination of many alternatives. One possibility was to ask the General Assembly for a special appropriation to cover all or part of the purchase price. As early as March 5, Loeb discouraged this solution. Legislative debate, by publicizing the society's interest in the collection, might arouse competing purchasers with whom Bay did not wish to deal. Furthermore, an extraordinary request for state funds "might have a bad effect upon the budget we have submitted for regular purposes."

A second possibility, to be used exclusively or in combination with a special appropriation, was to obtain donations from friends of the society. From mid-June, when the finance committee determined to make the purchase, through late July, Secretary Shoemaker and committee members made a concerted effort to solicit the entire purchase price from several wealthy prospects. The donor's name, the society was willing to promise, would appear on the collection with Bay's. This strategy failed to raise any money. By July 24, A. P. Green of Mexico, Judge Marion C. Early of St. Louis, Theodore Gary of Macon, J. C. Penney of New York City, and Mrs. Dulany Mahan of Hannibal, the widow of George Mahan's son, had declined to contribute. The merchandiser Penney, a Missouri native, explained: "The calls upon me are legion . . . and I cannot add to my present commitments." Theodore Gary wrote that "we are in no position to make any cash commitments at this time. . . . on account of the unsettled condition of general business." Shoemaker's private response to Gary's letter became his reaction to all the rejections: "It blasts hopes and confirms fears."

The finance committee's members reflected on and discussed a third method of financing the Bay purchase throughout the period that the society sought donations. As early as March 5, Dr. Loeb stated that, if other sources did not provide the money, "our Trust Fund offers the best plan. . . . I have always felt that this fund has been established for a purpose of this character." On August 1, Shoemaker gave President Rozier the same conclusion: the Membership Fund (Trust) should pay the entire cost of purchasing the Bay Collection "since that is what the fund was created for as I see it and as I believe you see it."

A second justification for making the Bay acquisition with the society's private funds reveals a lingering nervousness about the existence of this growing account. Not only did the historical society have $26,000 invested in government bonds in 1941, and the interest income that investment provided, but Shoemaker also estimated—correctly, it turned out—that "the society's membership receipts will . . . be $4,000 to $5,000 a year within the next several years." He and the finance committee members wished to avoid an embarrassment of riches. Still in effect was the 1933 law requiring state agencies to turn over their nonappropriated revenue to the state, legislation that the finance committee continued to argue did not apply to the State Historical Society of Missouri. If the society could spend its private monies for acquisitions that were beyond criticism, such as the Bay Collection or a significant work of art related to the state's history, the very act of diminishing the funds would protect them. As Secretary Shoemaker put it to Loeb: "If . . . the society bought the collection from the Membership Fund (Trust) then we have the strongest claim on budget officers, appropriation chairmen, and governors for continuing control of our private income and investments." Prompted by a complex mix of motives, then, the finance committee purchased the Bay Collection through the sale of some of its securities.

Bay's library, packed in shipping boxes, arrived in Columbia late in November 1941. Awaiting it was the special rare book room that the university's Ben Powell and Elmer Ellis had procured for the collection. Later in the decade, these two friends of the historical society would also obtain a partitioned section of corridor and an additional room on the library's third floor for the Thomas Hart Benton paintings and Daniel R. Fitzpatrick drawings. In the society's hands, the Bay Collection continued to be what Dr. Bay had made it: a continually expanding library specializing in the "Middle Border," to apply the Hamlin Garland phrase that Floyd Shoemaker used. In June 1941, the finance committee spent over $700 for the forty-volume set of Edward S. Curtis's *North American Indians*, which Bay's inventory lacked. Dr. Bay occasionally advised Shoemaker on the purchase of additions to the collection, suggesting in May 1943, for example, the acquisition of two maps. Bay himself made additional contributions to what he called "our collection." In his *Twenty-fourth Biennial Report* (1949), the secretary reported that the Bay Collection "now consists of 3,750 items," a growth of approximately 1,000 since 1941. The society made one of the more expensive additions to the rare book library in 1958, with the purchase of the first English edition of *Travels in the Interior of North America* by Maximilian, Prince of Wied. Printed in London in 1843–1844, the two-volume set contained eighty-one colored plates by Karl Bodmer, in addition to the text, a folding map, and an atlas.

On April 20, 1942, following its annual business meeting, the society ceremonially opened the rare book room, presenting the Bay Collection to those officers, trustees, and members present. Pearle McCown, the cataloger whose knowledge of this significant addition to the society's library was inferior only to that of Dr. Bay, defined it in her remarks as "one of the two most outstanding collections of Western Americana in this country," ranking behind only the Ayer Collection owned by Chicago's Newberry Library. Although U.S. participation in World War II was less than five months old on April 20, and the shock of the nation's jarring entry into the conflict had not disappeared, the annual dinner proceeded as planned that evening. The honored guest, J. Christian Bay, addressed the banquet. On April 23, while on the train returning him to Chicago, Bay wrote to thank Shoemaker for his "beautiful and elevating" visit to the society and Columbia. He was grateful "that a group of fine and live people have approved of what we jointly sealed and delivered." One of those people taught history at the university. A month after the annual meeting, Elmer Ellis wrote to his colleague Lewis Atherton: "The Bay Collection which Shoemaker secured seems to be a real one."

The financial impact of the purchase was "real," too, as the secretary and the finance committee members had already learned in March. Since

Floyd C. Shoemaker and J. Christian Bay examine one of the volumes in Bay's collection of Middle Western Americana during the official opening of the collection in the society's quarters on April 20, 1942.

1939, George Caleb Bingham's *Order No. 11* had hung in the society's reading room. The owner of the historic work, C. B. Rollins Sr., a son of Bingham's friend James S. Rollins, died in July 1940. In mid-March 1942, the several heirs to his estate offered to sell the painting to the society for $8,000, a full $2,000 less than the price requested in 1935. Simultaneously, a rare book dealer in Los Angeles offered for sale the Morse Mark Twain Collection, which, Shoemaker understood, "is reputed to be the second most complete in the United States." The asking price was $12,500. The secretary thought the owner would accept $11,000, and he initially proposed a cooperative purchase with the university library on a fifty-fifty basis.

After carefully analyzing either purchase or both of them for the finance committee, however, Shoemaker recommended against further significant expenditures from the society's discretionary funds. *Order No. 11* would absorb "nearly three-fourths of the society's investments in the Membership Fund (Trust)," he reported to Loeb on March 18, and the Morse Collection even more. Six days later, Shoemaker reported his projections of the future expenses of maintaining the Bay Collection. When added to the initial price of that library, these continuing costs "do not permit . . . [the society] to purchase either the painting" or the

Twain books and manuscripts. The State Historical Society of Missouri was an institution of limited means that had to make choices. The choice of acquiring the Bay Collection precluded other significant purchases for the present. Fortunately, the valuable Bingham was still available when the society again had sizeable amounts to spend on its collections.

In his *Semicentennial History* of the society, published in 1948, Floyd Shoemaker observed that the period since 1941 "was to be as noteworthy for its historical art acquisitions as for" other achievements. Indeed, the agency began systematically to create its noted art collection then. Equally noteworthy is the haphazard, almost accidental, way in which the finance committee began collecting paintings and drawings related in some way to Missouri's history, and the reluctance (at least initially) of some participants to embark on this endeavor. That reluctance grew less from the absence of a gallery in which to display valuable works of art than from other considerations. One was the society's proper mission. In March 1942, for example, Isidor Loeb admitted that he did not share the enthusiasm of others within the society's leadership circle for developing "historical museums and art collections. I felt that these were secondary" to the major purpose of the organization, which Loeb defined as "arousing interest in Missouri history through the collection of books, pamphlets and manuscripts, [and] the development of research and publication."

In 1942, Abbott Laboratories, an Illinois pharmaceutical firm, commissioned Thomas Hart Benton to paint a set of eight scenes interpreting U.S. participation in World War II. Collectively known as *The Year of Peril,* these widely reproduced works did not minimize "the kind of hard ferocity that men must have to beat down the evil that is now upon us," Benton remarked. The artist dedicated his paintings "to those new Americans" of the postisolationist era who found within themselves "new wills to see what is what and to come to grips with it, in this Year of Peril," 1942. At the midpoint of his career during World War II, the Neosho-born Benton was best known in Missouri for his murals painted in 1935–1936 in the House lounge at the state capitol. The controversy over the murals' subject matter and Benton's style remained alive during the war years.

In the spring of 1944, Estelle Mandel of the Associated American Artists, Inc., of New York, which had physical custody of Benton's

Year of Peril paintings, offered them to the society on behalf of Abbott Laboratories. On June 10, the finance committee voted its enthusiastic acceptance of the unexpected gift. In July, Benton added a ninth painting "as my personal gift" to the society: "a large portrait (4 × 5 feet) of a Negro soldier" commissioned, but not used by, the U.S. government in its effort to build public support for the war effort. In a letter to his friend L. M. White, Benton offered even more. "I would like to house what I have done" in the field of propaganda art "in an historical museum." Additional gifts, "however, will depend on your exhibition facilities. I don't want to load you with more than you can handle." By late August 1944, the society had received and the finance committee had inspected *The Year of Peril,* and it instructed Secretary Shoemaker to arrange a meeting with Benton in Kansas City, where he lived and worked most of the year.

President Loeb, no longer on the committee, was "most delighted" with the gift. White, now a committee member, expressed his "enthusiasm and personal admiration of Mr. Benton and his work." Floyd Shoemaker, ever more cautious as the years passed of innovations that might harm the society's interests, initially opposed accepting Benton's work. While the well-known paintings would be an asset to the society, they also might cause "some controversy which after all, will result only in more publicity" of the sort his institution did not need. Whether Shoemaker feared adverse public opinion or a negative response in state government is not clear, nor did the secretary name the possible reason for controversy. Perhaps it was the artist rather than the art. A meeting with Benton was necessary, the secretary wrote Loeb on June 30, to "make friends with him to be sure he didn't tear the roof off the banquet chamber" if invited to address the society's annual dinner meeting. But the paintings themselves may have triggered Shoemaker's anxiety. The historical society paid the shipping and insurance costs of moving *The Year of Peril* from New York to Columbia, and he urged that payment come from the Membership Fund (Trust). Should criticism of Benton's paintings develop, no one could charge the society with using its state appropriation on their behalf.

The committee's meeting with Benton in Kansas City on December 9, 1944, quieted Shoemaker's fears. The artist was "a very intelligent, considerate gentleman. . . . We agreed that there was no danger in our having an annual dinner and him for the speaker of the evening." The committee invited Benton to attend the 1945 annual meeting for the exhibit of his works. With reference to additional gifts of Benton's work, Loeb and White explained that when the state added the east wing to the university library building, the historical society would have the facilities to "permit adequate display of the paintings and possibly other works of art." Thomas Hart Benton was present on May 2, 1945, to help open the exhibit of his paintings *The Year of Peril* and *Negro Soldier,* although because of wartime austerities the society canceled its dinner. The artist returned on April 25, 1946, as speaker at the annual banquet.

The *St. Louis Post-Dispatch*'s editorial cartoonist Daniel R. Fitzpatrick presented the society with another art collection shortly after it had received Benton's gift. Born in Superior, Wisconsin, in 1891, Fitzpatrick attended the Chicago Art Institute and began drawing for that city's *Daily News* in 1911. Two years later he began a forty-five-year career with the *Post-Dispatch,* during which he won two Pulitzer Prizes. Fellow journalist L. M. White, a personal friend of the cartoonist, was responsible for Fitzpatrick's donations of his work in 1945 and 1952. By 1988 the society's Fitzpatrick Collection consisted of more than 1,500 items; however, the original idea was more modest.

The finance committee, in December 1944, approved White's proposal to obtain Fitzpatrick's World War II cartoons and others relating to Missouri issues. Both the Mexico editor and Thomas Hart Benton assured the artist that the state historical society, although it occupied crowded quarters, was a good place to deposit his work for preservation. By the end of the month, Fitzpatrick had agreed to make the gift. Shoemaker soon spoke of an editorial cartoon collection that included the work appearing in other St. Louis and Kansas City papers. On February 8, 1945, Isidor Loeb joined E. E. Swain, L. M. White, George Rozier, and Shoemaker to host Fitzpatrick for dinner at the Jefferson Hotel in St. Louis. The visitors went to the *Post-Dispatch* offices the following morning. After looking through several hundred cartoons, the society's representatives were still unable to make specific selections, so they finally requested all of them, and Fitzpatrick agreed to ship them to Columbia. By mid-March, the crated drawings began arriving, and by May the society had inventoried 1,273 of the artist's cartoons that had first appeared in his newspaper and in *Colliers* magazine.

Editorial cartoons create controversy. Like satirists who write fiction or essays—writers like Mark Twain, for example—their creators ridicule pretension and expose human folly. It is surprising, given the nature of Fitzpatrick's work, that only one objection to the acquisition of this first installment of the society's political cartoon collection exists in the documentary record. State senator Frank Briggs privately expressed dismay over the society's ownership of cartoons that had unspecified Missouri political events as their subject. Floyd Shoemaker personally assured the senator "that the society had no intention of publicly displaying those cartoons which were embarrassing to individuals now living." Daniel Fitzpatrick could not attend the 1946 annual meeting when he would have been a featured speaker, but, according to Shoemaker, his "cartoons will be on display . . . and will be the outstanding event of the day." The society continues to display them, from time to time, in its corridor gallery.

Perhaps the single most significant fine art acquisition of the 1940s was George Caleb Bingham's *Order No. 11,* also known as *Martial Law,* which the artist had painted between 1865 and 1868. As Secretary Shoemaker knew even prior to its purchase, "there seems reasonable probability of our society being able to eventually have an outstanding Bingham collection." He cited the artist's portraits of John Woods Harris, Vinnie Ream, and James Shannon, the genre painting *Watching the Cargo,* and Bingham's correspondence with James S. Rollins—all in the historical society's possession. Shoemaker compiled that list in May 1945 for a descendant of Bingham who wished to donate not art, but two family heirlooms, to the society. "We have on deposit . . . Bingham's outstanding historical painting 'Order Number Eleven,'" the secretary informed this correspondent, "which we hope eventually to purchase." In the spring of 1942, of course, the society had rejected the Rollins family's offer of the work for $8,000, both because it lacked funds and because Floyd Shoemaker considered it an expensive "white elephant." The painting's size—six by eight feet—made it too large for any but the most commodious exhibition hall, he believed. "It is entirely out of place in its present location and dwarfs everything in the society's reading room."

While that may have been true, the society still wanted the painting. Owning a replenished Membership Fund (Trust) account and having incurred only incidental costs in connection with the Benton and Fitzpatrick donations, the finance committee on May 2, 1945, instructed Shoemaker to "enter into negotiations with the owners . . . to see if it could be bought and, if so, at what price." The committee was willing to pay as much as the 1935 price, $10,000. There existed an appreciating market for Bingham's works: Shoemaker learned, for instance, that Thomas K. Smith of Boatmen's Bank in St. Louis had purchased the artist's *County Election* and *Verdict of the People* for $7,500 each. What the secretary had once regarded as a "white elephant" now assumed new value in his thinking. As aesthetically and financially worthy as were the works owned by Boatmen's Bank, no Bingham "has seized the public mind both over the years and in the present so much as 'Order No. 11.'" The painting was Bingham's angry protest against one of the most infamous actions in Missouri history, the forced evacuation of civilians from western border counties as dictated by Union General Thomas Ewing's "Order No. 11" in August 1863. Bingham's work was an investment as well as a historical document. Earlier in 1945, Thomas Hart Benton had advised the finance committee that the painting "was a buy at $10,000 and that some day it would be worth $50,000."

A number of heirs to the C. B. Rollins estate, most of whom lived in Columbia, owned a piece of *Order No. 11,* and the only real obstacle to closing the deal was their agreement on a price. By July 3, 1945, the society and the estate had agreed to a contract stipulating a price of $9,000, to be paid in three installments, the final one due two years later. That autumn, James Roth of Kansas City's Nelson Gallery of Art came to the society's quarters to clean the new acquisition and its other Binghams, as Benton had recommended. In November, the society purchased the artist's *Scene on the Ohio* (1851) from its owner in New York City for $500. In 1952, the society bought fourteen of Bingham's pencil sketches from two Rollins family members, but it was unwilling to buy every Bingham offered to it. The finance committee rejected, in 1946, two portraits that carried a $300 price tag. The expanding art collection also featured the works of other artists. In 1954, for example, the historical society purchased Walter de Maris's *The Westward March of America* (1846), which depicted a scene near the square in Independence.

The society made many other useful acquisitions during the 1940s and 1950s. Upon the adjournment of Missouri's Constitutional Convention of 1943–1944, for example, its officers deposited with the historical society the "verified verbatim steno type transcription" of its proceedings, in twenty-three volumes. Sarah Lockwood Williams enhanced her husband's scrapbook collection in 1945, and four years later the Missouri D.A.R. deposited genealogical records compiled by its local chapters. By way of purchases and gifts, the society's large collection of Missouri newspapers grew. Beginning in 1943, the *St. Louis Post-Dispatch* annually donated a microfilm copy of the paper. In 1950, Ed Swain gave his *Kirksville Daily Express* on film for the period 1906–1949. Five years earlier, the finance committee paid $1,000 for the library of the *Kansas City Journal,* including 2,097 issues of the paper, covering 1855 to 1942. Also in 1945, Shoemaker obtained the file of the *Richmond Conservator* from the 1850s to 1900.

On several occasions, the society declined to increase the collections. It rejected the forty-five volumes of the 1880 manuscript census schedules for Missouri in 1955, records that it already owned on microfilm. Friends of the society continued during this era to offer the staff information on manuscript collections: rescued courthouse documents here, church records there, a collection of personal letters somewhere else. And new ways of preserving the record of the past came to the staff's attention, including commercially marketed speeches on vinyl records and filmed copies of television programs. Although he inquired about them, Shoemaker made no attempt to build audio or video collections.

Considered together, what was the lasting significance of the major acquisitions of the years 1941 to 1945? To begin with, on the eve of its semicentennial, the society acquired an important rare book collection and began a serious art collection that, even as the agency turns one hundred, are major reasons for its uniqueness among historical societies. Most of its rare book purchases since 1941 have gone into the Bay Collection. The society's enhancement of the art collection since 1945 has concentrated on additional Bentons, Binghams, and editorial cartoons by artists other than Fitzpatrick.

One way to think about some of the society's special collections is to consider who, of all Missourians, has made the largest impact on American society, culture, and politics. On most short lists of such persons would appear the names of Harry S. Truman, Mark Twain, George Caleb Bingham, and Thomas Hart Benton. By means of its 1940s acquisitions, the society added important works by the two painters and to its Twain holdings and made an implied commitment to enhance those collections in the future. Only because of the presidential library system inaugurated by Franklin D. Roosevelt and endorsed by his successor, Harry S. Truman, has the society not specialized in materials relating to the career of Missouri's only president.

Their specialization in Twain, Bingham, and Benton gives the society's collections strength not in political, military, or economic history, but rather in Missouri's and the nation's cultural heritage. And, it is important to observe, this native literary and visual expression constitutes a democratic art. For who were these artists' subjects? Not the local ruling groups, if one excludes some of Bingham's portraits, but common Missourians living their everyday lives.

In Bingham's works one may view laborers on the rivers of the American interior or Missouri citizens participating in a political process that had meaning at the grassroots level. His *Order No. 11* depicted, as well as any serious American painting has, the destruction wrought by governmental tyranny. In Twain's masterpiece *Huckleberry Finn,* a reader can experience on several levels a nineteenth-century Missouri author and his lower-class characters sharing cultural traditions and human sympathies across racial boundaries that were still virtually impermeable in real life. Thomas Hart Benton, as Lyman Field affirmed in his address to the annual meeting in 1989, "disdained, without malice, high society . . . but he deeply loved what he called 'the solid underneath layer' of common folk," those he depicted in his work. Benton's prostitutes and blacks and farmers were part of the great unwashed multitude he celebrated, but that his critics found unacceptable in true art. Daniel Fitzpatrick's cartoons attacked urban political corruption in Missouri's two large cities and racial segregation throughout the state when both flourished, while they defended individual rights and promoted social justice. Later, in agreeing to publish Vance Randolph's *Ozark Folksongs,* the society would enter the realm of folk art, the noncommercial, vernacular, orally transmitted art of the folk, or people. What better ways existed, one might ask, for the State Historical Society of Missouri to fulfill the charge given it by the editors in 1898 and the state the next year, than to build these specialized collections during the 1940s?

II

At the same time that the state historical society successfully expanded its functions during the years 1941–1960, it failed to benefit from two other attempts to build collections of research materials. The society itself initiated the first of these projects. During World War II, as in the first global conflict twenty-five years earlier, Floyd Shoemaker and his staff published, between October 1942 and October 1945, a series of thirteen extended articles on "Missouri and the War" in the *Missouri Historical Review.* But the secretary wanted his agency to contribute a more lasting documentation of Missouri's war experience than these factual accounts. Thus, at war's end, the society launched the Missouri war letters project, which would never acquire a more formal title. An appeal for the public's cooperation, issued in November 1945, requested the donation "of war letters, diaries, and photographs of Missouri boys and girls in the armed services." The goal seems to have been a collection of as many as a hundred thousand items. This archive would do for historical research what newspaper correspondent Ernie Pyle and cartoonist Bill Mauldin had done for their wartime publics: document the average soldier's and sailor's experience in World War II. "Sketches of boot training in camp. . . . excitement, fear, heartbreak at railroad station partings and overseas embarkations . . . anecdotes pathetic, comical, heroic, of life in the armed service"—in requesting such sources, Shoemaker wanted the materials for a truly grassroots history of men and women at war.

The goal was admirable; the result proved disappointing. The fragmentary records of the war letters project suggest some causes for its failure. One problem was the late start. Other states preceded Missouri in initiating, as well as committed greater resources to implementing, the collection of first-person accounts by armed forces personnel. In 1942, Ohio's governor, for example, established the Ohio War History Commission to undertake that and other functions. The Ohio Archaeological and Historical Society aided the commission rather than sustained the entire project. That Secretary Shoemaker launched his project only at war's end—gaining the finance committee's endorsement three months after Japan's surrender—and that no other agency of state government contributed to it, may have doomed the effort from the start.

Shoemaker's plan for assembling war letters depended for its success upon private organizations, and he too-casually assumed their cooperation. Since his small budget and skeletal staff could not support fieldwork, he assigned mayors, local school officials, and veterans' groups the job of collecting the documents that the society's newspaper announcements would persuade citizens to contribute. He should not have been surprised when none of these individuals and organizations did his bidding. Shoemaker tried to do to others what he would not allow others to do to his society—determine its agenda and set its priorities. Veterans' groups like the American Legion, as Missouri Adjutant General John A. Harris pointed out in May 1946, were competing with each other to enroll the millions of returning veterans as members. They cared little about an archive of war documents.

Perhaps the fundamental cause of this project's failure was the "natural reluctance," of which Shoemaker was aware, of veterans and their families to surrender meaningful mementos of intense personal experience to an agency of government about which many knew very little. For some Missouri families, the last tangible contact with a dead father or son lay embedded in a crumpled letter mailed from the European or Pacific war theaters. Mrs. R. G. Allen of Weston, whose son R. Gorman Allen Jr. had died overseas, wrote to the society at the end of 1945. "Mr. Shoemaker, will these letters be returned to us? Our only boy is gone, so the letters we have from him and his crew will never be replaced by our dear son. Please tell me this." The secretary could only reply that the projected collection would be a permanent one, that he could not accept letters on loan, but that Mrs. Allen could send carefully made copies of the originals. Many others across the state, without writing to the society, must have rejected yielding valued personal possessions to the cause of historical documentation. On July 1, 1946, after more than six months' effort, Secretary Shoemaker admitted that "the number [of letters] we have acquired is pathetically small as compared to the goal we seek. We now have but several hundred." Within weeks of that date, traces of the war letters project disappear from the society's records, although in later years, such collections were occasionally received.

The second opportunity to enhance the society's collections occurred during the war. Members of the university history department who founded the Western Historical Manuscript Collection (WHMC) in 1942–1943 invited the society to cooperate, which it briefly did. But less than one year after its endorsement of the project, the finance committee ended its participation in this program to create a manuscript archive. From December 1943 until after Floyd Shoemaker's retirement in 1960, two separate manuscript collections resided in the university's library building.

History professor Elmer Ellis was the man most responsible for establishing the Western Historical Manuscript Collection. In 1942, he applied successfully to the Rockefeller Foundation for $15,000 "to establish a center of research and teaching on the history and culture of the Great Plains and Western Prairie regions." The University of Missouri supplemented that sum with an additional $5,000. In truth, Ellis told David H. Stevens of the foundation's Humanities Division, the project was not new, but rather aimed to "improve and greatly expand the center that already exists here in Columbia" in the university's and society's libraries. Although the collection would be regional in scope, Missouri—the "Mother of the West"—would be the hunting ground for undiscovered manuscript sources. "Missouri manuscripts, especially those in the old Missouri River towns which served as the starting place for Great Plains trails and migration, [are] probably the most important unexploited sources on Great Plains history." And Ellis expected to find in "the attics of the older families" letters "back home" from Missourians who had migrated to the California gold fields or Oregon agricultural valleys decades earlier.

The need to find and preserve such sources was pressing. Ellis wrote to Stevens of how the wartime "waste paper drive [was] making . . . substantial inroads into these records." He apparently knew that some people had thrown away collections of nineteenth-century letters in a patriotic effort to aid the nation's cause. In a memoir written in the 1960s or after, Professor Ellis recalled another "stimulation" or motive for founding the WHMC. Upon his retirement from the governorship in 1941, Lloyd C. Stark had offered his papers to the State Historical Society of Missouri. Secretary Shoemaker had "refused them on the grounds that the society did not have room to house them." The incident brought vividly to Ellis's attention how little effort existed in Missouri to collect, process, preserve, and make accessible manuscript sources. The state historical society ought to have performed these functions, Ellis implied. But the society's secretary "had little understanding or appreciation of the value of manuscripts," Ellis recalled years later. "His own historical experience had been in printed materials and the manuscripts he had in the society had come from local families like the Rollins where he could not very well say no." Shoemaker's training was in political science, Ellis might have added, not history.

The state historical society's records reveal that Elmer Ellis did not fully appreciate Shoemaker's attitudes toward and the organization's experience in the field of manuscript collection. He did not appreciate the degree to which severe limits—of space, of staff, of money, of all conceivable resources—dictated the society's decisions. In April 1941, Shoemaker wrote to former governor Stark that "I appreciate the worth of the collection" of the retired chief executive's papers. But he advised Stark that the state and his own family "would benefit more from your papers if they were retained by you until the society has more adequate and appropriate housing facilities." Should the governor insist, Shoemaker would store the manuscripts in a basement room, where there were no facilities for patrons or even Stark himself to use them. Alternatively, the secretary would try to locate space for the collection in parts of the library building assigned to the university. The only satisfactory solution was realization of "one of my cherished dreams," construction of the society's enlarged quarters in the promised east wing. Shoemaker was no pessimist: "It should be realized within the near future."

Also in 1941, the widow of former governor Herbert S. Hadley spoke with the secretary about accepting his official papers. Again, the requirements of accepting a collection were more than the society could meet. Hadley's "papers" included museum items, but the society had no museum. And the former Mrs. Hadley, now Mrs. Henry J. Haskell of Kansas City, wanted the governor's papers kept apart from the society's other manuscript collections. "She desires . . . a special room, a Hadley room. . . . She is willing to spend several thousand dollars fitting up such a room." Involved at the moment in outfitting a rare book room for the Bay Collection, Shoemaker apparently did not pursue the Hadley matter. The Stark and Hadley papers were among the earliest acquisitions of the WHMC.

In other cases, however, the society did acquire manuscript collections, and not only those which Shoemaker could not refuse, as Professor Ellis believed. In her unpublished "Sketch of History and Activities of State Historical Society of Missouri," dated 1933, Sarah Guitar wrote that in addition to published materials, the society actively sought "old letters, diaries, account books, and other valuable MSS [manuscripts]." Well before Ellis initiated his project, the state historical society obtained manuscript collections from some of the old Missouri River towns. Shoemaker enlisted Professor Jonas Viles's assistance in 1928 to evaluate "a large amount of manuscript material which had been offered for sale to us by a certain Mr. [William H.] Nixon of Boonville." The society purchased correspondence and a ledger book of Dr. John Sappington, the frontier physician of Saline County. In 1936, it bought from a farmer in the Rocheport area business records from Moses U. Payne's Columbia retail stores and his Great Plains wagon freight business. Secretary Shoemaker was not unmindful of the worth of such sources: "The day journals of Payne's stores are invaluable for a research worker in the field of history and economics."

The society worked closely with Professor Frederic A. Culmer of Central College in Fayette to acquire the papers, ca. 1820–1863, of lawyer and jurist Abiel Leonard. Shoemaker asked Culmer in July 1935 about material remaining "in the attic of the old Leonard home," Ravenswood, in Cooper County. He inquired: "Do you think it would be possible to persuade Mr. and Mrs. [R. Perry] Spencer to donate it to the State Historical Society of Missouri?" Through correspondence conducted in 1934, the society's chief administrator attempted to track down the nineteenth-century letters exchanged between John Hiram Lathrop, the first president of the University of Missouri, and James S. Rollins. He contacted Lathrop descendants in his search and enlisted the aid of society president George A. Mahan, who knew the family. Three years later, Shoemaker tried to persuade the sons of former U.S. Senator Francis Marion Cockrell to alter the conditions of a temporary deposit they had made of a portion of their father's papers. "We would be very glad to have you donate this material to our society for permanent preservation."

Shoemaker did not rely solely on his own efforts to acquire manuscript collections. In 1937–1938, the society welcomed the collecting project of Elmer Ellis's doctoral student and now junior colleague in the university's history department, Lewis Atherton. This bright young scholar's interest was western American business history, research that would fill his book, *The Pioneer Merchant in Mid-America* (1939), and other publications. Atherton received a University Research Council grant in 1937 to identify and acquire records either for the university library or the historical society. In contrast to what would be the society's perceptions during their experience with the WHMC five years later, Shoemaker and his finance committee saw no jurisdictional threat in Professor Atherton's efforts in 1938. As President Allen McReynolds wrote: "If the society is to serve any useful purpose, it is represented by affording opportunities for work of this kind."

In the Lewis E. Atherton papers and the society's own records are lists of entire collections and individual items acquired for the society by Atherton. Some of these resources came from the river towns. Atherton turned up some records of the Glasgow Savings Bank and Pritchett College in Glasgow, Howard County. J. B. Kennard of St. Louis offered some records of his business to the society through Atherton. Cash books and letter books of businesses in Hannibal and St. Joseph were among the items acquired in those important river towns. Professor Atherton, who would also collect materials for the WHMC beginning in 1943 and serve as its director twice in the 1950s, had a good working relationship with the historical society. Through his efforts, it acquired manuscript materials in which it was actively interested.

The society's finance committee, at its meeting of January 30, 1943, agreed to Elmer Ellis's request that it cooperate in the Rockefeller grant project. But it hedged its support with conditions clearly designed to protect the society's independence. In a 1980 oral history interview, Lewis Atherton made an interesting comment. Recalling the early years of the WHMC, he observed: "There were some people in the state historical society who, quite properly, were a little afraid that the state society might be gobbled up by the university." Shoemaker and the committee may have seen the new manuscript collection as a potential instrument of their subordination to their much larger neighbor and its department of history. Thus, their first condition concerned the matter that eventually triggered the society's break with the manuscript collection. The secretary must approve all of that organization's "publicity literature" when such releases mentioned the society's name. Second, the society's endorsement of the Rockefeller project did not imply that its director could "involve . . . the society . . . in any new or related activity or project." Finally, prospective donors of materials to the society must approach the society. Neither the history department nor the project director could accept manuscripts on its behalf.

Elmer Ellis, who entered military service in 1943, arranged for another of his graduate students, W. Francis English, to become director of the Western Historical Manuscript Collection and a part-time faculty member in the history department. English was an experienced high school teacher and administrator whose most recent assignment was as superintendent of schools in Fulton. During most of the WHMC's first year, 1943, as well as earlier and later, English and Shoemaker

A native of Carroll County, Lewis Atherton in the 1930s embarked on a distinguished career as a historian of the South and the American West. He was particularly active in acquiring manuscript materials for the society and served twice as the director of the Western Historical Manuscript Collection in the 1950s.

maintained friendly relations, personal and professional. While the secretary encouraged the director to submit portions of his dissertation for publication in the *Review,* English obtained members for the society among those he canvassed for manuscripts. As he spoke with potential contributors, English was careful to state that their materials could go to either WHMC or the historical society.

Less than six months after the society entered cautiously into its relationship with English's project, a problem arose. Governor Stark had donated his papers to the Western Historical Manuscript Collection, and its director used the society's name as well as the university's in accepting them. "Permission has not been given by the society," Shoemaker noted in a letter of July 13, "for you to accept material in its name." "You are entirely correct in your criticisms," English responded politely. In the autumn of 1943, English repeated his error in a folder intended to explain the purpose of the WHMC. Twice he referred to the State Historical Society of Missouri in ways that seem inoffensive and trivial, but that Shoemaker thought "were of great import." The brochure conveyed to readers a greater commitment and degree of responsibility for the manuscript project than the society had been willing to grant in January. The finance committee, at its November 5 meeting, instructed Shoemaker to draft a letter declaring the society independent of the WHMC. After experimenting with several drafts of varying specificity, the secretary settled on one dated December 7, 1943, which he sent to English and university president Middlebush. The society "dissociated" itself from the project and "discontinued" the use of its name by English.

It is tempting to criticize Floyd Shoemaker for seeking a pretext to cut his ties to a useful project that could have benefited his own active manuscripts acquisitions program. In his December 7 letter, the secretary recalled that, at the outset, "the society did not think it advisable to make the project a joint one." Its origins lay within the history department, and the foundation had made its grant solely to the university. Only Elmer Ellis's persuasive arguments had convinced the society to go along, in the hope that its support would help the project to a successful beginning. Ellis, too, recalled years later that "Shoemaker was not too happy about the whole idea, as he realized it reflected upon his administration of the state historical society."

It is possible that Shoemaker perceived a personal as well as a bureaucratic threat in WHMC. A "Memorandum on the Project for Collecting Manuscripts, etc.," probably written by Ellis in 1942 and addressed to his colleagues in the history department, envisioned the manuscript project as a vehicle for providing for Shoemaker's successor and affiliating the society with that department. "It would be my hope," the memo's author wrote, "that the man who holds this position [director of WHMC] would eventually . . . [be] the only logical successor for Shoemaker when Floyd retires. We should then be in the position here that we hope to reach, with the society tied in with the department." If Shoemaker detected any evidence of such thinking, his easily aroused fear of threats to the society's independence may not have been so far-fetched.

The society's reluctance to cooperate with the new manuscript collection during the Shoemaker years was only one of many examples of its fierce desire to remain autonomous. In the summer of 1942, before Ellis drafted his proposal to the Rockefeller Foundation, Isidor Loeb had suggested that the society cooperate with the University of Missouri library in acquiring and administering manuscripts. Shoemaker opposed the idea. Not only would the coordination of a joint project increase his workload, but he also saw a larger issue: "I favor the society keeping complete control, without outside suggestions, over its policy and activity in the manuscript field and fear infringement and pressure, however well meant, in any co-operative project." His statement predicted the failure of any joint operation of the Rockefeller project. It also expressed a continuing central theme of the society's history under Floyd Shoemaker's leadership.

Another opportunity for the society to become part of a historical research complex in Columbia failed to materialize in the early 1950s. For a time it seemed possible that Harry Truman would locate his presidential library and museum on the university's campus. Indeed, for several years the WHMC held Truman's senatorial papers. "We are delighted to have" them, Francis English wrote early in 1952, and "interested in the Presidential Papers" as well. But by that year the president was envisioning a "Cultural Center" to be located near Grandview, in the region south of Kansas City where he had been born. Containing all of his papers and other resources essential for the study of American politics, the center would be a major research facility enjoying "the wholehearted cooperation," Truman hoped, of universities in the central United States. The president's plans were not yet final in February 1954 when L. M. White wrote to Truman: "To have your library located close by [the state historical society], even on the same corner or across the street, would tremendously enhance" the society's resources and those of Columbia's other educational institutions. The Truman Library would make the city "a center for historical research." In May, Lewis Atherton and Elmer Ellis believed that Truman had "virtually decided in favor of M.U." as the library's location, but by July the president announced Independence as the site. The university eventually transferred Truman's senatorial papers to the Truman Library.

III

The decade of the 1940s was an extraordinarily busy time at the State Historical Society of Missouri. As the agency added significantly to its collections, it also brought innovation to its publications program. As of 1941, excluding the *Missouri Historical Review*, the society's major publishing ventures consisted of three documentary series: the journals and the debates of the 1875 Constitutional Convention and *The Messages and Proclamations of the Governors of the State of Missouri*. A 1949 press release explained the *Messages and Proclamations* series, saying that reference libraries, lawyers and judges, and students of the state's government required the official record of gubernatorial administrations, which was "not available elsewhere in a single library or reference unit." Having brought the state's governors to date in volume 12 (1930), the *Messages and Proclamations* series lay dormant until 1947. The society's staff, under the general editorship of Floyd Shoemaker and his successor, Richard S. Brownlee, completed the project in 1965, by which time volumes 13 through 20 covered the administrations of Henry S. Caulfield (1929–1933) through John M. Dalton (1961–1965).

Between 1941 and 1944, Isidor Loeb completed the editing of volumes 7 through 12 of the *Debates of the Missouri Constitutional Convention of 1875,* to complete that series. Loeb's scholarship made the accelerated publication schedule possible. Shoemaker in Columbia oversaw the staff's preparation of copy, worked with the printer, mailed packages of pages to Loeb in St. Louis, and encouraged his overworked colleague. In March 1943, the secretary sent half of the printer's copy of volume 10 to Loeb for proofreading, to be followed by the second half in two weeks. "You would doubtless have most of the first half off your hands by the time the second half arrives and could probably handle the second half by May 1." Fully aware that Loeb performed an important wartime job, Shoemaker feared that his former teacher would be unable to complete the publication "along the lines originally planned." "I cannot endure the thought of your not being editor of the *Debates* until the volumes are finished."

Loeb himself provided the society with a reason to hurry the remaining volumes to publication by 1943 or 1944. It was in those years that a convention of elected delegates met in Jefferson City to write a new Missouri constitution. Loeb reasoned that a reference work explaining why delegates to the 1875 convention had created the document that remained the state's governmental framework in 1943 would inform the current convention's work. The *Debates* did exactly that, and the historical society provided delegates with free copies of the set as well as the *Journal* of the 1875 body. Allen McReynolds, at Shoemaker's urging, wrote an article for the April 1945 issue of the *Journal of the Missouri Bar* that detailed the "Contribution of the State Historical Society of Missouri to the Constitutional Convention." Both as a key member of the convention and as a former president of the society, McReynolds testified that the combined fourteen volumes of debates and journals from 1875 had been of practical value to the delegates nearly seventy years later. "These works were a veritable mine of information, drawn upon continually in the study preparatory to the framing of a new document."

Although useful to experts in government, the 1875 documents did not interest the general public. In 1946, after deciding to retain only complete sets of the *Journal* and the *Debates,* Shoemaker had 336 of them on hand, totaling 4,704 individual volumes—"which takes up a large amount of shelving which is badly needed for other current and future publications." Other society publications during the 1940s and 1950s attempted to engage a larger audience with accounts of Missouri's past. *Missouri, Day by Day* (two volumes, 1943–1944), *Ozark Folksongs* (four volumes, 1946–1950), and the booklet *Historic Missouri* (1959) differed from the society's earlier books and were similar to features found in the *Review* in several ways. Two of the three publications were narratives—they told a story—rather than reprinted primary sources. Their subject matter was as much cultural and social history as political. And these books communicated with readers in a popular style, a trait that applied to the music of *Ozark Folksongs,* the vignettes found in *Missouri, Day by Day,* and the illustrations and text included in *Historic Missouri.* There is no clear evidence that the society's decision-makers were conscious of having made an important shift in their publications strategy in about 1942, but, in fact, they had.

Between February 1925 and December 1960, the society prepared and distributed free of charge to the state's newspapers a series of brief articles under the general title "This Week in Missouri History." Intended for a heterogeneous audience of adolescents and adults, the articles employed various formats over this long period to demonstrate the society's usefulness to Missourians, as well as to tie interesting occur-rences and personalities to a particular week in the year. In March 1938, Shoemaker noted that at least one newspaper in 74 of the state's 114 counties, plus the *Globe-Democrat* in St. Louis, carried the series. The service did more to develop "a statewide historical consciousness," the secretary told McReynolds that spring, "than anything [else] this society is doing." It was not pride of authorship that prompted Shoemaker to make large claims for the articles' influence, for staff members researched and wrote them. He was simply quite satisfied with this successful effort to reach large numbers of Missourians on a regular basis.

As early as 1941, the society's budget carried a line item for a book tentatively entitled *Missouri Historical Chronicle.* Later issued as *Missouri, Day by Day,* the publication's central concept was similar to that of the newspaper articles: brief, popular, informative pieces keyed to particular days of the year. The publication truly was a group effort by more than a dozen staff members, who failed to identify significant events for only a few days on the calendar. The volumes discussed more than one event for some dates. Able employees who remained with the society for relatively brief periods—Elizabeth Anne Hartley, Joyce Hatcher, and Sue Hetherington, for example—joined veterans such as Sarah Guitar and Roy T. King in gathering data from sources in the reference library for the articles.

Sally Brown, who continued to work on the project even after she left Columbia when her husband, Robert, entered the armed forces in 1942, wrote most of the articles included in *Missouri, Day by Day.* Shoemaker functioned as a motivator and overseer of what became a complicated long-distance process. He mailed books and notes to Brown, who wrote articles while living with family members in St. Louis and Muskegon, Michigan. She, in turn, sent him completed articles, suggestions for those in process, and requests for additional information. The society's correspondence reveals that Brown's role was crucial in the process of bringing *Missouri, Day by Day* to publication and that she ought to have received more credit than she did on the title pages of the two volumes. A part-time employee, Sally Brown earned seventy-five cents an hour in June 1943, after receiving a raise.

Although the society's staff designed these two volumes for a large popular audience, they did not sell well. As of May 30, 1946, the society had sold only 293 sets, well below expectations. At the end of his tenure as secretary, in December 1959, Floyd Shoemaker was still promoting the sale of the publication at a discount price of $3.50. The original price of the set had been $5.00. As was true of all the society's publications during the Shoemaker era, the finance committee mailed complimentary copies to state officials and many others within and beyond Missouri's borders. Publications, the agency's leaders knew, earned goodwill in high places. Governor Forrest C. Donnell, for example, "was elated over" volume 1 of *Missouri, Day by Day* when he received it during the summer of 1943.

One reason that Floyd Shoemaker chose the role of supervisory editor for *Missouri, Day by Day,* rather than that of coauthor, was his commitment to write and help market for a commercial publisher a new history of Missouri. While it would be unfair to suggest that the secretary created a conflict of interest between his roles as private author and the society's administrator by his work on *Missouri and Missourians: Land of Contrasts and People of Achievements* (two volumes, 1943), the books indirectly caused the organization he headed some embarrassment.

With the publication in 1944 of volume 12 of the 1875 convention debates, Shoemaker summarized his publishing accomplishments: "I will have sixty-one volumes produced by me as author, editor, or co-editor since I became secretary in 1915." He included in this total twenty-nine volumes of the *Review* and the documents series already discussed. Some of Shoemaker's earlier books had been narrative histories of the state, most notably *Missouri, Mother of the West,* cowritten with Walter Williams in the late 1920s. In September 1939, the secretary signed a contract with the same publisher, the Lewis Publishing Company of Chicago, to issue a two-volume history of Missouri. As he recalled after he had completed the project, Shoemaker originally doubted if he could simultaneously write the books and perform his duties for the society. But the publisher, B. F. Lewis Jr., wanted the volumes and was willing to pay the author's price, so Floyd Shoemaker grasped what he termed "one of the great opportunities of my life." As it turned out, the author spent more on research assistants than he received from Lewis. "I regard the money spent," he wrote in September 1943, "as the best investment I ever made." Shoemaker was "very well satisfied" with his work. He believed that his narrative and analysis did what no other history of the state had done—give social and economic history as much treatment as political and military events.

The embarrassment that this venture caused the society resulted from the alleged sales practices of a few of the Lewis Company's representatives. The firm's marketing techniques included the use of an "advisory council" of notable Missourians to endorse Shoemaker's history in advance of publication. Based on these recommendations and a prospectus, company representatives promoted the five-volume set (the last three of which contained biographical sketches written by Lewis's staff) at $35. On July 26, 1941, an angry Isidor Loeb informed the secretary of two instances in St. Louis in which Lewis personnel had apparently approached purchasers with the claim that the State Historical Society of Missouri was publishing *Missouri and Missourians.* "I am sure you will agree with me that such procedure will do great harm to the society and must be stopped." Again, in the summer of 1942, Shoemaker received complaints about the Lewis Company's sales tactics from a few of the society's members. A physician from Bolivar, for example, believed Shoemaker was "a victim of a fast-talking publisher who is promoting a shady deal on the public."

The author assured Loeb and others that the Lewis Company had a sixty-year record of integrity and that the few cases of misrepresentation were isolated and unimportant. He believed, indeed, that cases such as those cited by Loeb resulted from miscommunication between seller and buyer, rather than an intent to defraud. Whatever the truth, the controversy soon disappeared. But if the episode diminished public confidence in the society to even the slightest degree, it should have warned the secretary that his mixing of private and public roles created confusion among those only partially informed about his activities. In fact, his 1943 history was the last work that Shoemaker published apart from his society duties.

The most significant publication of the period 1941 to 1960, other than the *Missouri Historical Review,* was Vance Randolph's *Ozark Folk-songs.* The folklorist's extensive manuscript—3,645 typewritten pages containing 1,783 texts of songs and 880 different tunes—was a signifi-cant acquisition for the society as well as a notable publication. Just as the art and rare book collections acquired in the first half of the 1940s had done, Randolph's work gave breadth to the concept "Missouri history." The record of the state's past resided in the cultural as well as the business and political life of the people. It included melody and verse in addition to printed reports and handwritten correspondence.

The finance committee authorized the purchase of Randolph's orig-inal manuscript for $1,000 on December 9, 1944. It drew on the balance in the Membership Fund (Trust), once again validating the worth of that account. The society intended to commence publication of the several volumes as soon as possible, although the contract gave it exclusive rights to the material for ten years. Randolph would work with staff members to prepare his manuscript for publication. George Rozier negotiated with committee chairmen in the General Assembly to obtain a supplemental appropriation in 1945 that covered the expense of print-ing volume 1. It became clear early in 1946 that Randolph's abundant material would fill four published volumes rather than the anticipated three. The finance committee authorized printing one thousand copies of each.

The society's working relationship with Randolph proved at times to be difficult. Affecting the crusty cantankerousness that stereotype might attribute to a native hill person, Vance Randolph in fact was a Kansan, born in Pittsburg on February 23, 1892. Well-educated, he earned a bachelor's degree from Pittsburg State College in 1914, a master's degree from Clark University in Massachusetts in 1915, and experimented with teaching his chosen field, biology, in Pittsburg's high school. He intensely disliked the experience. After service in World War I, Randolph entered the University of Kansas's graduate school in 1922, at the age of thirty, to pursue a Ph.D. in psychology. He left after two years without the degree, sated with formal learning. It was then that he went to live permanently in the Ozarks, a region in which his family had vacationed during his youth and he had lived briefly after the war. The author of more than twenty books, he devoted his life to studying the culture of the Ozark Plateau and sharing his understanding with a national reading public. Randolph died in Fayetteville, Arkansas, on November 1, 1980.

Dr. Frances Emberson, who prepared Randolph's *Ozark Folksongs* manuscript for publication, had to work out several difficulties with the strong-willed folklorist. Her doctorate was in English, granted by the University of Missouri in 1935 for her study of *Mark Twain's Vocabulary*, and alone or with a collaborator she wrote several other studies of Twain's use of language. One problem that Emberson, working on behalf of the society, and Randolph had to resolve was whether the individual volumes in the *Ozark Folksongs* series should carry titles, and, if so, what they should be. After much discussion, the society overcame the folklorist's reservations about the titles Shoemaker and Emberson had suggested. A second problem was Randolph's dissatisfaction with the "most unfair" title page, which named the society twice but him not at all. "I spent twenty-five years of my life, and more than $5,000 cash, in getting that collection together," he complained. "I think my name should be played up on the title page in the conventional manner." The published title page thus named Randolph as collector and editor of the songs.

Minor problems such as these faded as strongly positive reviews of Randolph's volumes arrived. Shoemaker passed on to Governor Phil Donnelly in early 1948 the judgment of the reviewer writing for the *Mississippi Valley Historical Review*, the major professional journal of historians of the United States. In *Ozark Folksongs,* the reviewer wrote, "the State Historical Society of Missouri may well have produced one of the most distinguished contributions ever edited and put into print in this country."

Folk materials, of course, can cause embarrassment to morally or politically sensitive persons. The society's leaders debated the risks of offending groups of Missourians when Randolph offered to sell two additional collections of his work for publication. He submitted his manuscript "Ozark Superstitions" in 1945. Floyd Shoemaker's sensitive political antennae immediately sounded warning. Two chapters contained sexual material to which many readers would object, but the secretary detected "a more fundamental problem." The superstitions revealed in Randolph's manuscript, Shoemaker feared, exposed the "retarded development" of a large minority of Missourians who were already typecast as simple hillbillies. Because the society was a public agency, "it is not advisable to consider the publication of ["Ozark Superstitions"] in the near future." In Kirksville, E. E. Swain agreed. "It seems hardly right to use the taxpayers' money to hold them up to ridicule." On the other hand, George Rozier and Mitch White saw another issue, that of collecting and publishing important, accurate documents on the state and its people regardless of the potential temporary violation of regional sensibilities.

The society did not purchase Randolph's manuscript in 1945 or acquire a third one offered a decade later. On June 21, 1955, the finance committee decided not to purchase the two-volume collection of Randolph's "Unprintable Ozark Folksongs." The sexual and scatological references that made these songs "unprintable" foreordained a rapid negative decision. "I think the less we have to do with such matters the better," concluded White. Swain wrote: "I am just so old-fashioned it shocked me to read some of those things sung by 'Miss. _____' or 'Mrs. So-and-So,' as well as some of the male songs. Maybe my sense of 'scholarship' is dull." Randolph's collections had helped members of the finance committee to discover the outer boundaries of their definition of "history."

Several music publishers, through legal counsel, charged in the early 1950s that the society had violated the copyrights they held on selections published in *Ozark Folksongs.* Uncertain whether one such allegation was a "bluff" intended to extort money or a valid claim, and aware that the "ownership" of folk material was a vague and slippery legal matter, the society delayed resolution of the matter for several years. That was the advice of the lawyers among its own leadership and in the state attorney general's office. Finally, in 1952, the payment of a token sum to the firm with seemingly the most valid complaint settled the matter.

But the memory of what could happen when the society entered uncharted publishing waters lingered. Richard Brownlee denied the request of a California professor in the mid-1960s to reprint verses found in *Ozark Folksongs*. "Mr. Randolph presumed that both the words and music of all the songs in his publication were in the public domain. . . . Unfortunately, a number were not." In 1977, a publisher in New York asked that the society grant it permission to reprint the Randolph volumes. Since 1960 he had operated under instructions from the society's governing body, Brownlee responded, to refuse all such requests "because of the initial faulty copyright on the part of the society." It eventually allowed those copyrights to expire. Although the society experienced some distress over its publication of *Ozark Folksongs,* the venture was a success. The volumes made valuable source material available. W. K. McNeil's introduction to the 1980 reissue of the four volumes by the University of Missouri Press called it "Randolph's major work, one of America's most important folksong collections." The project also demonstrated the state historical society's willingness to innovate in the subject matter encompassed by its publications.

A booklet on the history of Missouri became one of the most widely distributed of the society's publications. As early as 1944, the finance committee considered the compilation of a sixty-four-page "illustrated pamphlet" on the state's history, to be distributed free of charge to interested parties. One anticipated audience was schoolchildren. The pamphlet, however, did not appear in the 1940s. Shoemaker put a staff writer to work in 1952 gathering material for such a booklet, which by now had been named *Historic Missouri.* At that time, the society envisioned the publication as forty-eight pages long with a price of twenty-five cents. It was not until the spring of 1959, however, that the society actually published *Historic Missouri.* Largely because of a successful sales campaign conducted through the Missouri State Teachers' Association and free distribution of the booklet to the historical society's members, the finance committee had ordered fifty thousand copies of the publication by September 1959.

The *Missouri Historical Review* during Floyd Shoemaker's final two decades as editor communicated with its large readership in a writing style and with visuals mindful of those employed in *Historic Missouri*. In fact, the quarterly was the model for the booklet. Its editor referred to the *Review* as a "history magazine," never as a scholarly journal. While the Wisconsin and other state societies also applied the term "magazine" to their journals, it is clear that Shoemaker took great pains to fashion a publication that readers of all sorts, only a handful of whom had a specialist's understanding of history, found easily accessible. His continuing campaign to maintain the society's national lead in membership went hand in hand with the accessibility of the *Review*'s contents. By 1957, it reached over ten thousand members and doubtless had many more readers and browsers than that. While scholarly articles appeared in the magazine's pages, Shoemaker did not consider them to be the principal features of any given issue.

Instead, the *Review*'s central attractions from volume 35 (October 1940–July 1941) to 54 (October 1959–July 1960) were several regular departments. Shoemaker and his staff "research associates" researched the topics and wrote the copy that appeared in these featured series. A positive aspect of this approach to filling the pages of what amounted to a small book four times each year was that staff members, many of whom held master's degrees in journalism or history, wrote for the *Review* as well as edited submitted work. Such satisfying labor may have helped to offset their meager pay.

The April 1941 issue of the quarterly included three continuing features. One was the "Missouriana" department, begun in July 1931. In April 1941, this miscellany included a sixteen-page presentation of the historic markers positioned along U.S. Highway 36; a piece on St. Louis publisher Joseph Pulitzer; a table of statistics on Missouri's population growth since 1870; and a series of interesting historical facts about the state presented under the heading, "Do You Know or Don't You?" The second feature was, and is, at the society's centennial, the *Review*'s oldest continuing department: "Historical Notes and Comments." In April 1941, it included news of the society, such as recent additions to membership, obituary notices of deceased members, and the society's recent acquisitions. The feature also publicized the "activities of county and regional historical societies," and by doing so served as a statewide clearinghouse of information and loose network of organizations. Following the notes and comments section appeared "Missouri History Not Found in Textbooks." This feature reprinted some current, but mostly old, newspaper articles and editorials on historical subjects.

Departments like these continued to inform readers throughout Shoemaker's volumes of the *Review*. In October 1944, "The Missouri Reader" replaced the "Missouriana" section. Into the 1950s, it presented primary source accounts of various groups "in the valley"—the Mississippi Valley, that is. Documents edited by staff members and academic historians from a number of colleges revealed the lives of native peoples, French explorers, and the Lewis and Clark Expedition, for example. In April 1951, the *Review* added a fourth ongoing feature: "This Week in Missouri History." It consisted of articles the society still provided, now on a bimonthly basis, to newspapers, plus relevant illustrations from the society's collections. In July 1956, "This Week . . ." became "Vignettes of Famous Missourians," reprints of newspaper articles to which the society had by this time given a biographical focus. Also appearing on an irregular schedule in the 1950s was a series of articles detailing one of the society's new responsibilities: "Missouri's Program for Highway Historic Marking." The last issue of the *Review* on which Floyd Shoemaker's name appeared as editor was that of April 1960. It contained three familiar departments: the "vignettes" of notable persons, the notes and comments news section, and "Missouri History Not Found in Textbooks."

If these features provided continuity for readers of the *Review*, the articles in each issue brought variety to its pages. The featured speaker's address before the annual luncheon appeared each year, a practice that brought the thoughts of notables such as J. Christian Bay and Bell I. Wiley to members unable to attend the meetings. The *Review* served as a meeting ground for the university's history department and the historical society, as professors Lewis Atherton and Francis English, in particular, wrote and edited several contributions. Out-of-state academics also found a Missouri readership through the journal. In April 1951, for example, a political scientist teaching in an Iowa college and the head of the journalism department at a Mississippi institution published articles.

With its articles and regular features filling approximately 150 pages in each of four issues annually, the cost of printing the society's quarterly represented an increasingly large budget item. In the 1941–1942 biennium, the society budgeted $5,400 for printing the *Review* and miscellaneous printing. In the 1951–1953 budget, the figure increased to $14,000. The society requested $29,000 for 1959–1961, nearly $15,000 per year just for printing the *Review.*

As it had earlier, the State Historical Society of Missouri participated in the anniversaries of a number of events during the 1940s and 1950s. Centennials abounded in those decades because a century before Missouri had served as an important staging area for western development. In 1943, Secretary Shoemaker spoke in Independence, along with Senator Harry Truman and others, at the Oregon Trail Centennial. In 1958, the society took part in a caravan that traced the route of the Butterfield Overland Mail in Missouri. The most meaningful commemoration for the staff, officers, and members of the society, however, was the observance of its own fiftieth anniversary in 1948.

One way in which the agency marked the milestone was through its publication of Floyd Shoemaker's *The State Historical Society of Missouri: A Semicentennial History.* In four chapters and accompanying lists and appendices, Shoemaker assembled from widely scattered sources a wealth of data and a useful summary of accomplishments. In one sense the book was autobiographical. Most of what the author recounted had occurred during his years as assistant librarian and secretary since 1910. Many reviewers, who praised the book as one of the few available histories of state historical societies, viewed the Missouri society's achievements as a monument to Floyd Shoemaker's lifework.

The semicentennial observance consisted of more than a book. Shoemaker's history, in fact, substituted for the original plan for celebrating the society's founding. In May 1947, the finance committee "tentatively" endorsed the secretary's suggestion "of a seven or ten day historical tour to Eureka Springs and back." A caravan of automobiles would carry surviving founders of the society from the Missouri Press Association, past and current officers, and other friends back to the Arkansas resort that was the society's birthplace. Rejecting the tour as excessively costly and complicated, the finance committee decided, in March 1948, that Shoemaker should, instead, write a history of the organization for the October *Review.* Too lengthy for an issue of the quarterly, the account of the society's development grew through the spring and summer of that year to become *The State Historical Society of Missouri: A Semicentennial History, 1898–1949.*

The book was ready for distribution at the society's birthday party, celebrated at the annual luncheon on October 15, 1948. Four of the eleven surviving members of the press association in 1898 attended, as did many former trustees and officers. All of these groups contained many newspaper editors, and one theme of the festivities was the key role played by the state's journalists in the historical society's impressive growth over five decades. Speakers at the luncheon included Dean Elmer Ellis of the university, former society president Allen McReynolds, and Milo M. Quaife. Quaife was an Iowan who had earned an M.A. in history at the University of Missouri in 1905 and had later headed the State Historical Society of Wisconsin. All spoke of the evolution of Missouri's state-funded historical agency since 1898 and its contributions to the state. Printed in the January 1949 issue of the *Missouri Historical Review,* these addresses remain valuable assessments as the society turns one hundred.

IV

During the 1950s, the State Historical Society of Missouri revived and amplified the program of erecting highway historic markers inaugurated by George Mahan's gift two decades earlier. And it initiated an inventory of Missouri's historic sites. This expansion of functions was deliberate and cautious, for it involved a rethinking of the society's mission. As L. Mitchell White observed in 1958, "research is our field," a goal clearly promoted by acquisition of the Bay Collection and the continuing program of microfilming newspapers. Under a broadening definition of "research," the collection, preservation, and display of historic artwork also provided researchers with documents for understanding the past. The society now applied that same rationale to the study of material culture—the objects in the built environment—which included historic buildings.

As the society's decision-makers considered expanded roles, they implicitly considered the question of whom the society served. Should it be only those who conducted research in its print collections? Such patrons constituted a limited audience. But informing tourists pausing at a roadside marker and supporting local preservationists by collecting and publishing information on historic homes and public buildings put the society into contact with other constituencies. These functions did enlarge the society's public during the 1950s, but they cost money. Could the society's expanding budget absorb the costs of new programs, or would the General Assembly add supplementary funds for them? The answers to such questions did not lead the society to a sweeping reassessment of its mission. Although it accepted some new roles, it resisted such radical departures from its traditions as the establishment of a museum in Columbia to house artifacts and the management of historic sites at locations across Missouri.

The society's launching of a statewide program of highway historic markers was the easiest new role to accept. Not only had its marking of U.S. 36 succeeded, but also the post–World War II boom in automobile ownership and leisure use had created a popular demand for history along with other roadside attractions. While a few pioneers like Virginia had begun to note historic sites on highway markers in the 1920s, nearly three-fourths of the states administered programs by the late 1940s. Although in retrospect it seems inevitable that Missouri would place markers along its major roads and that the state historical society would participate in the program, Floyd Shoemaker at first resisted the prospect. When a society member suggested the subject in a 1947 letter, the secretary told George Rozier: "I am not very enthusiastic on the subject." During several auto trips through Virginia, he recalled, "I found nothing interesting in . . . [that state's] fine historical markers with very few exceptions."

Yet in that year the society began the long process of developing a highway marker program for Missouri. The 1947 annual meeting adopted General Paul M. Robinett's resolution requesting that the Executive Committee "consider the inauguration of a state-wide historical marker program with special reference to highway marking." Responding favorably to this call for action, the finance committee unsuccessfully requested a special appropriation in 1949 to begin the program. By that year, however, Secretary Shoemaker had laid the necessary factual foundation for a successful appropriation request in 1951 in his "Preliminary Report on Historical Markers along U.S. Highways." Based on his survey of other states' marker projects, to which forty-five of the other forty-seven states had responded, this valuable compilation of data guided the society's own program. Shoemaker presented his findings to the American Association for State and Local History meeting in Burlington, Vermont, in September 1949.

Having secured knowledge of other states' experience from the survey and an appropriation for highway marking from the legislature, the society still faced decisions preliminary to the placing of markers in the ground. One was a division of labor with the state highway department and its chief engineer, Rex M. Whitton. A meeting of the highway commission and the finance committee on November 15, 1952, resulted in a working agreement. The society would pay for the markers, research and write the text, create a standard design for the markers, and suggest a general site for each one. The highway department, for its part, would determine the precise location of the markers and prepare roadside turnouts or parking areas there, install the markers, maintain the sites, and locate markers on official Missouri highway maps. In a letter of November 18, 1952, Whitton informed the society that the highway commission "was very enthusiastic about this project." However, that enthusiasm did not continue until completion of the program. In March 1959, with seventy-five markers in place across the state, Whitton wished to end the cooperative endeavor: it was "increasingly difficult to find suitable locations for these markers. . . . the present method of selecting sites has become somewhat of a burden to the department." Nevertheless, the two agencies found ways to work together to complete the program.

As essential as the highway department's participation in the project was a process for selecting the sites to mark and determining what to say about them. The society's criteria for making these decisions were reasonable and wise, and they satisfied most, if not all, communities and interest groups. By the late 1950s, Shoemaker, the finance committee, and the society's staff had decided to limit the total number of markers to 121—a single marker for most counties. And since the limitations of money and staff allowed work on only a portion of the total in any biennium, the highway department did not place the last markers in the ground until 1964, well into Richard Brownlee's term as director. Shoemaker's "guiding principle" in site selection was "the state-wide importance of the site. . . . 'historical' is considered in its broadest meaning." The term encompassed facts of geologic, geographic, and archaeological significance, as well as specific historic events and broad social, economic, and political generalizations suggested by the area's past. The *Review* articles that presented the markers to the society's members, written by Ruby M. Robins, head of the project beginning in 1953, stressed that their inscriptions were "accumulative." That meant that they carried "a wide range of information on sites of interest, historic events, outstanding achievements, and characteristics of the land within the orbit of the marker."

As the secretary reported to finance committee members while they selected the first group of twenty-eight marker sites in 1952, not everyone was satisfied with overview marker inscriptions. In Louisiana, Shoemaker announced, former Governor Lloyd Stark had moved a log cabin built by his grandfather in 1816 "to the highway location opposite the Stark Nursery office. . . . He is willing to give the land for a [vehicle] turn-out. . . . Stark and the highway [department] staff are plugging strong [*sic*] for a marker." Shoemaker insisted on an inscription that discussed Louisiana and the vicinity, with only one paragraph about the cabin and Stark's business. In Trenton, "the alumni and their descendants of Grand River College," an early coeducational institution no longer operating, "are plugging for a marker." Shoemaker preferred "an accumulative marker for Trenton . . . with a paragraph" on the college. That inscription would include information on area notables Governor Arthur M. Hyde and General Enoch Crowder, among other material. Such were the politics of marker site selection. The society held to its policy of general inscriptions covering numerous phenomena written in what the *Review* called a "telegraphic" or condensed style.

Working with the markers' manufacturer, the Sewah Studios of Marietta, Ohio, the society developed an attractive design. The inscription appeared on both sides of the marker, beginning just below Missouri's Great Seal. The Sewah Studios cast aluminum markers fifty-four by seventy-two inches, provided two metal posts for mounting, and rendered the inscription in twenty-three-karat gold leaf on a field of blue baked enamel. The society's first group of sites included Ste. Genevieve, Fort Osage, and the Mark Twain birthplace at Florida, Missouri. During the dozen years that the marker program brought recognition to Missouri's counties and towns, representatives of the society appeared at numerous roadside dedication ceremonies. With justifiable pride in their past, communities became genuinely caught up in the marker program. Of all the outreach programs attempted by the society, surely this has been one of the most successful. It fell short of reflecting the history of all Missourians chiefly by neglecting the unique experiences of Native American and African American racial minorities and women. In the 1950s, such neglect was nearly universal among historical societies and other official custodians of the past.

Probably from the state historical society's earliest years, but increasingly after World War II, various parties attempted to enlist the society's support in plans to save, restore, and operate historic sites. The term *historic site* can refer to a structure—a house, public building, or similar enclosure—or terrain, such as the land on which military forces clashed, associated with significant happenings or personages. While the society's highway markers recognized multiple aspects of an area's history, a designated historic site memorialized a specific family or event or architectural achievement. The State Historical Society of Missouri, in contrast to its willing acceptance of the highway marker program, successfully resisted pressures to involve it in historic site purchase or management.

The society's records include a copy of Senate Bill 701, introduced in the Fifty-fifth General Assembly on March 11, 1929, by Senator Lon S. Haymes of Springfield. The proposal gave the society the power to "acquire by purchase, gift or condemnation and hold such real estate as comprises such places and sites of historical interest." It would bear the "cost incident to the acquisition, preservation, reconstruction and maintenance of such places." The legislature did not transform into law Senator Haymes's bill, which would have significantly modified the historical society's mission. The Missouri Constitution of 1945, in Article III, Section 48, authorized the government to preserve "the memorials of the history of the state," and to acquire such sites and objects by "gift, purchase or eminent domain." An editorial in the September 22, 1946, edition of the *St. Louis Post-Dispatch* suggested the society as one existing agency that might execute the constitutional provision. The General Assembly eventually assigned the responsibility for acquiring and administering historic sites to the State Park Board, and by the mid-1950s that agency operated a half-dozen parks dedicated wholly or in part to memorializing history. But from time to time legislators and citizen groups suggested that the society ought to perform that duty.

The finance committee and Secretary Shoemaker refused to incorporate such initiatives into the society's mission. With reference to Section 48, for example, Shoemaker argued in 1951 that the society should move

The dedication of the New Madrid County highway marker was held on October 26, 1954. Among those attending the ceremony were (left to right) Mrs. Orville Chandler, Mrs. Vincent Rost Jr., Mrs. S. L. Hunter, Mrs. Roy Boeker, and Mrs. Leo Hedgepeth. These women represented local organizations involved in the dedication ceremonies.

to implement the provision only if the legislature directed it to do so. Until that time, the society's leaders should "stick to our original position taken in 1947 to have nothing publicly to do with the matter." That was also the agency's response to groups and individuals who requested its assistance in preserving specific sites. Such appeals arrived with some regularity. In 1950, Governor Forrest Smith urged Shoemaker to act to save the deteriorating building in Marshall, Texas, that had functioned as the Confederate Capitol of Missouri in exile. The governor failed to mention what resources the society should employ in the rescue effort. Responding to a 1954 request that the society save the drugstore in Arrow Rock used by pioneer physician John Sappington, President White declined, "Unfortunately, the State Historical Society of Missouri has no museum for the collection and preservation of the material you mention and it has no funds for the preservation of the drug store itself." White suggested that the Saline County Historical Society undertake the project. When the Clay County Historical Society asked, in 1955, that the society recommend state purchase of the Watkins Woolen Mill complex of buildings, the finance committee declined for the same reason it refused to ask the park board to add the Sappington cemetery to Arrow Rock State Park three years later: for one state agency to lobby another was poor public policy.

The only instance in which the society expressed a genuine interest in accepting a gift of property that might qualify as a historic site occurred in 1957. The heirs of A. P. Green of Mexico offered that industrialist's estate, consisting of a large home and five acres of grounds, to the historical society. Uncertain how it might best use the structure—apparently "for offices, archives, or for research" rather than for a museum, according to its minutes—the finance committee conditionally accepted the Green family's offer in September. But the condition caused eventual withdrawal of the offer: that the Greens contribute $15,000 annually for maintenance of the property. The society's budget was unable to meet that obligation. For President L. M. White, a friend of the Green family in Mexico, money was the major reason that the society and other state agencies should leave the "preservation of historical sites" to others. Local historical societies were among the organizations that found purpose and meaning in such projects. Entering the field of preservation would, at the very least, distract the state society from other, more worthy activities. At worst, White feared, "it might destroy or tend to destroy" the organization, "which operates under, I believe, the smallest budget of any organization of its kind in the country."

Complicating the society's reasoned consideration of the historical preservation issue was Floyd Shoemaker's inexplicable aversion to Charles van Ravenswaay. Born in Boonville in 1911 and educated at Washington University during the early depression years (B.A., 1933, M.A., 1934), van Ravenswaay became one of Missouri's and the nation's leading advocates of material culture study and historic preservation. He headed the WPA project that produced the volume *Missouri: A Guide to the "Show Me" State* (1941), a celebration of as well as guidebook to the physical evidence of the state's varied cultural heritage. Following military service in World War II, van Ravenswaay was director of the Missouri Historical Society in St. Louis from 1947 to 1962, of Old Sturbridge Village in Massachusetts from 1962 to 1966, and the Winterthur Museum in Delaware from 1966 to 1976. These assignments allowed him to pursue his fundamental belief, expressed in a 1958 speech, that people learn history from "the three dimensional, visual souvenirs of our past. . . . Perhaps of all the forces for positive historical education, historical buildings are the most immediately effective." His conviction implicitly challenged the assumption underlying the State Historical Society of Missouri's collections of printed research materials—that we learn about the past from the written word. Floyd Shoemaker may have taken another of van Ravenswaay's assertions in the 1958 address as a more direct criticism of his policies: "One is forced to ask why Missouri has been so backward in developing an integrated historic preservation program." As his experience with the Western Historical Manuscript Collection had already demonstrated, Shoemaker did not always accept criticism as the path to improvement.

Van Ravenswaay was a member of the society, and the documentary record reveals that the two men were capable of cordial relations. But Shoemaker had long mistrusted a man whom he seemed to consider a rival. For the cause of historic preservation in Missouri, that attitude was unfortunate. Conceivably, the societies they headed could have fashioned a cooperative effort in this field with the St. Louis organization assuming the lead role in historic preservation, allowing Shoemaker to focus, as he preferred to do, on his agency's established commitments. But as early as 1937, his view of van Ravenswaay as a competitor and foe predicted the impossibility of cooperation in the postwar years. In the summer of that year, the secretary came to believe that the young Boonville historian had "stolen the march on me" by obtaining manuscript material from a woman in Potosi. With the aid of a society member, the newspaper editor in that town, Shoemaker persuaded the donor that the state historical society was the best repository for her family's ledger books and other business records.

But Shoemaker remained suspicious of van Ravenswaay's motives and actions. In the spring of 1942, van Ravenswaay helped Roy Williams, a member of the finance committee, to plan J. Christian Bay's visit to Missouri. Shoemaker described him to Loeb at that time as "a most polished, educated gentleman . . . but he doesn't like this society although he has gotten much from it and his heart is in the Missouri

Historical Society . . . of which he is a trustee." In 1953, now head of that organization, van Ravenswaay urged the creation of a state historic sites commission, which Shoemaker apparently interpreted as a criticism of his own lack of achievement. The St. Louisan's appeal, the secretary believed, was "filled with emotion and pseudo logic and some truth." Others shared his beliefs. L. M. White responded to van Ravenswaay's 1958 speech on historic preservation by urging George Rozier to place a letter in the *Post-Dispatch* "drawing attention to what the state historical society was doing along this line."

What the society was doing in the field of historic preservation was important. At its meeting of June 22, 1957, the finance committee authorized a survey of historic sites in Missouri. A news release described the project as "an inventory, to be continued until completed, of the nature, location, and condition of notable historic buildings extant in the state." This collection of data would serve as the "initial step . . . to the preservation of Missouri's historic sites." Polly Batterson and later Dorothy Caldwell directed the survey, the success of which depended on the cooperation of local historical societies, preservation groups, and individuals. They gathered information on sites and reported it on the society's forms. By 1963, when the state historical society published the *Missouri Historic Sites Catalog*, edited by Caldwell, local preservationists had submitted information on 2,391 sites and photographed 1,716 structures. This library of factual information on Missouri's built environment, unprecedented in its comprehensiveness, was a valuable resource. The achievement was part of a nationwide renewal of interest in site preservation, stimulated in part by federal government actions. On the positive side, Congress and President Truman created the National Trust for Historic Preservation in 1949. A major threat to historic districts and individual structures, however, was the 1956 interstate highway system. The American Association for State and Local History cited the latter as a reason for a renewed effort to save historic buildings, to which the society's survey and report was a response.

V

Although incomplete when Floyd Shoemaker retired on May 5, 1960, the historic sites survey was one measure of the changes that he had experienced during forty-five years as secretary and a half-century in the society's employ. Many of the buildings being threatened by highways and other instruments of economic change had been relatively new in 1910, including the fifteen-year-old Jesse Hall that contained Shoemaker's first office. Not yet concerned with highway markers, historic structures, or collections of political cartoons, the organization that Shoemaker inherited from Francis Sampson devoted its energies to building an unrivaled collection of newspaper and book sources on Missouri history. That original goal remained the society's central purpose in 1959, when Secretary Shoemaker determined that he had made his contribution and would step aside.

His state and his profession amply rewarded Shoemaker's achievements. At the society's annual meeting in October 1956, the finance committee unveiled an oil portrait of the secretary, which from that date has hung on a wall in the society's quarters. Central College in 1942 and the University of Missouri in 1954 awarded the society's administrator the honorary degree of Doctor of Laws. The American Association for State and Local History presented Shoemaker with two individual awards of merit, and the Missouri Press Association gave him its distinguished service award. Of all the tributes he earned, Shoemaker expressed the greatest pride over the title "Mr. Missouri," which many had applied to him before 1955, when the Sixty-eighth General Assembly officially bestowed it in a joint resolution.

The secretary submitted his letter of intention to retire on September 15, 1959. At the retirement luncheon, held on April 6, 1960, Professor Lewis Atherton delivered an eloquent tribute to Shoemaker's contributions to the study of Missouri history. A second outstanding summary and evaluation of "Mr. Missouri's" career was Richard Brownlee's annual report to the society's members in the fall of 1972, shortly after Shoemaker's death. Calling him a "man of vision who originally set the direction for the society," Brownlee spoke of "the debt that our state, our society, owes Floyd Shoemaker. . . . he has left a great legacy for future generations to use and enjoy." Brownlee, more than any other single person, was the direct heir of the strengths and shortcomings of Shoemaker's legacy.

4

The Society under Richard S. Brownlee II, 1960–1985

or the first time in forty-five years, the State Historical Society of Missouri acquired a new top administrator in 1960. A careful observer of Richard Smith Brownlee II's conduct of his office—the official title of which the finance committee changed to "director and secretary" on July 9, 1960—soon would have perceived subtle but important changes in the society's operations. Brownlee was not a protégé of Floyd Shoemaker. Familiar with the society and a specialist in Missouri history, the new director came from outside the organization, and he began his administration with a mandate for change from the finance committee. From the last Shoemaker years into the early 1960s, change occurred. During that time, the fresh ideas and firmly held convictions of Dr. Richard Brownlee brought new leadership qualities and policy orientations to the agency.

Much about the society, of course, remained the same during the Brownlee years of 1960 to 1985. Significant continuities underlay change. The art and rare book collections that the new director enhanced were those suddenly acquired or gradually built under Floyd Shoemaker. George Rozier challenged the finance committee in 1963 to look for "some major acquisition or project which the society might undertake, similar to the Bay Collection." But the deliberate accretion of existing collections, rather than the purchase of a large existing library or gallery of paintings, characterized the acquisitions policy during Brownlee's tenure. Still acutely conscious of its limited resources, the state historical society continued to reject requests that it assume new functions. In July 1962, for example, members of the finance committee refused an appeal that they sponsor a conference on historic preservation, with its attendant "obligations and problems." A caution about innovation pervaded all aspects of the society's operations. From the 1960s into the 1980s, the agency continued its modest book publication program, concluding its last multivolume series in 1965 while initiating no new ones, but issuing individual volumes of quality.

Given continuities like these, of what did the transformation wrought by Richard Brownlee consist? With the encouragement and support of the finance committee and the assistance of an able staff, the new director set out to accomplish three broad goals. First, he reconciled and integrated his agency with the University of Missouri, a process well underway when state government reorganization mandated a budgetary merger in 1974. Second, Brownlee applied the highest standards of the historical profession to the society's work. Third, the new director consolidated the organization's programs of service and outreach.

I

In the fall of 1957, Floyd Shoemaker was seventy-one years of age, in his forty-second year as secretary, and his forty-seventh year with the society. Although beyond normal retirement age, he successfully applied at that time for a "continuance of service" agreement with the Missouri State Employees' Retirement System. It is clear to one who has read major portions of his correspondence from the late 1920s forward, and who has followed his detailed administration of the society's business as reflected in the finance committee's minutes, that Shoemaker's effectiveness diminished beginning in the mid-1950s, if not earlier. The lengthy, informative, analytical correspondence of earlier years disappeared, and in its place appeared brief, businesslike letters that revealed much less about the society's workings or the secretary's thinking. The finance committee, which depended on Shoemaker for its agendas and policy recommendations, met less frequently, to the frustration of at least one member. "Before I left" for several months in Florida, L. M. White wrote to George Rozier in March 1959, "I called the historical society three times and each time Shoemaker was absent, sick. . . . We should have a meeting and some matters should be discussed." The committee failed to deal with whatever issues White had in mind.

Secretary Shoemaker's desire to hire an assistant, who would assume some of his responsibilities and perhaps emerge as his logical successor, suggests that the veteran administrator recognized his diminishing capabilities. That search began in 1956, and it constitutes the first phase of the transition from Floyd Shoemaker to Richard Brownlee. Thus, Donald H. Welsh came to the society in March 1957 as assistant editor. A Montana native and a professor at a South Dakota teachers college before coming to the society, Welsh was the first full-time staff member to hold the Ph.D. He earned the degree in 1955 in the University of Missouri's history department, upon completion of his dissertation, "Pierre Wibaux, Bad Lands Rancher."

As his former professors made clear, Welsh was the department's choice in 1956 for the immediate opening and as Shoemaker's ultimate successor. Both Francis English and Elmer Ellis had departed their history classrooms for administrative duties in Jesse Hall, but they recommended Welsh to Shoemaker and encouraged their former student to accept the job if the society offered it to him. "I believe you would find this society a real challenge and a chance for professional development," English wrote in November. University president Ellis added: "I can assure you that both Lewis Atherton and I would be very happy to have you here in that position. . . . everyone concerned wants you here." Atherton was the most forthcoming, telling Welsh on November 6 that Shoemaker's tenure as secretary was drawing to a close. "You might possibly succeed him as head of the society." The history department's Americanists, Atherton revealed, "feel that we will have considerable influence in shaping the future of the society." One of their goals was to unite the Western Historical Manuscript Collection with the society. "You are definitely our first choice" for the job opening, Atherton assured Welsh, "and we are greatly pleased that you are also Mr. Shoemaker's first choice."

The university's history department did not shape the state historical society's future through Donald Welsh any more than it had by means of the WHMC's director in the early 1940s. But another Atherton student, Richard Brownlee, became the department's candidate to replace Shoemaker in 1959, and it was he who brought the department and the society into an unprecedented working relationship after 1960.

The incomplete documentary record fails to satisfy many questions about the selection of Floyd Shoemaker's successor in 1959. Even though Welsh was on staff as assistant editor in the spring of that year, Shoemaker pressed the finance committee to fill a new position, that of "assistant secretary." In March, he favored Clement L. Silvestro, executive secretary of the American Association for State and Local History. The committee brought Silvestro from Madison, Wisconsin, to Columbia "for a conference" with Shoemaker in early April. The visit, which the secretary held on the earliest possible date, prompted Ballard Watters of the committee to observe: "You are anxious to have an assistant and immediately." But Silvestro was not interested in even the top job at the society, according to Irvin H. Wyllie, once on the Missouri history faculty and in 1959 at Wisconsin. Wyllie's "private guess" was that Richard Brownlee was a likely prospect to succeed Shoemaker, a guess confirmed by Lewis Atherton in a letter of April 14, 1959. "Shoemaker would like to pick his successor," Atherton wrote to Wyllie, but "Brownlee has told him and indirectly some members of his board that he intends to be a candidate for the post when it becomes vacant." Responding to Shoemaker's continued insistence, the finance committee and the secretary interviewed three candidates for the position of assistant secretary on Saturday, April 18. Two of them were Donald Welsh and Brownlee.

But the committee did not hire an assistant secretary in the spring. Instead, Floyd Shoemaker, on September 25, 1959, announced his retirement, effective on the forty-fifth anniversary of his acceptance of the office of secretary, June 5, 1960. From that date until his death in 1972, Shoemaker, still on salary, held the title "secretary emeritus and consultant." Speculation can never substitute for documented fact, but in the absence of fact, speculation suggests possibilities. The finance committee may well have offered the veteran secretary a post-retirement income and a continuing, though mostly honorary, role in the society's affairs in return for abandoning his search for an assistant secretary and yielding his leadership position to a new secretary. At any rate, Mitch White, chair of the finance committee, announced Brownlee's selection as the new chief administrator in a press release dated October 8. The secretary-elect appeared at the December 3, 1959, meeting of the committee to plan his apprenticeship. Although he "would have no responsibilities or authority" until June 5, beginning on February 1,

1960, he "would participate in the work of each department . . . in order to familiarize himself as fully as possible with all the activities and duties in each." The present and future secretaries, the committee planned, "could spend an hour a day together discussing the society, its history, policies [and] problems."

Richard Brownlee, although he came to his new job from outside the agency, was well prepared to assume direction of his state's public historical society. Through his own academic career and family heritage, Brownlee had a rich knowledge of and close identity with Missouri's past. A youthful-looking forty-two years of age when he assumed office, Brownlee had been born on March 12, 1918, in Brookfield, a few miles west of Shoemaker's boyhood home of Bucklin, in Linn County. The Brownlees were of Scottish descent. An ancestor, James, left Scotland for Northern Ireland in the 1740s, and his son, George Brownlee, settled in Pennsylvania shortly after the American Revolution. A restless people with a preference for frontier settlements, the Scotch-Irish helped pioneer the interior of the United States. Making their way from Pennsylvania to Kentucky and Indiana, Richard's branch of the Brownlee family arrived in Missouri well before the Civil War. William H., the great-grandfather of the society's new director, was an early settler of Linn County.

Richard Brownlee's expertise was Missouri's experience during the Civil War. As is true of many longtime Missourians, his family heritage placed him on both sides of the conflict. On his father's side, a great-great uncle, John Sandusky, fought with Sterling Price's Confederate army at the Battle of Corinth in Mississippi in 1862. In the Shore family—the family of his mother, Margaret—Brownlee's great-grandfather, Thomas Spenser, "was a Union man and ran a store and hotel at Laclede throughout the war." As he helped to lead Missourians in observance of the Civil War's centennial during his earliest years at the historical society, Dick Brownlee could speak with knowledge and sympathy of the war that cast family members against each other. "Wasn't it a tragedy," he commented in 1968, "that young Linn County men were so divided."

The new director's associations with the University of Missouri were equally deep and meaningful. His grandfather, his father, Ellis, and uncle Rollins, as well as other relatives, had graduated from the institution. At the age of seventeen, in 1935, Brownlee enrolled at the university and joined the Rho chapter of the Sigma Nu fraternity, with which the male

Richard S. Brownlee, a native of Brookfield, became the society's third director, secretary, and librarian in 1960. A noted scholar on the guerrilla war in Missouri during the Civil War, Brownlee worked cooperatively with university officials, stressed professional standards in the society's publications and public services, and consolidated its varied programs.

Brownlees also had a long association. He earned a B.A. degree in 1939 and a B.J. degree the following year and then used his journalism training in advertising to land a job with the Coca-Cola Company. Those born during World War I lived to fight the second global conflict, and so it was with Dick Brownlee. Entering the army in January 1941 as a private, he emerged as a captain when discharged in December 1945. Three years before his discharge, Brownlee and Alice Rowley of New Haven, a 1942 graduate of the university, married. Their two children, Richard III and Margaret, would extend the family's ties to the state university in Columbia.

Brownlee's journalism background made him a coprofessional of those who had founded the State Historical Society of Missouri. He held jobs with newspapers in Lebanon and Warrensburg before returning to the university for graduate study in history beginning in the summer of 1947. With Lewis Atherton as his major professor, Brownlee completed most of his course work by 1950, when he received his master's degree. He held a graduate teaching assistantship in the history department from 1947 until 1950 and was a part-time faculty member during the 1950s.

Between 1950 and his designation as the society's director a decade later, Brownlee served as assistant director of the Division of Continuing Education at the university, in which position he administered adult extension classes as well as taught some of them. One of his courses, both in the extension program and for the history department, was Missouri history. Brownlee earned the Ph.D. in 1955 with completion of his dissertation on Missouri's Civil War Confederate guerrilla units. His thesis became the book *Gray Ghosts of the Confederacy* in 1958.

Richard Brownlee seemed to recognize that in replacing a legend— "Mr. Missouri"—he would encounter some awkward moments, particularly since some of Floyd Shoemaker's longtime associates believed that he had remained in office too long. Brownlee understood their feelings. "I know this has not been an easy time for you," he wrote to George Rozier a few days after the press releases announcing Shoemaker's retirement and his own hiring. "I want you to know the great admiration I have for the way you had to handle a delicate situation." In the months of transition, Shoemaker formed a positive impression of his successor's qualities and prospects. "He comes of a fine family, has had good scholastic training, and is the author of a most readable book," Shoemaker wrote on October 21, 1959. "I shall do all I can to help him when he reports for duty this winter." Brownlee chose not to sit at the head table at Shoemaker's retirement dinner, held on May 18, 1960. He believed that the retiring secretary alone should be the center of attention. Shoemaker appreciated the gesture: "He is a cultured, considerate gentleman."

Richard Brownlee's closest associates in the work that lay ahead, the society's president and the members of the finance committee, expected him to re-energize the society. They were pleased with his early efforts. "Dick will certainly do a good job," George Rozier predicted five weeks into the new administration. "The work of reviving and re-activating the society is already under way." Two weeks after Brownlee's inauguration, Mitch White praised his abilities: "His enthusiasm, ambition and all those fine, useful qualities the years sometimes numb, simply radiated from him. I am more impressed than ever that our choice was correct," he confided to Rozier. Of the society, White commented: "It seems to me that what was fast becoming a 'ghost' will soon be taking on the flesh of healthy progress." In December 1962, two and one-half years into Brownlee's directorship, White retained his enthusiasm. Recent achievements, he told the society's head, revealed "a progress which hasn't been achieved for many years in the past." The Mexico editor believed that Brownlee had "caught us up when we were drifting backward and [had] given the society the needed impetus to progress again." Rush Limbaugh, former president and now permanent trustee of the society, writing at the end of October 1960, confessed that Brownlee had "sold himself completely to me" in his agenda for the historical society published in the current issue of the *Review*. "I have not seen from the pen of anyone a finer confession of faith and declaration of purpose."

That declaration of intent foresaw change for the society. After recognizing the agency's "position of strength" attained through past leadership, Brownlee shared with the society's members "a look into the future as I see it." While he conceded that the impending move into its new quarters would disrupt the society's functions in the short run, the society would enjoy adequate space for the first time since the mid-1930s. Brownlee not only praised his staff but also promised them greater intangible recognition and financial reward than in the past. The society's large membership created an ever-growing demand for staff services, which modern office procedures and equipment would help to alleviate. The *Missouri Historical Review* went to each of the fourteen thousand members, and it could never fully satisfy all of them. But its new editor, Brownlee, pledged a new commitment to scholarship, while retaining "popular information of appeal to our general readers." After promising the continued growth of collections, the maintenance of "a sound and steady publication program," and the reinvigoration of relations with local historical societies, Brownlee formulated the society's mission in his own words. "The state society is not a museum and it is not a social organization of antiquarians. It is a center for serious historical research and a heavily utilized service institution for citizens of the state of Missouri." A sound knowledge of their past, he assured his readers, was more necessary in the current cold-war context than it had ever been before. Under his leadership, the State Historical Society of Missouri would dedicate itself to making the past serve and enlighten the present.

Director Brownlee earned the admiration of the finance committee and realized his goals for the society in part through sheer hard work. His energetic leadership and ready acceptance of personal obligations contrasted sharply with his predecessor's avoidance of speaking commitments and committee assignments during the late 1950s. The conditions that Brownlee discovered at the society's quarters during his first years in office demanded considerable energy. "I will be so glad when we get settled and can really devote time . . . to the normal conduct of our business," he wrote to Mitch White in January 1962 about the impending move into a portion of the society's new quarters. "It seems to me all we have done for a year and a half is to transact our affairs on top of moving and general confusion." Three years later the director explained to former president Roy D. Williams the workload that his assistants carried. Five persons, including Brownlee himself, all with other tasks to perform, handled the one hundred letters that, on average, arrived daily. "Of these almost fifty percent require research and [a] written answer." Brownlee was one of the three-member editorial staff that published the *Review* four times annually. Running "a major magazine production," the society produced a total of sixty thousand copies for each volume in the early 1960s.

One of "the many new and unfamiliar tasks" that Brownlee faced was the preparation of a budget and presentation of its requests to the General Assembly. In 1996, trustee Virginia Young recalled that Brownlee was an excellent representative of the society before the Coordinating Board for Higher Education, of which she was a member in the 1970s. Earlier, he had learned the budget-building process from veterans George Rozier and Elmer Ellis of the finance committee. And, as Floyd Shoemaker had done, Brownlee shared data with the administrators of comparable historical societies to assess varying levels of state support. "As I suspected, Missouri has fallen far behind you," he revealed to W. D. Aeschbacher, director of the Nebraska State Historical Society in mid-June 1960, "and your figures should give me some wonderful ammunition" for use in Jefferson City.

The society's director readily offered his own talents and his agency's resources to many public and private groups devoted to promoting Missouri history or the interests of libraries. In 1963, for example, Brownlee was the state chairman for the observance of National Library Week. In his September 1968 report to members at the annual business meeting, the director reviewed his own recent "activities." He had been a member of the Missouri World's Fair Cultural Commission, formed to create an exhibit for the New York exposition of 1964–1965, and the Civil War Centennial Commission, both of which had recently concluded their work and deposited their records with the society. He also "served actively . . . on" the First State Capitol Restoration Commission, formed to save the original capitol building in St. Charles; the State Records Commission; the State Park Board Historic Sites Advisory Committee; and the Father Marquette State Tercentenary Commission. Brownlee also judged entries in the D.A.R. National Scholarship Contest. In 1969, he joined Missouri's Sesquicentennial Commission to plan the 1971 celebration of 150 years of statehood.

The director left his office not only to attend meetings, but also to speak to groups across the state. Jim Goodrich has estimated that Richard Brownlee gave nine hundred talks to groups that had an interest in Missouri history and the work of the society during his twenty-five years on the job. He averaged three speeches a month during the three hundred months of his directorship. Not only Brownlee, but also Goodrich and other staff members, appeared at the meetings of local historical societies. In 1971, Missouri's community and county societies numbered 117. Local history promoted by nonprofessionals was a growing movement of large proportions in the post–World War II years, and the State Historical Society of Missouri fostered it by staff presentations and other means. In his annual report of October 4, 1969, Brownlee noted the organization of ten new local societies during the past year. "I am happy to say our society was influential and helpful in the formation of eight of these, and all are affiliated with us."

By early October 1963, the society's director had filled his speaking schedule up to the spring of the following year. "It is almost impossible for me to conduct my duties here satisfactorily without limiting my public appearances," he told a representative of the Phelps County Historical Society. A sample of Brownlee's speaking engagements in 1962 will suggest the range of groups that heard him: the Washington (Missouri) Museum Society, the Old Settlers Reunion at Huntsville, the highway marker dedication at Aurora in Lawrence County, the Joplin District Rotary meeting, the Missouri Press Association gathering in St. Louis, the Social Science Workshop banquet in Kirksville, the Truman Presidential Library murals dedication in Independence, and the General Pershing Home dedication ceremony in Laclede. When he delivered formal addresses, Brownlee had a versatile arsenal of talks from which to select prepared remarks. Presentations such as these represented

Brownlee's scholarship as well as the society's public relations efforts: "Colonel John Smith 'T.,' Missouri's Most Dangerous Pioneer"; "Problems in Research and Writing Missouri History"; "Your State Historical Society of Missouri"; "Opportunities for Research and Writing in State and Local History"; "Gray Ghosts of the Confederacy"; "The Battle of Pilot Knob"; "The New Story of Order Number Eleven"; "General Ulysses S. Grant in Missouri"; "The Missouri Dream"; and talks on Missouri women during the Civil War and cholera in the state. On May 12, 1961, the society's director addressed a joint session of the Missouri General Assembly to formally open the Civil War centennial.

A major preoccupation of the leaders who served with Director Brownlee from 1960 to 1985 concerned the society's financial status. Their experience included years of income satisfactory to meet the agency's goals and obligations, as well as years when resources fell short of sufficiency. Changes in the American economy and fluctuations in state support were among the factors that contributed to the historical society's financial uncertainty during the 1970s and early 1980s.

Table 4.1 presents data on the society's state appropriations during the years that Richard Brownlee administered it. The annual state grant was by far the largest source of income available to fund programs, but membership dues, the sale of publications, and gifts of cash and of book and art properties were significant supplements to state support. Over the twenty-five Brownlee years, the net appropriation more than quadrupled. It surpassed the half-million dollar mark for the first time in the 1985–1986 fiscal year, the last budget that the director had a hand in preparing. The data reveal nine years in which the state grant of funds represented at least a 9 percent increase over the previous year, and the society's records during good years contain appropriate expressions of gratitude and satisfaction. In his annual report for 1962–1963, for example, Brownlee praised Governor John M. Dalton and the legislature for their support. "[We] have today sufficient funds to enable us to satisfy the increasing demands for our services," he concluded. The finance committee's minutes for May 5, 1978, read: "The society has received one of its best appropriations in recent years."

But revenue shortfalls at the state level and rampant inflation in the national economy jeopardized the state historical society's ability to perform its mission during periods in the 1970s and 1980s. Ten percent increases in state funding failed in some years to equal even

Table 4.1 State Appropriations for the State Historical Society of
Missouri, 1961–1962 to 1985–1986

	Appropriation	Percentage Change over Previous Year
1961–63 (24 months)	$235,669	+20%
1963–65 (24 months)	315,609	+34%
1965–66	174,928	– 6%
1966–67	186,134	+ 6%
1967–68	194,979	+ 5%
1968–69	204,814	+ 5%
1969–70	212,754	+ 4%
1970–71	212,506	0
1971–72	234,661	+10%
1972–73	236,776	+ 1%
1973–74	248,744	+ 5%
1974–75	262,068	+ 5%
1975–76	280,308	+ 7%
1976–77	295,232	+ 5%
1977–78	326,349	+11%
1978–79	361,470	+11%
1979–80	387,179	+ 7%
1980–81	439,694*	+12%
1981–82	407,964†	– 7%
1982–83	420,127‡	+ 3%
1983–84	427,105	+ 2%
1984–85	474,498	+11%
1985–86	532,468	+12%

Note: Years given as fiscal years (July 1 to June 30).

Source: Biennial reports to the governor.

* Net appropriation. Original appropriation was $453,293, with 3% ($13,599) withheld by governor.

† Net appropriation. Original appropriation was $453,293, with 10% ($45,329) withheld by governor.

‡ Net appropriation. Original appropriation was $442,239, with 5% ($22,112) withheld by governor.

higher rates of inflation. After informing the finance committee that the appropriation for 1970–1971 would remain at the 1969–1970 level, Brownlee noted that the cost of publishing the *Review* had appreciated considerably from the previous year. The director reported to members attending the October 25, 1980, annual meeting that during the past five years, "the cost of books, serials and related library supplies have increased from fifty to ninety percent." In March 1981, "in view of the severe economic conditions" facing state government and therefore its agencies, the finance committee withdrew its request for five new staff positions. Governor Christopher "Kit" Bond had ordered a 10 percent reduction in 1981–1982 state agency appropriations. The more than $80,000 that the state's poor financial outlook forced Governor Bond to withhold from the society's appropriation in the three years from 1980–1981 to 1982–1983 caused the elimination of three and one-half full-time equivalent staff positions. Nineteen and one-half employees in 1984 carried a workload greater than twenty-three staff members had handled in 1981.

Since the 1920s, the Membership Fund (Trust) had supplemented the state appropriation. It helped the society to bridge the gap between reduced state funding and program obligations in hard times and made possible what the legislature did not, even in the best of times, provide for: the purchase of special collections or works of art. The society's leadership, for example, used membership dues revenue to "make up [for] the withholding" of $45,000 in 1981–1982. At its meeting of January 6, 1966, the veteran members of the finance committee and the society's director reviewed for the benefit of two new members the past uses of membership trust funds. These included the acquisition of research materials such as rare books and supplies and equipment requiring immediate purchase or not funded by state appropriations. The society also had used trust funds to meet unexpected printing or mailing costs, to hire short-term employees for specific projects such as newspaper indexing, and to cover employees' travel expenses as they represented the society outside of Columbia.

Examples of trust fund expenditures give insight into the functioning of the society during Richard Brownlee's tenure and convey the significant degree to which the agency was able to supplement the state appropriations. In the period from July 1, 1961, to December 31, 1966, while the society disbursed $779,999.91 from its state appropriations, it spent $111,347.43 from the Membership Fund (Trust). The supplementary dollars amounted to 12 percent of the total expenditure of $891,347.34, a notable strengthening of the society's ability to fulfill its mission. Nearly $38,000 from the trust fund supplemented $212,506 from the state's general revenue fund in 1971, constituting 18 percent of total expenditures that year.

In 1964, the finance committee authorized several translating, indexing, and cataloging projects designed to make the collections more accessible to researchers. The indexing of early St. Louis French- and Spanish-language newspapers, as well as the *Columbia Missouri Statesman,* was among the projects. Over $1,500 from the trust fund purchased two card catalog cabinets for the newspaper department's indexing project in August 1967. Between 1962 and 1966, trust fund monies paid for a substantial program of cleaning, repairing, and framing art properties. The society purchased the microfilmed 1900 federal census and its index for Missouri with money from the fund in 1978. The largest single program that the Membership Fund (Trust) supported over the years was the microfilming of newspapers. Enjoying a cash balance in the fund of $69,000 and government securities amounting to an additional $90,000, the finance committee on September 7, 1984, determined to "reestablish and beef up programs" recently weakened by state withholding. It designated $20,000 to supplement the $22,600 in state funds earmarked for microfilming newspapers.

Although the committee first considered obtaining not-for-profit status with the Internal Revenue Service (IRS) in February 1970, the financial woes of the early 1980s finally compelled it to act. Gifts of cash or materials that would benefit contributors at tax time also would help the society to make up for lost state income. In the first half of 1982, the committee employed a Columbia accounting firm to prepare the application for tax-exempt status, and during the summer it filed the papers with the IRS. The federal agency approved the application in January 1984. The society, by the following June, had prepared a statement for potential donors. "Gifts to the society are deductible for federal and state income, estate and gift tax purposes," the invitation read. "Contributions are greatly appreciated and are used for the purposes of the society." The Friends of the Libraries of the University of Missouri–Columbia and the State Historical Society, in 1983, gave the society gifts of cash and books. During the 1982–1983 fiscal year, members and other individuals gave 923 volumes, worth almost $34,000, to the state historical society.

The society's admission to the tax-exempt category no doubt helped to persuade some of its friends to make significant donations. But those who know its history well realize that the generosity of individuals and families has always enriched the State Historical Society of Missouri, even before the existence of federal or state personal income taxes. Unlike most other agencies of Missouri government, the society performs work that stimulates the sympathies and emotions, as well as the intellect, of thousands of citizens. Perhaps no other fact about the society's story is more essential to a complete understanding of its evolution over one hundred years.

II

Since its founding in 1898, the State Historical Society of Missouri had enjoyed a remarkably cooperative relationship with the University of Missouri, in which most of the tangible benefits flowed from the larger to the smaller educational partner. Their inability to unite in sponsoring the Western Historical Manuscript Collection in 1943 and after had not significantly diminished this mutually supportive interaction, since Floyd Shoemaker's discontent with the project focused solely on members of the history department. Just as Isidor Loeb until 1925 and Walter Williams until 1934 had personified the positive ties between the university and the historical society, so also did Elmer Ellis and Lewis Atherton during the Brownlee years. The society's presidents during the years 1974–1977 and 1980–1983, respectively, both men were leaders of the finance committee, whether they held the presidency or not, by virtue of their persuasiveness and experience as professional historians. That Richard Brownlee and James Goodrich, the society's directors from 1960 through the 1990s, were Atherton doctoral students was additional evidence of the integration of the two centers of historical study located on the university's campus in Columbia.

Two construction projects—one completed in 1961, the other in 1987—demonstrate a new stage of the society's integration with the university during the Brownlee and Goodrich administrations. Except for its expansion into several additional rooms in the university's library during the 1930s and 1940s, the society in 1960 occupied the same space into which it had moved in 1915. Although spacious then, neither the society's nor the university's quarters were even adequate in 1956 when university president Elmer Ellis and his staff began planning for the long-delayed east wing. The pre–World War I plan for completing the library building projected the society's new home in the east wing, but several depressions, two world wars, and numerous obstacles of lesser import had delayed physical expansion. Ellis fulfilled the promise of that plan. As university president, he took personal charge of the library expansion project, and during the planning phase in 1956 and 1957, he did everything possible to give the society the home it wanted.

As Floyd Shoemaker awaited the library building's east wing, he contended with recurring problems in the existing facility. One was heat. In June 1954, he complained to the director of the university library, Ralph H. Parker, about steam pipes that raised the temperature in two newspaper and microfilm storage rooms. The secretary feared damage to important research materials. While his solution to that problem consisted of open windows and a fan, in 1955 and 1956 the society paid for several window air conditioners for use in a building that still lacked a central cooling system. These units made more comfortable the main-floor reference library reading room and the basement cataloging room, which "in warm and hot weather is almost unbearable." On December 13, 1954, a faulty plug on an electric fan caused a fire in the society's basement acquisitions room. Although quickly contained, the blaze destroyed a limited amount of office equipment and current periodicals. But it highlighted a continuing concern about quarters so crowded and uncomfortable that they required moving air, summer or winter.

Help was on the way, in the form of a $75 million construction bond issue approved by voters in January 1956. The authors of this Second State Building Fund designated monies for a number of new or reno-vated and enlarged structures on the university campus in Columbia, including $3.5 million "for completing, furnishing, and equipping" the university library, which would include new quarters for the state historical society. That amount was $500,000 less than the university had requested.

President Ellis's role in providing the society with a new facility was crucial. As planning proceeded, he frequently consulted with Secretary Shoemaker and the finance committee, on several occasions walking from Jesse Hall to the veteran secretary's library office with blueprints and documents in his arms. From the spring through the late summer of 1957, as negotiations continued on the size and location of the society's space, Shoemaker and his colleagues considered several alternatives. One plan placed most of the society's operations on the third floor of the new addition, a remote location made accessible by an elevator for the exclusive use of the society's staff and patrons. At that point, Ellis had promised the College of Agriculture and various science departments that their relocated libraries would occupy the east wing's ground floor, just steps away from the white campus and their classroom buildings. A second vision of the historical society's future located it in a new two-story annex building, to adjoin the south half of the 1936 west wing of the existing library and connected to it through first and second floor entrances. Dissatisfied with both of these alternatives, the finance committee approved a third scheme at its August 6, 1957, meeting. It gave the society the entire ground floor of an enlarged version of the east wing, nearly all of the ground floor of the old building, and book stacks on the first and second floors. Later refinements to that plan included a main entrance off of Lowry Street to the north rather than one to the east facing Hitt Street. On Ellis's recommendation, the university's curators approved this plan on August 26. The university's president explained the building project to the society's members gathered for their annual meeting on November 1.

The State Historical Society of Missouri dedicated its new quarters and held an open house on the day of the 1961 annual meeting, Saturday, September 16. It was "a smashing success in every way," Richard Brownlee wrote to the George Roziers in Jefferson City on the Monday following the big day. The society had been unable to move all of its materials by dedication day. The extended move, begun in January 1961, concluded in the spring of 1962. In November 1962, with that job completed, Brownlee enthusiastically reported to state senator Omer H. Avery: "We have finally moved into our new quarters and are developing a research center that Missouri can be proud of." In "a few years," he predicted, the society would become "one of the great research centers of the nation."

Appropriate, well-equipped, and wisely managed space, if not a prerequisite to greatness in research and in other areas, certainly facilitated the achievement of that goal. The society's new facility did not include the auditorium that Shoemaker and his finance committee had lobbied for, but it contained the first art gallery in the agency's history and an art storage space. Indeed, for the first time ever, the society functioned in quarters that planners had designed for its needs, and not generic space that any university library function could conveniently utilize. Visitors to the society's home on dedication day toured rooms suited for the Bay Collection, for the editorial staff, for newspaper storage and use, for the reference library, and for administrative offices. Governor John M. Dalton, long a member of the society and, by virtue of his office, now also a trustee, delivered the address at the luncheon on September 16. He and members of his audience recognized that space was only a means to achievement, not itself the desired goal. Its old facility, after all, had not prevented the state historical society from becoming, in Dalton's opinion, "Missouri's greatest cultural and educational organization." But now that the state had solved the space problems of the past, an even brighter future lay ahead.

That the 1961 solution to the society's space problems was only temporary probably surprised no one among the agency's staff or leadership. Spacious enough to house the various collections and functions at the moment of planning in 1957, the new quarters soon failed to accommodate the entire art, book, newspaper, and manuscript holdings that grew rapidly during the Brownlee years. In the fall of 1961, Governor Dalton requested that all state departments and agencies project their financial needs for the next decade. At its November 10 meeting, just weeks after dedicating the new facility, the finance committee instructed Director Brownlee to demonstrate to the governor "that within ten years the society and the university library will need a warehouse building to store manuscript materials not being used." In 1966, the society converted an existing room into an additional, badly needed art storage space. To permit the removal of shelving from about half of the newspaper reading room in favor of additional patron work space, the society in 1978 discarded the bound volumes of the *Kansas City Star* and *Times* from 1908 to 1949. The $11,000 purchase price of these papers on microfilm became the cost of the reclaimed space. Richard Brownlee had begun conversations in 1977 with Dr. John Gribben, the current director of the university library, on ways to enlarge their shared facility. Both institutions, Brownlee informed the finance committee on July 1, "are out of space in the present building."

In the 1960s, in quarters designed to meet its storage and public service needs, the society could, for the first time, mount significant exhibits on historical topics as well as provide researchers with source materials. These Columbia schoolchildren examine a Smithsonian Institution traveling exhibit about Frederick Douglass.

During the late 1970s and early 1980s, the university and the society petitioned Missouri's legislature for the funds to construct a separate storage building, occupying, in some plans, land just south of Ellis Library across Conley Avenue. In a letter of February 17, 1978, President William R. Denslow formally requested a portion of a proposed storage building for the society's growing collections, while Director Brownlee was already meeting with a university planning committee. But in its spring 1978 session, the General Assembly failed to fund the project. By the end of that year, the university had included an on-campus storage facility in its 1979–1980 capital improvements budget request. A committee of Elmer Ellis, Lewis Atherton, and Brownlee worked with Columbia state senator Warren Welliver, a close friend of the society, and university president James C. Olson, a professional historian, to acquire twelve thousand feet of storage space in the proposed structure.

In the spring of 1979, however, the House of Representatives refused to appropriate construction funds for the project. In a third effort to gain space, the university proposed the construction of a combined health sciences library and storage facility in 1980–1981. Although President Olson guaranteed the society a share of the shelving in this building, Brownlee feared that reduced state revenues would kill the project. He was correct.

When the expansion of Ellis Library became a reality in the mid-1980s, the society found it necessary to assert the continuing relevance of its historic claim to a location in the university's general library building. Occupying important decision-making positions at the University of Missouri were administrators such as the chancellor of the Columbia campus, Barbara Uehling, and her deputy chancellor and director of institutional research and planning, Duane Stucky, who, unlike former presidents Williams, Middlebush, and Ellis, had not spent their entire careers in the institution's classrooms or executive offices. Particularly troubling were statements included in the November 18, 1981, "preliminary draft" projection of the state historical society's need for, and claim to, space in an expanded Ellis Library. The product of the consulting firm MIRA, Incorporated of Minneapolis, Minnesota, the report made an alarming assertion: "University officers have indicated to the consultants that, while there is no obligation that the society be located in the Ellis building, there is an expectation that alternative space on campus would be furnished the society if it is relocated." In a cover letter to Director Brownlee, Dr. Thomas R. Mason of MIRA reiterated his understanding that the university would find quarters for the society "on or near the Columbia campus" if the university's collections displaced it from Ellis Library.

The society's leaders, guided by Brownlee and finance committee members Ellis and Atherton, carefully documented their firm refutation of an apparently radically altered university policy. Restrained and businesslike in tone, the agency's response concealed frustration and disappointment that unidentified university officials seemingly had abandoned a nearly eighty-five-year commitment with little thought and no consultation with the society. In the Elmer Ellis papers deposited in the Western Historical Manuscript Collection are copies of court papers, minutes, and other documents dated from 1898 to the 1970s. The society's leadership assembled the evidence in this packet to prove that state government, through General Assembly appropriations for building construction and governors' signatures on such bills, and the university itself had from the society's initial location in Jesse Hall committed to a policy of shared library facilities.

Why had state and university officials done so? Elmer Ellis stated one reason in a March 1, 1982, letter to Chancellor Uehling: the society's print, manuscript, and art collections "are essential to the distinguished character of our [university] library." The university and society libraries complemented one another. Years before, they had agreed not to duplicate their acquisitions. The society's holdings were "an essential and useful part of the general library in the fields of humanities and social sciences," helping to make it "one of the very best between Chicago and California." If such arguments were not persuasive, Ellis cited the Omnibus State Reorganization Act of 1974, which "placed the state historical society under the university for budgetary purposes only." Subsequent to that law and designed to clarify the new relationship, the two organizations had signed a written statement that included the stipulation that "the society shall remain in its current quarters."

Lewis Atherton, the society's president in 1982, reinforced Ellis's argument with a forceful letter to Duane Stucky dated March 22. The troubling statement in Thomas Mason's report was simply incorrect. The documentary record proved "that from 1913 to the present the Ellis building was designed originally, and enlarged at later periods, for joint occupancy" of the historical society and the university. The finance committee, Atherton asserted, believed that "its right to its present quarters are without question." The university could not relocate the society and claim all of the library building's space. Atherton's point-by-point review of the evidence concluded with as fully substantiated a conclusion as any he had ever made in a monograph. The society would openly negotiate with the university over the future uses of the central library building, including future additions, but its home would remain in that building.

And so it did. Responding to Ellis's letter on March 8, Chancellor Uehling assured the president emeritus: "It is certainly not our intention to displace" the society's collections, "only to raise the question as to whether the specific location accorded them is the best." On June 29, 1982, President Olson assured Dr. Atherton "that the state historical society will be a full and complete partner in the present planning of the Ellis Library addition and any future planning that will involve the space presently assigned to the society." If anyone in the university administration explained how the planning consultants had acquired a contrary notion in 1981, that explanation does not rest in the society's archival records.

On March 22, 1982, Richard Brownlee appended President Atherton's letter to a report entitled "Facilities Program Plan for the Libraries and Departments of The State Historical Society of Missouri" and sent both to university officials. This twenty-four-page document was the society's first significant attempt at long-range planning. Jim Goodrich, who in 1982 was the society's associate director and associate editor of the *Review,* headed the self-study that produced the report. As his summary statement revealed, it was the momentary misunderstanding with the university and its consulting firm that led the society into the planning process. "Thorough study of the preliminary MIRA Report revealed erroneous assumptions and projections." To accurately present its case to library expansion planners, the society "embarked upon an extensive, time-consuming study to arrive at its projected needs for the next twenty years." Peering into the future, the report anticipated a salaried staff that would grow from thirty-three and one-half persons in the society and in the joint manuscript collection in 1982 to sixty-eight in the year 2002, and a facility totaling 54,472 square feet in the latter year as compared to 32,006 in 1982. The detailed text of the report, together with its tables and diagrams, provided a carefully crafted profile of Missouri's publicly supported historical society that even in the late 1990s constitutes informative reading.

By the time that the south addition to Ellis Library opened in 1987, President James Olson had retired, Interim President Melvin D. George had come and gone, and a new president, C. Peter Magrath, had assumed office. But against the fluidity in the university's administrative structure stood an old principle, freshly affirmed. When Melvin George, in August 1984, sent a diagram of the library's expansion plan to Dick Brownlee "marked Exhibit A showing the area identified for the state historical society," his letter added a significant statement. "This plan continues the commitment of the university to provide space for the society within the Ellis complex. . . . Please be assured that it is the intention of the university to maintain the very fine relationship we have had with the state historical society." The complicated and extended planning and negotiation that resulted in the addition to Ellis Library, much of it conducted for the society by Jim Goodrich, included significant new book storage space for the agency. The historical society also acquired improved climate control and security systems in the existing art storage room, the gallery, and the Bay rare book room. Like the construction projects that had enlarged the society's quarters on three earlier occasions, the 1987 addition at least temporarily relieved the crowding and congestion naturally experienced by a dynamic organization.

Construction projects during the Brownlee years brought the society and the University of Missouri into an unprecedented working relationship while reinforcing a long-standing commitment. Similarly, the eagerness of both institutions to merge their manuscript archives under Richard Brownlee's direction reconciled old differences while it integrated ongoing functions. During the 1950s, with Elmer Ellis and Francis English now deans, Lewis Atherton provided leadership to the Western Historical Manuscript Collection. Retaining a full teaching load in the history department, he served as WHMC's acting director from 1951 to 1953 and director from 1957 to 1963. And it was Atherton who arranged for his doctoral student, James Neal Primm, to direct the archive when he left that position in 1953, and who hired Nancy C. Prewitt in 1952 to provide daily management of the collection.

At the finance committee's meeting of November 10, 1961, Elmer Ellis proposed consolidating the two manuscript collections. As the founder of WHMC, the incumbent university president, and a committee member, Ellis was the most appropriate person to move formal action on a matter that no one really opposed. George Rozier, who had been the society's president in 1943 when it withdrew its support of the university's manuscript archive, won approval of his suggestion that Director Brownlee first conduct a "space utilization study" to determine where, in the society's expanded quarters, the enlarged manuscripts department would locate. Even Rozier could not question the desired results of merger as Ellis phrased them: "economy of space, ultimate efficiency of administration, [and] removal of all feeling of competition and confusion to the public." On December 1, 1961, after hearing Brownlee's plan for housing and integrating the two archives, the finance committee approved the merger. Dick Brownlee would serve as assistant director of WHMC until such time as Atherton stepped down, which occurred in 1963, when the society's director became director, too, of the joint collections. In both new positions, Brownlee received a university salary, which symbolized in a tangible way the unifying of the two manuscript research facilities.

The joint collections grew again in 1968, this time through expansion onto the university's campuses in Rolla, Kansas City, and St. Louis. By that date the University of Missouri's multicampus system was five years old. Faculty and administrators in the state's two largest cities, as well as on the Rolla campus, saw local opportunities for manuscript collection and utilization. St. Louis chancellor James L. Bugg Jr., for example, had pressed the central university administration for funds to establish an independent manuscript archive on his campus in 1967. The alternative solution selected by the university and the society was the expansion of the existing joint collection in Columbia. The same motives that had favored merger in 1961—efficient operation, centralized coordination, no destructive competition for collections—now argued for four-campus expansion. Ellis, Atherton, and Brownlee met with the four chancellors and their representatives throughout 1968 to create a detailed plan that, in the absence of adequate funding, the university did not fully and immediately implement. Indeed, as late as the spring of 1980, university president James Olson appointed a four-campus committee to solve a persisting problem: "the collections still seem to be regarded as separate," as the finance committee's minutes put it.

At the end of the society's first century, however, the four-campus Western Historical Manuscript Collection functioned smoothly as a single archive, with James W. Goodrich as its director and an associate director at each location. A microform *Guide to Collections* (1985) provided researchers with a subject index to 3,414 manuscript collections at the four locations. A one-day courier service that whisked materials from one site to another allowed WHMC to function as a single archive. The collection in Columbia, as the oldest, was also the most comprehensive. But it, as well as those at the other branches, built special strengths. In Columbia, these included the German Heritage Archives and the National Women and Media Collection. While the Kansas City and St. Louis archives focused on collecting materials relating to the political, social, and economic history of those metropolitan areas, the Rolla collection specialized in the history of the Ozark Plateau region and the history of science and technology. What Francis Sampson and Floyd

By the early 1970s, the Western Historical Manuscript Collection comprised both the university's and the society's manuscript holdings and had nominally become a four-campus-wide operation. Professionally trained manuscript specialists and graduate assistants arranged the documents and wrote finding aids for use by researchers.

Shoemaker had begun early in the century, and the university's history faculty had promoted in the 1940s, had grown into a major regional manuscript archive by the 1990s.

Graduate students, by means of their individual research, helped to forge closer ties between the university and the historical society during the same years that facilities expansion and archives consolidation commanded the attention of Dick Brownlee and the finance committee. The department of history's increased graduate student enrollment helps to explain the growth in student use of the society's resources beginning in the late 1950s. So, too, do the improved relations between the society and the history department during Brownlee's administration, the increasing richness of the society's collections, and the society's new physical facilities. In addition, those graduate students whose assistantships gave them part-time work in the society's departments, especially the WHMC, became familiar with available resources that suggested interesting research topics.

The note on sources following this account includes a bibliography of Ph.D. dissertations and books that rest in part on research in the society's collections. The list is by no means complete, and not all of the items on it came out of the University of Missouri's history department. But the bibliography fairly represents a large number of seminar papers, master's theses, and doctoral dissertations researched by students at the society. A strong U.S. history faculty with nineteenth- and twentieth-century specialties directed this work. Among those who had come to Missouri in the 1940s or earlier were Lewis Atherton, W. Francis English, James L. Bugg Jr., and Walter Scholes. Joining them in the late 1950s and 1960s were Americanists Richard S. Kirkendall, Allen F. Davis, Harold D. Woodman, Noble E. Cunningham Jr., Arvarh E. Strickland, Charles B. Dew, David P. Thelen, and Susan L. Flader. Later additions to the faculty who encouraged their students' work in Missouri history included David Roediger, Susan Porter Benson, and Steven Watts.

Atherton's enthusiasm for the field of American western history and the standards he set in his own teaching and publications inspired the largest number of graduate students whose work appears in the note on sources. Among those who made use of the society's sources on Missouri and the West were Atherton's doctoral students John V. Mering (dissertation completed 1960), James D. Norris (1961), Lewis O. Saum (1962), William E. Foley (1967), Eugene Forderhase (1968), Charles T. Jones Jr. (1969), Jerome O. Steffen (1971), Ralph E. Glauert (1973), George H. Kellner (1973), and James W. Goodrich (1974). The society's rich sources in Missouri's Civil War experience provided material for the dissertations of Wilbert H. Rosen (1960, James Bugg director), Robert E. Shalhope (1967, Atherton), and Donnie D. Bellamy (1971, Charles Dew). Some of Richard Kirkendall's students who did not focus their research on the Truman presidency chose political topics that the society's resources could support, including Franklin D. Mitchell (1964), Lyle W. Dorsett (1965), Gary M. Fink (1968), and Ronald W. Johnson (1973). Students who entered the rapidly expanding field of African American history, in the Missouri context, found the society's resources significant to their work, including George Everett Slavens (1969, Atherton), Larry H. Grothaus (1970, Kirkendall), Lawrence O. Christensen (1972, Atherton), Margaret L. Dwight (1978, Strickland), and Antonio F. Holland (1984, Strickland).

Each of these studies contains words similar to those included by Paul E. McAllister in his dissertation on antebellum Missouri politics: "It has been a pleasure to research" in the society's facility. "The staff of Dr. Richard Brownlee provided much assistance. . . . I owe a special note of thanks to Mrs. Nancy C. Prewitt and her staff" at the manuscripts collection. "They were always gracious, cooperative, and helpful during my many hours of research in their collections." Why does the state of Missouri support a historical society? Thank-yous of this sort provide one compelling answer.

A Type III Transfer under the Omnibus State Reorganization Act of 1974 assigned the state historical society to the University of Missouri "for the purposes of budgeting and public reporting," as President William Aull III described the limited change in June of that year. As Director Brownlee and the finance committee followed the development of state government restructuring in Jefferson City in 1973 and 1974, they expressed satisfaction with their new relationship with the university. The minutes of March 22, 1974, expressed the committee's consensus expectation: "a most cordial relationship guaranteeing the society's entity and self-government." Aull and university president C. Brice Ratchford signed the transfer agreement on June 14, 1974.

Although the State Historical Society of Missouri retained its autonomy under state reorganization, one notable and embarrassing misunderstanding of its status occurred. Routinely featured, as were other state agencies, in the *Official Manual of the State of Missouri,* the society virtually disappeared from the 1975–1976 edition. In three short paragraphs, the staff of Secretary of State James C. Kirkpatrick presented a capsule description of the allegedly former agency, "now a part of the University of Missouri." Dick Brownlee, in a letter to an apologetic Kirkpatrick on March 10, 1976, reported that the finance committee "was disturbed and unhappy over the error." Later editions of the manual restored the society to its position as an independent agency of state government. It was a small misunderstanding, one of many caused by state reorganization, but important to correct. As Brownlee put it, those responsible for the society's well-being "did not desire to have

Missouri's oldest cultural and research institution absorbed by another agency."

A major legacy of Richard Brownlee's leadership was the integration and reconciliation of his organization with the university. He also attended to a smaller, yet significant, act of reconciliation early in his administration. On March 20, 1964, he delivered his lecture "John Smith 'T.,' Missouri's Most Dangerous Pioneer" to members of the Missouri Historical Society gathered on the campus of Washington University in St. Louis. Under Brownlee and Director George R. Brooks of the St. Louis society, a new era of cooperation thus began between the two organizations, despite their names that confused the public and history of cool relations. "There is no reason why we shouldn't have pleasant contacts with the Missouri Historical Society," L. Mitchell White commented to Brownlee in February 1962. "I know that is your thinking."

III

While he integrated his agency more fully with the university, Director Richard Brownlee also applied professional standards to the society's functions and departments. This process was quiet and subtle; also it was without precedent. Unlike Floyd Shoemaker, Dick Brownlee was the product of a Ph.D.-granting, research-oriented university history faculty. His successor, Jim Goodrich, emerged from the same process and environment. The expectations that their mentors at the University of Missouri established for their doctoral work in the 1950s, 1960s, and 1970s had advanced far beyond that prevailing in the World War I era when Shoemaker took his graduate work.

Whereas Secretary Shoemaker often had applied idiosyncratic standards of judgment to the work of the society, Director Brownlee applied professional criteria universally accepted by colleagues nationally to personnel matters, publications, and the society's other business. Given a half-century of the society's earliest years to shape the organization, Shoemaker inevitably had made it a reflection of his own personality, an instrument of his individual preferences. First Dick Brownlee and then Jim Goodrich ran a bureaucracy, in the best sense of that term: an efficiently run state agency that employed impersonal—and therefore even-handed—and universally recognized standards of professional performance to authors and their work, to employees, and to elected leaders. Although Shoemaker became a celebrity of sorts—no one named his successors "Mr. Missouri"—those that followed him were competent administrators and content to be known as such. This is not to diminish Floyd Shoemaker's considerable achievement, but rather to observe that, over time, the historical society reflected the maturation of the history profession in this nation.

His own scholarship was one area in which Richard Brownlee performed the role of professional historian. The early years of his administration coincided with America's observance of the Civil War centennial. As a student of that conflict in Missouri, the director had many opportunities, between 1961 and 1965, to share his expertise with his fellow citizens. On May 12, 1961, for example, Brownlee addressed a joint session of the General Assembly in the capitol's House chambers on Missouri's divisive war experience. The 1961–1962 *Official Manual of the State of Missouri* featured the director's account of the 1864 Battle of Pilot Knob in Iron County.

The most important product of Brownlee's scholarship was his *Gray Ghosts of the Confederacy: Guerrilla Warfare in the West, 1861–1865.* Published by the Louisiana State University Press in 1958, the study was a revised version of his 1954 doctoral dissertation. By "west," Brownlee meant large regions of Missouri's interior, the borderland that it shared with Kansas, and areas such as Texas to which some guerrilla units, like William Quantrill's, withdrew during winter months. After completing the first chapter of the dissertation during the unbearably hot and dry summer of 1954, Brownlee reported to Lewis Atherton, his dissertation supervisor, that he had completed his research in various archives. He continued: "The writing went easily for me. . . . As you suggested, I am approaching the whole subject as a series of historical problems, and the material is lending itself readily to such treatment."

Brownlee's study was original, authoritative, and relevant to many Missouri families. The young scholar's documentation both confirmed and undermined the stories that participants living in areas affected by guerrilla warfare had handed down to their children, and that they, in turn, had passed to the next generation of post–Civil War Missourians. In something of a departure from family and community lore, Brownlee rejected the view that Confederate irregulars like Bill Anderson and the

James brothers deserved forgiveness, even admiration, because intolerable circumstances had forced them to commit their bloody deeds. They, as well as the equally vicious Kansans who opposed them, were "men of free will" to whom the historian assigned "personal responsibility" for their actions. Professor Dudley B. Cornish's review of *Gray Ghosts* in the June 1959 *Mississippi Valley Historical Review* expressed the generally positive scholarly reception that greeted Brownlee's study. Cornish called it "a masterful analysis of the war in Missouri," the strength of which was the author's "detailed explanation of the roots of guerrilla warfare and its development" under Quantrill and others. Reviewers might have added that *Gray Ghosts* contained the most clearly written and carefully reconstructed explanation in print of the events that motivated George Caleb Bingham to paint his *Order No. 11*, the crown jewel of the society's art collection.

Although he planned at least one other book in his field of expertise, Brownlee's all-consuming duties as the society's director prevented completion of that project. The director drew his essay on the Battle of Pilot Knob from his research on General Sterling Price's raid of 1864. "I was half through" the manuscript of that book "when I took this job five years ago," Brownlee wrote in 1966, "and have never had time to bring his army on past Jefferson City." In 1963, Brownlee had cited his heavy workload as the reason he must decline university history professor James Bugg's request that he write the book on the Civil War and Reconstruction in a proposed multivolume history of Missouri. As a referee for the University of Missouri Press, Brownlee found one way to contribute to historical scholarship in the midst of his society commitments. In 1964, he wrote detailed positive evaluations of William A. Settle Jr.'s manuscript on Jesse James, William Parrish's work on Missouri during Reconstruction, and Perry McCandless's book of readings on Missouri history.

As editor of the *Missouri Historical Review*, Brownlee had his greatest opportunity to apply the highest of his profession's standards to the work of the society. In October 1960, less than six months into his administration, the director easily won the finance committee's support of his plan to enhance the quality of the contributions published in the *Review*. Perceiving a "real need for scholarly materials" in the quarterly, Brownlee phased out some of the regular features that Shoemaker had published in favor of a greater number of articles per issue. With some contributors of unacceptable manuscripts, the editor was firm but polite. "Your research is not documented and does not include footnotes," he wrote to the author of an account of a murder case in 1966. "You have used certain techniques of a novelist in ascribing conversations, events and conditions." As he worked through successive revisions of his essay on the "Battle of Moore's Mill" with the *Review*'s editor, Judge Hugh P. Williamson of Fulton wrote to Brownlee in the same year: "You are teaching me a great deal about historical research." Evidence of the society's success in publishing quality pieces in its journal was an award that it shared with author Dorothy V. Jones in 1970. Jones's article, "John Daugherty and the Pawnee Rite of Human Sacrifice," which appeared in the April 1969 issue, won the Western History Association's prize for the best scholarly article in the field of western history.

Beginning during Brownlee's tenure, the society used its own awards to promote and recognize excellence in historical research and publication. As early as July 1962, the finance committee discussed the awarding of a cash prize from the Membership Fund (Trust) and a certificate to the author of the best article appearing in each volume of the *Review*, as judged by a panel of academic historians. The organization's president bestowed the award at the annual luncheon when the society inaugurated this award later in the decade. During the Brownlee years, a public historian, James M. Denny of the Historic Preservation Program, Missouri Department of Natural Resources; a librarian, Robert W. Frizzell of Illinois Wesleyan University; and an assortment of university scholars won awards. The Civil War, Missouri race relations, and recent American politics were among the subjects of prizewinning articles. Floyd Shoemaker's generosity made possible a second award. In his will, the former administrator created a trust fund that generated a cash award for, in alternate years, the high school senior and college junior who wrote the best paper on a Missouri history topic. The society gave its first Shoemaker award to University of Missouri student Patrick J. Dexter at the October 1974 annual meeting.

A highlight of the luncheon following each annual meeting was a guest speaker, a version of whose paper usually appeared in the *Review*. Some speakers, however, informed the audience in a talk that was not simultaneously a scholarly paper. Missouri native General Maxwell D. Taylor, in his "Military Influence on the Formulation of Foreign Policy" in 1969, and C. Brice Ratchford, University of Missouri president, who spoke on his institution's future in 1971, delivered such addresses. So did Clarissa Start Davidson in 1972. A feature writer for the *St. Louis Post-Dispatch,* her talk on the "Women of Missouri" was a venture into the emerging field of women's history. But most of the annual luncheon speakers were scholars, the great majority from teaching institutions, and by subsidizing their work and placing them before an audience of its members, the society promoted some first-rate monographic studies. Among the speakers were William E. Parrish, professor of history at Westminster College (1970), James C. Olson, chancellor of the university's Kansas City campus (1975), Whitfield J. Bell Jr., librarian of the American Philosophical Society in Philadelphia (1976), and William E. Foley, professor of history at Central Missouri State University (1982).

In several ways, the *Missouri Historical Review* commemorated notable events. The quarterly was one of the vital ties between the state society in Columbia and local societies across Missouri, and often it recognized their milestones. The October 1970 issue, for example, included a brief but informative article on the Johnson County Historical Society's fiftieth anniversary. An April 1966 article reviewed Missouri's participation in the New York World Fair of 1964–1965. Both Richard Brownlee and society art curator Sidney Larson had helped to prepare the state's cultural exhibit for that exposition. When the society joined in the celebration of the Missouri Press Association's centennial in 1966–1967, the *Review* noted the event and recalled the editors' role in founding and nurturing the society. Several articles in 1971 informed readers about events that the state held to commemorate its sesquicentennial, including the dedication of Missouri's recently restored first capitol in St. Charles.

Perhaps the *Review*'s most permanent contribution to the commemorations of the 1960s and 1970s was its several special issues. Volumes 55 through 57, appearing between October 1960 and July 1963, included a number of articles and edited documents on the crisis of the Union in Missouri. The July 1971 issue honored the state's sesquicentennial with a group of six articles commissioned for the occasion. In addition to contributions by Bill Foley, David March, and Lewis Atherton, Floyd Shoemaker's article in this collection turned out to be his last publication. Joining discussions of traditional political and economic subject matter were essays by Jerena East Giffen on Missouri women in the 1820s and by Arvarh Strickland on slavery at the time of state-hood.

The society's own seventy-fifth birthday in 1973 occasioned a special anniversary issue in October of that year. Richard Brownlee and his two assistant editors, James Goodrich and Mary K. Dains, wrote a brief history of the society up to that time and also reprinted articles that had appeared in early issues of the *Review,* including one by Francis Sampson from July 1907. For the nation's bicentennial, the three editors assembled hundreds of photographs and prints, most from the society's files, in the July 1976 issue. Informative captions transformed the miscellaneous illustrations into an interesting and popular visual history of the state. Finally, on the centennial of Harry Truman's birth in 1984, the *Review*'s April issue carried three articles on the state's best-known public figure.

A survey of the *Missouri Historical Review*'s contents during Brown-lee's editorship—that is, from volumes 56 (1961–1962) through 79 (1984–1985)—reveals an impressive growth in the variety of subject matter that attracted scholars. Although often-visited fields such as po-litical and military history did not disappear, and although contributors did not depart radically from traditional research methodologies and sources, the *Review* published an unprecedented number of articles on Missouri's minority racial and white ethnic groups. That trend, of course, reflected changing research interests among historians nationally. Surprisingly, only a few of the quarterly's contributions during these years revealed the growing interest in women's history. The twenty-four volumes surveyed included twenty-six articles on African Americans, both during and after slavery. Two of these were two-part essays. Joining this largest category of studies of Missouri's multiethnic past were seven articles on the Germans, five on Native Americans, four on Jews in Missouri, and one on the Irish. Finally, three studies of Missouri's best-known antebellum religious minority, the Mormons, appeared in these issues of the journal. In January 1958, the *Review* had published, posthumously, W. K. Moore's 1945 essay, "An Abortive Slave Uprising." Moore presented the tale "of a few deluded slaves" who failed to carry out a slave revolt in Lewis County. They should have known better than to have tried, the author argued. The flowering of social history in the pages of the society's quarterly in the 1960s and after quickly moved beyond such antiquated simplicities.

The society continued, under Director Brownlee's leadership, its limited book publication program. Since budgetary constraints prevented it from becoming a major publisher of books in Missouri history, the society discontinued one ongoing series. At its meeting of September 7, 1971, the finance committee learned from Brownlee that it would cost $40,000 to publish, in two volumes, the public papers of Governor Warren E. Hearnes. After extended discussion, the members concluded that, whereas the messages and proclamations of the governors series had performed a useful service for administrations whose records were otherwise inaccessible to Missourians, citizens could more easily locate the papers of modern chief executives. One depository for such documents was the new State Archives in Jefferson City. The committee voted to end the gubernatorial papers series, initiated by the society in 1922.

The society did publish five volumes during the period 1960–1985. A varied collection designed to serve several constituencies, the list included Dorothy Caldwell's *Missouri Historic Sites Catalog* (1963). In 1964, the society issued *Missouri Newspapers: When and Where, 1808–1963*. In this useful reference work, compiler William Howard Taft of the university's School of Journalism produced a comprehensive listing "of nearly six thousand publications that have appeared in the state and where they are located." The society's newspaper librarian, Kenneth Holmes, provided Taft with important assistance, and the society's funds gave essential financial support. Dick Brownlee told a number of his correspondents in the spring of 1964 that "in a research sense it is my opinion that" Taft's volume was "the most important work the society has ever published." It served as a catalog of titles in its own newspaper library, a guide to papers that it hoped to obtain on microfilm, "and its dissemination to other libraries should bring a greatly increased use of our library."

The state historical society's last publication under Floyd Shoemaker's editorial direction had been the illustrated booklet *Historic Missouri* (1959). Since it was out of print and out of date, the society replaced it in 1977 with *Historic Missouri: A Pictorial Narrative*. In 1969, the editorial staff had been revising the original booklet, but Brownlee was dissatisfied with the result. "The manuscript was turning into sort of a short history" of the state, he told the finance committee in May, when what he wanted was "a more pictorial treatment" for use primarily in schools. For unknown reasons, the project languished until 1976, when the *Review*'s special July issue marking the American bicentennial became the model for the revised version of *Historic Missouri*. In July 1977, the society began distributing thousands of copies of the publication at a popular price.

The society's most important publication, during Director Brownlee's or any other era, was the 1980 English translation of Gottfried Duden's *Report on a Journey to the Western States of North America and a Stay of Several Years along the Missouri*. This was the first complete English translation of Duden's first edition, which had been published in 1829. The society's volume also included, in an appendix, the author's revisions for the 1834 edition of his work. Carefully translated and edited, authoritative, and permanent in its value to scholars and informed general readers, the Duden project also had the most involved publishing history of all the society's titles. The finance committee inaugurated it on Elmer Ellis's suggestion in 1964. The society distributed complementary copies of the just-printed volume at its annual meeting on October 25, 1980. On that occasion the society's associate director, James W. Goodrich, devoted his luncheon address to the project and to Duden's *Report*.

German immigration had begun to alter Missouri's population make-up in the 1830s, and from that decade forward, Missourians of German origin had played an influential role in the state's history. The state historical society long had displayed an interest in the accounts by German visitors to Missouri, which, circulating in their native land, had encouraged emigration. In 1917–1918, the *Review* had carried a multi-installment translation of parts of Duden's *Report* by William G. Bek, a University of Missouri graduate who had been one of Ellis's professors at the University of North Dakota. Besides the thirty-six letters that constituted Duden's influential publication, these promotional pieces included Friedrich Muench's *Der Staat Missouri: Ein Handbuch für Deutsche Auswanderer* and Gert Goebels's *Langer als ein Menschenleben in Missouri*. Brownlee and the finance committee originally hoped to publish a trilogy of all three works. The society's leadership abandoned that plan as well as others when it encountered several changes of editors and translators and delays in the editorial process.

The committee's minutes and a few surviving letters provide only a bare outline of the Duden project's history. In 1965 and 1966, Brownlee spoke of Thomas M. Davis of the university's English department as the editor of the trilogy, and he hired Friedel Maasdorf of the German language faculty to translate the texts into English. But soon Davis dropped out of the discussions. By midsummer 1966, Maasdorf reported that she could not complete her work. During the latter months of that year and into 1967, Brownlee attempted, but failed, to obtain a grant from the recently established National Endowment for the Arts or the National Endowment for the Humanities to fund the project. The committee, in August 1967, authorized Elsa Nagel, associate professor emeritus of German, to translate Duden's, Muench's, and Goebels's works, and by July 1969 she had completed the first and was working on the second of them. The minutes of October 2, 1970, recorded the finance committee's hope that "by winter . . . all of the translations would be completed" and its decision to identify the volume's editor. For that position a committee of Brownlee, Ellis, and Atherton selected one of Professor Atherton's doctoral candidates, George H. Kellner. A native German speaker, Kellner was completing a dissertation on Germans in antebellum St. Louis while teaching at Rhode Island College. He planned to complete the editing of the Duden manuscript by January 1, 1972.

Although he had made progress on the manuscript, and the published volume would credit him for his contribution, Kellner left the Duden project in the spring of 1975. From that point on, Lewis Atherton, on behalf of the finance committee, played a leading role in guiding the manuscript to publication. So did Jim Goodrich of the society's staff, who now became the book's general editor. It was he who researched and wrote numerous citations and arranged for an interdisciplinary team of University of Missouri faculty—experts in atmospheric science, fisheries and wildlife, and geography, as well as history—to help him complete the annotations of Duden's text. And it was Goodrich who reminded them when their contributions had missed deadlines. German professor Adolf Schroeder also contributed generously to the explanatory notes that filled appendix 2.

The University of Missouri Press published Duden's *Report* for the society. The volume that the team of diverse specialists produced pleased both organizations. Although the finance committee intended, as late as December 1980, to publish Friedrich Muench's and Gert Goebels's promotional accounts, that plan died sometime in the early 1980s. In addition to the monographs published during Brownlee's tenure, the society began issuing its useful *Directory of Local Historical Societies* in 1966. The directory, first issued annually, became a biennial publication in the 1980s.

The greatest challenge to Richard Brownlee's program of raising the professional standards by which he and others judged the society's performance lay in the area of staff remuneration. There existed an inherent contradiction between his high expectations of quality publications and expert patron services on the one hand and the low wage policy that he had inherited on the other. In his first budget proposal, for the 1961–1963 biennium, the society's new director wrote: "The most serious problem facing the society is the maintenance of an adequate professional staff and standard remuneration for that staff." These were "specially educated and trained historians and writers," he reminded legislators, with degrees in library science, journalism, and history. "The salaries for these highly trained specialists have declined to a point where the society is totally unable to compete with other libraries and educational institutions, or, for that matter, even with the public schools." During his years as the society's chief administrator, Brownlee supported his strong words with a determination to raise staff salaries and benefits.

In his report to the annual meeting in September 1963, Director Brownlee noted that increased state appropriations have "enabled us to obtain professionally trained people and to pay them with more adequacy." The society recognized the low salaries endured by its "loyal staff" and was "slowly but surely bringing about conditions of some equality." More than two years later, in January 1966, in a report to the finance committee, Brownlee sounded less optimistic. Recent resignations and long-vacant positions forced him to identify "the recruitment and keeping of a professionally trained staff" as one of the "crucial problems" facing the society. He had been unable, in four years of trying, to hire a full-time cataloger. Staff turnover resulting from "limited salaries" caused inefficiencies in the historical society's operations.

It was the budgetary integration of the society and the university, beginning in 1975, that encouraged hope for a solution to the salary problem. By June of that year, following an evaluation of each staff position, the university placed the society's employees in its job classification system; where necessary, new position titles were added to the system. The goal was to equalize pay between university and society personnel who performed comparable duties. The society's staff, who had participated in the university's group life and health insurance plans since early 1960, now gained full access to that institution's benefits plans. In 1971–1972, the society expended $145,120 for salaries. The budget that year contained no line item for benefits. The cost of salaries in 1975–1976 was $175,037, and that of benefits $6,644. In Richard Brownlee's last fiscal year, 1985–1986, his agency paid $326,318 for salaries and $39,453 for staff benefits.

When Donald Welsh joined the society in 1957, Floyd Shoemaker created a new position for him, one that Richard Brownlee maintained and then enhanced. Welsh became the first assistant editor of the *Review*, with duties reaching far beyond the publication. James E. Moss replaced Welsh in August 1961. When Moss left for another job in the summer of 1966, his title was assistant to the director and associate editor of the quarterly. Jim Goodrich, Moss's replacement, came to the society as associate editor, a position that Dorothy J. Caldwell and Mary K. Dains also occupied during the Brownlee years. When Jim Goodrich replaced Dick Brownlee as the society's director late in 1985, he had also held the titles of assistant and associate director. These new posts created a path of professional advancement and recognition absent from the society's first six decades as an employer of trained historians and librarians. Only Jim Goodrich has traveled that path of succession to the society's top post.

The graduate degrees that they had earned helped to measure the expertise of Director Brownlee's staff. Welsh and Goodrich earned their Ph.D. degrees in the university's history department, while Moss, Dains, and Caldwell held the M.A. from the same institution. A native of Poplar Bluff and a Navy veteran of the Korean War, Moss studied business as an undergraduate and completed his master's degree in history in 1958. Before joining the society, he taught at Christian College in Columbia and worked with Brownlee in the university's extension division. Kathy Dains earned an M.A. in American history in 1964. Her extensive list of publications included the two-volume work *Show Me Missouri Women,* a collection of biographical sketches that she edited. Dorothy Caldwell's career with the society extended from 1955 to 1972. To her B.S. degree in education (1926) and B.F.A. in music (1930), she added a B.J. (1949) and M.A. (1954) in journalism. As committed to historic preservation in her private life as she was in her society assignments, Caldwell was a leader in efforts to restore the historic Missouri river town of Rocheport.

Marie Woods represented the clerical staff that provided the society's professionals with essential support. Raised on a farm near Pierce City in southwest Missouri, Woods learned secretarial skills at Springfield Business College. From 1929 to 1943, she was secretary to three presidents of Central Methodist College in Fayette. From 1943, when Floyd Shoemaker brought her to the society, until her retirement in 1974, she served as secretary, then administrative assistant, in the director's office. Upon her retirement, the Missouri House of Representatives recognized her dedicated service to the state's history in a resolution. The society bestowed upon Woods its Distinguished Service Award in 1974. She was the first woman to receive it.

IV

In January 1966, Richard Brownlee identified the retention of a professional staff as one of three critical problems facing the society. The other two problems involved rapid, even uncontrolled, growth. By the end of 1965, the society's membership had swelled to over sixteen thousand. In addition, the number of those who used the society's collections also had increased dramatically since he took office in 1960. While growth was evidence of the society's success, the director also emphasized that it strained limited resources.

Richard Brownlee achieved his third goal for the State Historical Society of Missouri, consolidation of the outreach and service programs, as he struggled with the consequences of growth. Consolidation meant stabilizing and strengthening existing programs. It meant effectively managing the properties and functions that the society had accumulated in previous years, which now showed the effects of increased use, rather than launching new ones. Its behavior was that of a mature organization.

While the Missouri highway historic marker program had been a realm of innovation for the society in the 1950s, for Dick Brownlee it was a task to complete and maintain. When the society began its marker program, the system of interstate highways did not exist. The interstate system had begun to divert a considerable amount of the state's long-distance automobile travel away from the network of numbered U.S. and state highways by the mid-1960s, and therefore away from the markers. During the same years, the Missouri highway department relocated many sections of the two-lane thoroughfares along which the historic markers stood, and others, such as segments of U.S. 40, simply disappeared as nearby Interstate 70 replaced it. "We are having a tremendous problem with our markers because of highway re-location," Brownlee wrote to a friend in Osceola in 1964, "and the fact that none of the new roads have access drive offs." The society had already relocated a few markers to courthouse lawns in county seats, and that process would continue. In 1983, the finance committee authorized the Bethel German Communal Colony to move the society's marker from the original highway location to the colony's property.

A second maintenance problem was the restoration of damaged markers. In 1980, for example, a truck hit the marker at Altenburg in Perry County. While a local organization had paid the premiums on an insurance policy that replaced that marker, the one removed by thieves from Missouri 21 near Hillsboro in Jefferson County in 1983 lacked such protection. Only in 1985 did the society's finances permit replacement of that marker, at a cost of $2,900. Its policy was to consider repair and replacement needs on a case-by-case basis.

Under Brownlee's direction, as in earlier years, the society played a facilitating rather than a supervisory role in the preservation of Missouri's historic sites. When asked to promote the cause of a threatened structure—for example, the Missouri State Fruit Experiment Station at Mountain Grove in 1968—Brownlee cited the society's "policy of not formally endorsing the preservation of any specific historical site in Missouri." To support one such project would encourage numerous other requests, some involving "sites of dubious historicity." On the other hand, the director wrote to a correspondent in 1967, "We are intensely interested in every sound proposal and will assist in research functions to the best of our ability." Material in the society's collections could validate or undermine a site's claims to historical significance. As Brownlee informed many who contacted him, the General Assembly, in 1959, had made the Missouri State Park Board the custodian of state historic sites.

The society's most important contribution to the work of the park board was Dick Brownlee's service as chairman of the agency's Advisory Council on Historic Sites and Buildings in the 1960s. The group's task was to evaluate the merit of proposals and make recommendations to Joseph Jaeger, director of the park board. During Brownlee's tenure as head of the council, the group evaluated some sites, including the Daviess County rotary jail at Gallatin and the site of Civil War Fort Wyman in Rolla, as lacking "primary statewide historical significance." It also advised against state acquisition of Congressman Champ Clark's home at Bowling Green. By contrast, the committee recommended state maintenance of the Rozier-Valle House at Ste. Genevieve, which had been "connected with historically important Missourians since its building and represents a unique type of architecture for the area."

While the society played an ancillary role in the preservation of historic sites, one of its central responsibilities, that of managing and protecting its own collections, grew as its holdings increased in value, age, and size. Its responsibility also grew as added numbers of people used the society's resources. In part, patron interest responded to the more spacious research facilities. "I am certain that you will be pleased to know," Brownlee commented to Governor Dalton in mid-1962, "that research in our new quarters has nearly doubled in the past year." Research also grew as more Missourians learned of the society's resources, as interest in genealogy expanded, as people increasingly made inquiries by telephone—and, doubtless, for numerous other sound reasons.

Whatever complex of causes produced it, Brownlee, as early as the fall of 1963, spoke to the annual meeting about "a phenomenal and desirable growth in the utilization of the society's resources." In the first half of that year, 3,501 researchers visited the society's book, newspaper, and manuscript libraries, while the staff answered over 4,000 requests by mail. Over 3,000 persons viewed exhibits in the art gallery in 1962–1963. In early 1966, when Brownlee perceived another "phenomenal increase" in the number of researchers and mail inquiries as a growing problem for a staff "swamped with work," he presented the finance committee with new statistics. While 4,776 researchers had visited the newspaper library in 1964, 8,380 had done so in 1965. The manuscripts library welcomed a greater number of patrons during the first three months of 1965 than it had throughout 1964.

While the reports of increased patronage became routine, Brownlee remained concerned about his staff's ability to meet the heavy demand for services. Budgetary limitations, when they did not force employee reductions, maintained or only slightly increased staff numbers. Nor could the society acquire the computer technology that would have multiplied the ability of a small staff to serve a growing clientele, or that would have allowed patrons to serve themselves. Brownlee's 1979 report to members summarized Missourians' use of the reference library in 1978–1979: 12,800 visiting researchers, 2,800 letters requesting help, and 1,300 telephoned requests. The staff of the newspaper library had helped 12,000 patrons in person, 4,000 by mail, and 800 over the phone. In that year, the Columbia branch of the joint manuscript collection "had served over 1,000 patrons with in-depth research." In an effort to summarize the full range of the society's user services, Brownlee revealed in his 1980 annual report that all divisions had assisted 28,000 visiting patrons during the 1979–1980 fiscal year, dispatched 15,300 letters, and answered 4,200 telephone calls—in every case providing answers to questions about Missouri's history. In his 1984, and last, report on the state of the society, Richard Brownlee reported that "over 40,000 patrons of the society . . . had been served" by the staff during the past fiscal year.

A variety of maintenance activities and management decisions, of which the public in most cases was unaware, prepared the collections for their numerous users. A persisting issue was researcher access to materials on Saturday mornings and weekday evenings. In November 1966, the finance committee voted to close the reference and newspaper libraries on Saturday mornings, when only a handful of visitors appeared, in favor of having a full staff present on weekdays. The decision inconvenienced some, including a master's degree candidate at Lincoln University who lived in St. Louis and who could visit Columbia only on weekends. "I would suggest that it would be better to close for one full day during the week, in order that the society can be open on Saturday mornings," he wrote. State Senator Roger Wilson, in the spring of 1980, inquired about "possible evening openings of the society's libraries" on behalf of patrons who could not visit during regular business hours. Until the state government's darkening financial outlook made such a request impolitic, the finance committee planned to ask the legislature for five additional staff positions in 1981, to permit expanded services. To those who requested increased access to the society's research materials, Director Brownlee could only apologize for the inconvenience and cite staff—that is, budgetary—limitations.

The routine of day-to-day management demanded decisions, large and small, about how best to spend the society's funds. By the fall of 1963, the society had framed all of its Thomas Hart Benton lithographs and John J. Audubon engravings. Three years later the finance committee decided to continue framing many of the society's maps so that the staff could more easily exhibit them. A decade later the committee allocated additional funds from the trust account to encapsulate for preservation selected atlases and books. With the support of a grant from the Clifford W. Gaylord Foundation, the society authorized art curator Sidney Larson to restore Bingham's *Order No. 11* and Benton's *Exterminate* in 1984–1985. The replacement of old and the acquisition of new equipment was a continuing need. In 1971, for example, the newspaper library installed a new microfilm reader-printer at a cost of $2,100 in place of one ten years old that "was obsolete and damaging film."

One of the society's major ongoing commitments was to microfilm current and back issues of newspapers and pamphlets in the reference library. Many of the older titles suffered deterioration from repeated use and advanced age. On several occasions during Director Brownlee's tenure, the finance committee authorized $5,000 expenditures from the Membership Fund (Trust) for microfilming newspapers. From its state appropriation, the society spent even larger sums for microfilming. In the nine fiscal years from 1971–1972 to 1979–1980, it expended over $100,000 for the microfilming of its own materials and purchased additional resources already on machine-readable film. When the General Assembly rejected the university's third proposal for a library storage facility in its 1981 session, Dick Brownlee received the finance committee's approval to earmark additional trust monies for microfilming portions of the collection. Sources stored on microfilm consumed less space than shelved pamphlets or newspapers. These expenditures included $23,000 to enhance the newspaper microfilming program, for which the legislature had denied a requested increase of $10,000 in the state appropriation. The committee authorized up to $19,000 additionally to microfilm deteriorating serials.

The confluence of two factors in 1982 and 1983 threatened the society's important newspaper microfilming project. As Director Brownlee grimly informed the 1983 annual meeting: "For the first time since the program was started in the 1930s, funds for microfilming current newspapers had been eliminated because of withheld appropriations." The second difficulty was inflation. The society's microfilming service increased its rates 46.6 percent in 1982–1983 over the previous year. A temporary stopgap was the expenditure of $14,000 from the trust fund for newspaper microfilming, which the finance committee approved in September 1982. The state's editors, acting through the Missouri Press Association, generously responded to a more significant solution. Brownlee's plan was to ask editors to pay for the cost of a negative microfilm copy of their newspaper, while the society would pay for the less expensive positive copy. In the past, the society had paid for both. The plan would save up to three-fourths of the cost of current newspaper microfilming. By its September 9, 1983, meeting, the finance committee knew the outcome of the initiative: 66 percent of the state's newspaper publishers had responded favorably, contributing $18,116 of the year's total of $27,159 needed for the newspaper microfilming program. Brownlee's 1984 annual report contained more good news: "Improved state appropriations had allowed the society to once again fund all of its programs, including the newspaper microfilming program."

In managing some of its most valuable holdings—namely the art and rare book collections—the society faced several problems of security. The protection sought for its treasures covered impersonal threats from fire, water, and improperly conditioned air. But a 1964 incident reminded Dick Brownlee throughout the remainder of his career that the society also needed protection against human threats. On March 10 of that year, a part-time "trusted employee" of the Western Historical Manuscript Collection, who was also a university history department graduate student and teaching assistant, confessed that he had stolen and sold over one thousand letters and other documents. An alert manuscripts dealer in New York had recognized a soon-to-be-auctioned letter as one that the society had once owned and phoned the society's director to inquire. The historical society recovered only a portion of the missing manuscripts, but the disturbing experience did create a new awareness of its vulnerability.

Security systems to guard against various threats, insurance coverage, and the changing value of the fine art and rare book collections in an inflationary economy were interrelated matters. The society had paid $17,500 for the J. Christian Bay Collection in 1941. In 1974, it insured that collection, to which numerous rare titles had been added, for $282,788.50. An appraisal of the fine arts properties completed in the spring of 1979 revealed a total value in excess of $3.6 million. The society's George Caleb Bingham collection alone was worth more than

$2.25 million. The annual premium on a new blanket insurance policy for the art collection cost over $2,000 in June of that year.

With such valuables stored in its quarters, the society required effective security and climate control systems. Indeed, without them insurers would refuse to write policies on the collections. Twice during the 1970s and 1980s, the society discovered that moisture had caused minor damage. Some paintings showed the effects of excessively humid air in the gallery and art storage area in 1975, and a fungus damaged a small number of books in the Bay room in 1981. Between 1975 and 1978, the society spent well over $23,000 to improve the physical security of its quarters and the climate control equipment in the art and rare book rooms. As the improvements neared completion, Brownlee reported to the 1977 annual meeting that "for the first time in our history" the society enjoyed adequate protection of its valued collections.

As Richard Brownlee often observed, he presided over one of the nation's great specialized research facilities. Under his guidance, the book, newspaper, art, and manuscript collections grew from the strong foundations laid by the society prior to 1960. To say that the state historical society's newspaper and art holdings represented unique strengths does not in the least diminish the reference library's rich resources, the rare book collection whose core was the J. Christian Bay purchase, or the society's and university's joint manuscript archive. As they had prior to the society's designation as a not-for-profit, tax-exempt organization in 1984, gifts continued to be an essential means of growth. Director Brownlee informed a benefactor in 1966 that the society received "more than a thousand" donations a month. Friends of the society displayed conspicuous generosity in their gifts of artworks and manuscript collections during the Brownlee years. Even in periods of static or reduced state financial support, donations and purchases made with membership trust funds allowed the collections to keep pace with the increased demand for them.

Floyd Shoemaker and his finance committee had begun the society's art collection without adopting a policy statement that explained why visual art was appropriate resource material for an organization that lacked a museum or a gallery. Under their direction, the art collection grew in an incidental fashion as, for example, the Rollins family decided to sell *Order No. 11* and L. M. White persuaded Daniel Fitzpatrick to deposit his editorial cartoons with the society. While Dick Brownlee was director, however, and to complement its new art gallery, the society's leadership systematically built collections both of fine and popular visual art. It expressed a rationale for collecting art from time to time, but did not linger over justifications. In a 1964 *Review* article on the society's paintings, the editorial staff affirmed "that works of art provide one of the most important sources for documentation of the American scene." Librarian Laura Peritore, in her 1979 report on the society's cartoon collections, pointed out that these newspaper editorial statements were artifacts that reflected history, but could also be independent causal forces in history. Students of art, too, could observe the evolution of Benton's, Bingham's, or Fitzpatrick's technique or subject matter by analyzing the society's holdings.

Throughout the period, the agency sought to enlarge its already significant collections of George Caleb Bingham's and Thomas Hart Benton's works. The addition of seven Bingham portraits, by gift and purchase, solidified the status of the society's Bingham collection as one of the largest anywhere. The portraits included those of James S. Rollins, the "father" of the University of Missouri and defender of the Union during the Civil War, and of Confederate General Joseph O. Shelby. A small acquisitions budget prevented purchase of Bingham's *John Quincy Adams* in 1968; the price tag on the former president's portrait was $25,000. In 1972, the society purchased hand-colored original prints of Bingham's genre paintings *County Election* and *Stump Speaking*. The Rollins family, descendants of James S. Rollins, Bingham's patron, presented the society with a major gift in 1983. It donated John Sartain's original engraved plate for the folio engraving of *Order No. 11*. To commemorate the hundredth anniversary of Bingham's death, Sidney Larson delivered an address on the artist at the 1979 annual luncheon, and the society mounted a special exhibit of his works.

Thomas Hart Benton, who lived until January 19, 1975, continued to be a generous benefactor of the State Historical Society of Missouri. It honored the artist, in turn, with its distinguished service award in 1969 and with special exhibits of his art in that year and in 1981. The second of these featured the watercolors and drawings that Benton had executed for collectors' editions of three Mark Twain books published between 1939 and 1944. The society also purchased several of Benton's lithographs, including *Hoeing Cotton* and *Youth Music*. As of 1975, the historical society's collection of Benton lithographs totaled 88. Over the years, the Neosho native gave 203 of his works to the society, whose collection was one of the most extensive in the United States.

While Binghams and Bentons were the art collection's special features, Brownlee and the finance committee encouraged the donation of other artists' works. One project suggested by art curator Sidney Larson, which the committee first discussed in 1969 and launched in 1972, was the contemporary artists collection. Brownlee requested the donation of a representative painting, sculpture, or work in another medium from those on a lengthy list of living Missouri artists, and many responded. By the fall of 1975, fifty-two artists had contributed pieces to the collection. At its meeting on March 7 of that year, however, the finance committee tempered its initial enthusiasm for contemporary art. It directed Brownlee to "be highly selective" in obtaining such works in the future "in order to keep the society's art program in proper balance with its historical mission." The society had never lost sight of that mission, of course, as the gift of a portrait of former governor Trusten Polk in 1960 and the purchase of nineteenth-century lithographs by Thomas L. McKenney and James Hall in 1971 demonstrated.

Editorial cartoons and photographs fit the society's inclusive definition of art as readily as did paintings. In the 1960s, L. M. White, who had prompted Floyd Shoemaker and his colleagues on the finance committee to inaugurate the cartoon collection in the 1940s, continued to use his friendship with newspaper artists to enlarge it. White's goal, as he expressed it three weeks after Brownlee had assumed office, was "the largest collection of original newspaper cartoons . . . in the world." By the end of 1961, the new director had contacted sixty-two editorial cartoonists across the nation about giving samples of their work. Brownlee reported to Daniel Fitzpatrick in September 1964 that recent additions, including one by the *St. Louis Post-Dispatch* artist himself, give the society "the largest and most famous collection of original cartoons in the nation." Joining the contributions of individual cartoonists such as Tom Engelhardt of the *Post-Dispatch,* S. J. Ray of the *Kansas City Star,* and Don Hesse of the *St. Louis Globe-Democrat,* was the Peter Mayo Collection in 1964. A Chicago architect, Mayo had assembled a comprehensive collection of American newspaper art, supplemented by examples from the foreign press as well. Mayo's collection included over sixteen hundred original editorial cartoons dated from 1813 to 1964. This treasure trove included the

Thomas Hart Benton, a longtime and generous friend of the society's, was named the 1969 recipient of its Distinguished Service Award. The award was presented to Benton, who had been unable to attend the annual meeting, at his home in Kansas City in April 1970. Society President T. Ballard Watters (right) presented the certificate and medallion to Benton.

work of Thomas Nast, John T. McCutcheon, and Rollin Kirby. In 1979, the society owned over fifty-eight hundred original cartoons. The staff of the editorial department managed the society's extensive collection of historic photographs, selections from which illustrated the *Review*'s articles. Contributions to that collection in 1964 included photographs of St. Louis and the Ozarks taken by Charles Trefts. A year later, the society received a collection of photos taken by G. Houston George in 1917 when he traveled by automobile from Flint, Michigan, to Odessa, Missouri.

The society enhanced its holdings of original manuscript material in the Western Historical Manuscript Collection in several ways. Donors included Senator Stuart Symington, Governor John M. Dalton, Congressman Jerry Litton, medical missionary Dr. Tom Dooley, Methodist Bishop Ivan Lee Holt, and writer Homer Croy. The Dr. E. B. Trail collection of pictures and manuscripts on the subject of Missouri steamboating came to the society in 1963. Trail, as Brownlee pointed out, was "most likely the only person left on the Missouri River who has any personal knowledge of his subject." In 1978, Missouri alumnus Morris E. Dry donated his eight-thousand-piece sheet music collection to the society. On several occasions the society also acquired manuscript materials on microfilm. Purchases included the entire Lyman Draper Collection, owned by the State Historical Society of Wisconsin, in 1960; series 1 and 2 of the American Church Records, in 1966 and 1971, respectively; the service records of Missouri Federal and Confederate soldiers, in 1970; and the records of Missouri postmasters by county, 1930–1971, in 1972.

The most important manuscript project that engaged Director Brownlee and specialists from the Columbia branch of the Western Historical Manuscript Collection was their work with the Ste. Genevieve District Papers in 1978 and 1979. Researchers had made little use of these twenty-eight thousand uncataloged eighteenth- and nineteenth-century documents, some written in French and Spanish, and the records were increasingly subject to physical deterioration. In the late summer of 1978, the society offered to bring the collection to Columbia "for the purpose of professionally arranging, cataloging, making finder cards and microfilming both finder cards and the original documents." Local officials agreed. On November 8, 1979, the director led a delegation to Ste. Genevieve to return the original papers and one microfilm copy to the county court. The society retained one copy of the microfilmed records for research use. Cindy Stewart and Laura Bullion of the manuscripts staff joined Brownlee in describing for Ste. Genevieve residents the collection's contents and explaining the process by which they had cataloged and preserved the manuscripts. This project stands as one of the finest examples in the society's history, of both the preservation of valuable historical records and of creative cooperation with local citizen-historians.

The microfilming process also brought to the newspaper library numerous files of nineteenth- and early-twentieth-century newspapers. When their owners did not give the papers to the society, it borrowed

Among the significant manuscript collections acquired by the Western Historical Manuscript Collection during Richard Brownlee's tenure were the papers of U.S. Senator Stuart Symington. The senator presented the first increment of his papers to the manuscript repository in 1964. Left to right, Albert M. Price, society member; Ralph Parker, director of the university library; Senator Stuart Symington; and Richard S. Brownlee. Price became treasurer of the society in 1968.

them for filming. The society also borrowed some schedules of the 1850 through 1880 censuses from the Missouri Historical Society in 1972 for microfilming. Among the friends of the society who donated personal collections of books were Lewis Atherton, James C. Olson, Jean Tyree Hamilton of Marshall, and Irene Fitzgerald, professor emeritus of education at the university. The latter gift established the Fitzgerald Collection of Missouri's Literary Heritage for Children and Youth in 1982.

Overseeing the increase of collections was, for the most part, an internal administrative function that attracted little attention. Managing the tremendous increase in membership that the society continued to experience in the early Brownlee years became a public matter when the finance committee took steps to control membership numbers. As early as his fall 1963 annual report to members, Brownlee characterized some consequences of growth as a "serious concern." One of these was the administrative burden of sending each of fourteen thousand members dues statements and annual meeting announcements, the cost of which consumed a good share of the one-dollar annual membership fee. A second concern was the production of "almost 57,000 *Reviews* each year, a major magazine publication operation." Unanticipated in budget requests made to the legislature, the addition of four thousand new members between 1962 and 1966 created increased costs that the Membership Fund (Trust) absorbed.

The finance committee proposed, and those members present for the annual meetings approved, dues increases for annual members from one to two dollars in 1966, and from two to five dollars in 1981. Life memberships also increased in cost. The context, and therefore the rationale, for each increase was different. The first signified the end of the era of membership growth for its own sake launched by Secretary Shoemaker in the 1920s. The society remained first in membership of all state societies in the 1960s, and proud of it. But that position had become less important than the liabilities of large size. By September 1968, membership had fallen from approximately sixteen thousand to about fourteen thousand. Brownlee and the finance committee members "felt the loss was normal and desirable." As the director phrased it in his annual report of that month, the modest dues increase of 1966 had reduced the number of "inexpensive gift membership[s]" that some Missourians had given to friends and family members. The dues hike, "as was intended, curtailed a run-a-way growth which was approaching a thousand new members each year."

The 1981 increase in the cost of annual membership, and of life memberships from $40 to $100, was a response to reduced state appropriations and years of increases in the cost of doing business caused by relentless inflation. As President Lewis Atherton framed the problem in a letter to finance committee members in February: "State revenues for the coming year are of crisis proportions and the society's future may be threatened seriously." Before those who attended the annual meeting voted on the fee increases, Director Brownlee suggested that increased revenue from dues "might assist the society in becoming more self-sufficient." Indeed, the Missouri General Assembly had strongly suggested that the society generate a greater proportion of its annual financial support from its members, relieving the state's general revenue fund of some of the stress that it experienced in the early 1980s. Representative Everett W. Brown, chairman of the House Appropriations Committee, represented that view to the director and the society's elected leaders. Aware that the society's dues were comparatively low among state-supported historical societies, and that some legislators wished to make deep cuts in the society's appropriation, Brown urged the agency to shift more of its costs to those who benefited most directly from its services, the membership. Legislators believed, Brown wrote, that "the amount of $5.00 would not cause the society to lose members."

In that prediction the lawmakers were wrong. The staff's monitoring of membership trends traced a deep decline in annual members following the 1981 dues increase. From January to May 1982, compared with figures from the same months in 1981, the society experienced a 55 percent decrease in new members, a 121 percent increase in those who terminated their memberships, a 44 percent increase in those who missed the deadline for renewing but still might do so, and a 4.5 percent total decrease in membership, from 13,751 to 13,134. At the December 2, 1983, finance committee meeting, Director Brownlee reported a 12.9 percent decrease in members during the first eleven months of the year, from 12,552 to 10,922. By June 1984, the society had experienced a 28 percent reduction in members since the dues increase took effect, a total of 3,453. Society leaders agreed that the severe recession of the early 1980s joined the fee increase as a cause of membership decline.

The higher dues did produce what legislators wanted, increased revenue. Membership revenue in 1982–1983 was $39,417, compared with $33,324 the previous year. All things considered, however, Brownlee wrote to Everett Brown in February 1983, "I believe the increase to have had disappointing results." What the statistics could not do was to identify the people who had dropped their affiliation with the society. Many, Brownlee believed, "are older people who simply could not afford the increase." Such persons had often "in the past . . . given the society valuable books and documents concerning our state's history."

Although not operated for profit, the State Historical Society of Missouri was a large and complex business. If that reality was not evident during Floyd Shoemaker's years as secretary, it was quite obvious during Director Richard Brownlee's tenure as the society's chief administrator.

When Brownlee retired in 1985, the transition to his successor Jim Goodrich proceeded more smoothly and naturally than had been the case twenty-five years earlier. Goodrich would assume direction of an efficient, professionally run, as well as substantial, organization.

5

Completing the First Century
under James W. Goodrich, 1985–1998

ichard Brownlee, an outsider to the society but a scholar in Missouri history, was familiar with its work when the finance committee chose him as Floyd Shoemaker's successor in October 1959. James W. Goodrich, an employee of the State Historical Society of Missouri since 1967, commanded detailed knowledge of the agency's operations when he replaced Brownlee in December 1985. That working knowledge guaranteed that the transition from one director to the next would be so smooth as to be nearly imperceptible.

An easy transition implies continuity of philosophy and policy, and in its broad interpretation of the society's mission, the Goodrich administration was in harmony with its predecessors. Indeed, in a letter of November 27, 1989, addressing the society's mission and his own priorities, Goodrich echoed one of Floyd Shoemaker's and Richard Brownlee's fundamental assumptions. He wrote: "One of the reasons the state historical society has achieved past successes is that [it] . . . has been prudent in its approach to its mission." It had avoided "inadequately funded" commitments in the past and should continue to do so.

Yet, although Executive Director Goodrich was cautious about innovation, he soon launched policy initiatives that gave a distinctive character to the last thirteen years of the society's first century. The numerous innovations that marked the Goodrich years, rather than setting major new directions for the society, instead increased its effectiveness as a public service agency. The reappearance of Saturday hours, workshops held on annual meeting day, an oral history program, cosponsorship of History Day in Missouri—in these and other ways, the society under Jim Goodrich made its services and resources more accessible than ever before to students of Missouri history and seekers of genealogical data.

I

Beginning with Richard Brownlee's resignation as director in 1985, considerable change occurred in the ranks of the society's elected leadership and professional staff. Suffering from poor health, Brownlee informed the finance committee on March 8 that he would leave his position on September 1. Among the honors bestowed by the trustees upon the departing director was the Distinguished Service Award for 1985 and, later, a portrait painted by art collection curator Sidney Larson. Brownlee's death on February 14, 1990, came only months after those of two mentors. Lewis Atherton's passing on March 25, 1989, and Elmer Ellis's on August 27 of that year removed two of the society's most significant friends and officers.

With the concurrence of University of Missouri officials, who employed the society's director as head of the joint manuscript collection, President Francis M. Barnes III had named a search committee by the date of the June finance committee meeting. Those who would evaluate applicants' files and recommend Brownlee's successor were Barnes as chair; William Aull III; Jean Tyree Hamilton; Dr. James C. Olson, president emeritus of the university; Stuart Symington Jr.; Dr. Arvarh Strickland of the university's history faculty; and Thomas W. Shaughnessy, university librarian. All but Shaughnessy were trustees of the society.

The "position announcement" that was circulated by the committee, the first for a director in the organization's history, constituted a commentary on the society's mission as well as a description of the job. The new director must hold the doctorate, it read, and have at least two years' experience "in an historical society or archival organization." An interest in Missouri history was optional. Among the successful candidate's desired skills were some that went beyond the expected abilities to lead, administer, and direct. These special qualities included "vision," the ability to project the society's roles and needs into the future. And they included the skills required to "design, fund and implement creative and effective programs of research, publication, and service linking the historical resources of the society, university and state to their various constituencies." The announcement seemed to be a mandate for innovation, if funding for new programs existed. October 1 was the deadline for receipt of applications.

While the search process moved forward, trustee Virginia Young, a trained librarian, served as acting director, a position she assumed on October 7. Young was the only woman to serve as director, in any capacity, during the society's first one hundred years. During the search period, Nancy Lankford, the joint manuscript collection's associate director for the Columbia facility, served as acting director for the entire four-campus operation.

Associate Director Jim Goodrich was "the obvious choice" to succeed Brownlee, Elmer Ellis wrote privately on May 9, and indeed Goodrich was among the candidates for the position. The society's second-in-command had major accomplishments to his credit: as the general editor of the Duden volume in the late 1970s, as the chief representative of the society's interests during the Ellis Library expansion process of the early 1980s, and as one of those most responsible for preparing the society's quarterly since the late 1960s. During Brownlee's last years in office, Goodrich took on other responsibilities for the ailing director. After Brownlee had announced his retirement plans to the finance committee on March 8, 1985, for example, the associate director reported on strategies to boost the society's membership.

Although Goodrich was a strong internal candidate, the search committee conducted an open, nationwide canvass for a new chief executive. Trustees Ellis and Atherton, in the interest of a competitive search, encouraged one other qualified candidate to apply. The committee's only exclusionary decision was that there would be no "appointment relationship" between the university's history department and the new director. The search committee received approximately twenty-five applications for the directorship during the summer and fall of 1985. At least one other serious candidate beside Jim Goodrich, an accomplished Missouri history scholar, came to Columbia for an interview with the search committee. That applicant dropped out of the running for personal reasons.

Jim Goodrich became secretary, director, and librarian of the State Historical Society of Missouri on December 7, 1985, when the finance committee unanimously endorsed the search committee's nomination of the former associate director. The university administration had already approved Goodrich's appointment as director of the joint manuscript collection. The new director's titles also included that of editor of the *Missouri Historical Review.* In January 1988, the administrator's title became executive director.

While Richard Brownlee represented a family with deep roots in the state's past, and while he acquired his scholarly interest in Missouri history in part through a personal identification with his subject matter, Jim Goodrich did neither. Goodrich, as with most other Missouri historians, professional or amateur, found Missouri's past compelling enough to command fascination and sustain attention without the aid of ancestors who had participated in its events. Born in Burlington, Iowa, on October 31, 1939, Goodrich attended public schools in Kansas and Missouri, graduating from Sedalia's Smith-Cotton High School in 1957. Involved in dramatic, musical, and yearbook activities, it was Goodrich's high school football achievements that led to an athletic scholarship at the University of Kansas in 1957. But a knee injury brought a halt to his playing days, and Goodrich transferred to Central Missouri State University in Warrensburg. He graduated from there in 1962 with a B.S.Ed. degree in social studies. In 1962, the future executive director did his practice teaching in a classroom across the hallway from a history teacher and future society trustee, Lawrence O. Christensen, at William Chrisman High School in Independence. They would meet again and renew their friendship as graduate students at the University of Missouri–Columbia.

Jim Goodrich began his graduate studies in history at the University of Missouri in Columbia in 1962 and received the M.A. degree in 1964. He gained a working knowledge of the Western Historical Manuscript Collection as a graduate assistant between 1964 and 1966. That experience helped Goodrich to earn appointment as the first state archivist for the Records Management and Archives Service in the office of Missouri's Secretary of State in 1966. Dick Brownlee announced to the finance committee on November 11, 1966, that "he had been able to employ James W. Goodrich as associate editor of the *Missouri Historical Review*" and assistant to the director. Returning to Columbia with his

James W. Goodrich, a graduate of the University of Missouri–Columbia Department of History, became executive director, secretary, and librarian of the society in 1985. Goodrich acquired numerous significant additions to the society's collections, focused on public service, and made the organization's resources more widely available to researchers.

family, Goodrich began his duties with the society on January 2, 1967. Linda M. Andreoli of Akron, Ohio, a Stephens College student, married Jim Goodrich in 1963. The couple became the parents of two daughters, Lisa and Kimberly.

During his early years with the society, Goodrich continued work on his doctoral degree, which the university conferred in May 1974. Goodrich was a student of Lewis Atherton, like Dick Brownlee specializing in the nineteenth-century history of the American West. Materials located in the society's manuscript archives first sparked Goodrich's interest in "The Waldo Brothers and the Westward Movement," the title of his dissertation. Seven brothers of this Virginia family migrated westward between 1819 and 1830 to improve their economic circumstances. Each, for varying lengths of time, had settled in Missouri. The author used these family members as vehicles to explore the Athertonian subject of western entrepreneurship. Although clearly persons of secondary importance in the sweep of American western history, the Waldos served as useful case studies of the classic western roles of pioneer merchant, town promoter, trader, and land speculator. Since primary source material on the Waldo brothers was sparse and widely scattered, and much of what existed remained in private hands, Goodrich gained valuable experience by working with a variety of archives and families. And as a historian of the western United States, he enhanced his value to the state historical society, which, from its earliest days, had included western history within the scope of its mission.

Executive Director Goodrich, whose association with the society reached the thirty-year milestone in 1997, assembled a lengthy and impressive professional résumé. His publications included a number of articles in the society's *Review,* including "In the Earnest Pursuit of Wealth: David Waldo in Missouri and the Southwest, 1820–1878" (January 1972) and other results of his dissertation research. Some of his *Review* pieces were annotated original documents, which colleagues such as Donald B. Oster of the University of Missouri at Rolla and Lynn Wolf Gentzler of the society's staff coedited. In 1986, Goodrich coedited with Howard Wight Marshall, and contributed to, the volume *The German-American Experience in Missouri.* Writing entries in biographical dictionaries and regional encyclopedias helped this scholar to keep current in all eras and fields of Missouri history. For example, Goodrich contributed articles on Bennett Champ Clark to *The Harry S. Truman Encyclopedia,* on Manuel Lisa and Andrew Henry to the reference work *American National Biography,* on Brownlee, Ellis, and Atherton to the *Dictionary of Missouri Biography,* and on several Missourians to the *Encyclopedia of the Confederacy.* A part of Jim Goodrich's friendship with Dick Brownlee grew from their shared passion for duck hunting. For years they enjoyed memorable hunts at the Dalton Cutoff in Chariton County, where Goodrich continues to carry on the tradition. Another expression of Goodrich's interest in waterfowling are the several articles that he has published in sporting periodicals on duck decoys.

Jim Goodrich served his dual professions of historical study and librarianship in other ways. In 1984, he began his extended membership on the State Historical Records Advisory Board, and one year later on the State Records Commission. In the 1980s and 1990s, Goodrich filled several planning roles for the annual Missouri Conference on History, and he delivered papers or served on panels at such gatherings as the American Association for State and Local History (AASLH), the Missouri Valley History Conference in Omaha, and the Missouri Committee for the Humanities in St. Louis. He received specialized training from and served on committees of the AASLH from the 1970s through the 1990s. As had Floyd Shoemaker and Richard Brownlee, Goodrich represented the society before numerous local historical societies and civic groups in Missouri. As of 1996, he had made well over three hundred presentations to such groups. One of them was a talk, in December 1991, on the history of New Madrid at the dedication of the new annex to that city's historical museum. Jim Goodrich exceeded all of his predecessors in the director's office in his active commitment to community service. Throughout the years, he has been a member of more than a score of committees and commissions charged with activities that range from city bond issues and fund-raising for Columbia's private colleges to recognizing the historic contributions of that city's African Americans. For two terms, 1977–1981, he served on the Columbia City Council.

On behalf of the state historical society, its executive director engaged in a mix of activities that both touched the agency's origins and anticipated its future needs. As if to recall the Missouri editors' founding of the society in 1898, Goodrich periodically spoke at journalism conferences. His subject was "Special Library Collections" in July 1987, as a featured speaker at the Working Journalists Program organized by the university's School of Journalism. In April 1989, Goodrich addressed the Missouri Associated Dailies meeting on "The State Historical Society's Newspaper Collection."

As he had done prior to Dick Brownlee's retirement, Jim Goodrich continued to represent the society in ongoing planning for Ellis Library expansion. Although discussion of Phase II expansion abounded, no actual construction project followed in the wake of the 1987 addition, which had created critically needed space. As early as the spring of 1988, however, Goodrich reported to the finance committee that "space will once again soon be [at] a premium." Materials that the society had stored prior to completion of the 1987 project had already filled the stack space provided by that construction. Executive Director Goodrich's meetings with various university officials between 1988 and 1992 resulted in assurances by the latter that Phase II expansion would meet the society's reasonable space requests. A December 1988 meeting, for example, produced the figure of 18,000 square feet for the society and the joint manuscript collection from the total of 100,000 to 120,000 square feet of new space in the Ellis complex.

As in the early 1980s, however, discussions with university administrators over space in Ellis Library raised concerns. In the summer of 1992, Goodrich sent copies of the documents tracing the society's historic relationship with the University of Missouri to President George Russell, after he learned that Russell "had formed a committee to evaluate the society's relationship with the university." No further mention of the matter appeared in the society's records. Nor, after 1992, did references to Phase II construction, as Russell decided not to pursue the project. By that date, talk of facilities expansion focused on the off-site storage of library materials. Goodrich reported to the September 18, 1993, annual meeting that the university's planned request for state funding "of an off-site storage facility for the libraries of the four-campus system" would include space for the society. At the time, the society and the Western Historical Manuscript Collection's branches already were storing some of their research materials in off-campus facilities. As the state historical society's first century ended, the problem of crowded quarters was as real as Francis Sampson and a youthful Floyd Shoemaker had found it to be in the original Jesse Hall location.

Under Jim Goodrich, as under earlier directors, the society was anxious to make its resources available to groups of Missourians with an appropriate project or need. Such an organization was the Missouri Law Enforcement Memorial Foundation. The foundation's goal was to accomplish what similar groups had done in other states and nationally: document the deaths of law officers in the line of duty and erect a monument in their honor. In 1988, having already assembled some of the relevant data, the foundation requested that the society conclude the research on murdered law officers by compiling a definitive list and assembling supporting information. The private group's funds and one-time state monies helped to underwrite the supplies needed and the salary of reference specialist Elizabeth Bailey, who took charge of the project. By mid-1990, Bailey had completed the work, and in the April 1992 issue of the *Review,* she reported her findings: 488 male and 2 female Missouri law enforcement personnel had died while performing their duties between 1836 and the end of 1991. Jim Goodrich participated in several of the Missouri Law Enforcement Memorial Foundation's observances, held in Jefferson City on the capitol grounds site of the monument bearing the officers' names. The society became the depository for the foundation's collection, which, sadly, continued to grow.

In a myriad of activities of which these are only suggestive, Directors Goodrich and Brownlee enjoyed the support and counsel of an able group of advisers from 1960 into the late 1990s. All of the society's trustees, who met each autumn, fit that description. But those few who served as the agency's presidents and as members of the finance/executive committee (the name changed in 1988) deserve special recognition. Some of those who constituted the society's top leadership group were professionally trained historians whose careers included university teaching and scholarly publication. Each of the members who were not professional historians also brought unique and relevant experience to their high office, which enabled them to contribute actively to the historical society's mission. In no single instance were these individuals mere figureheads occupying honorary positions.

As new members joined the society's policy-making body, some of the most important leaders of earlier times passed away. L. M. White died in Florida on January 16, 1965, of injuries he suffered when struck by an automobile two days earlier. George Rozier, who remained a member of the finance committee until 1983, died in October of the following year. His thirty-nine-year tenure on the committee ranks second in length only to Isidor Loeb's forty-one years. Tables 5.1 and 5.2 introduce the names and summarize the roles of the society's top leadership group since 1960. Although not a trustee, Albert M. Price of Columbia, the agency's treasurer since 1968, has given long and able service to the society in an important post.

The finance committee undertook a major project early in the Goodrich years when it revised the society's constitution and bylaws. With the exception of specific changes made by amendment, the documents remained as the society's founders had written them in 1898. President Francis "Bud" Barnes, in March 1985, appointed a committee chaired by trustee Robert C. Smith to study these papers that established the organization's mission and governing structure, and to propose revisions. The society's members present at the October 17, 1987, annual business meeting ratified the changes that Smith's group had suggested and the finance committee already had approved. Among the most noticeable changes were the substitution of *executive director* for *director* as the official title of the society's chief administrator and the assignment of the name *executive committee* to what had been the *finance committee*. Until this point in the society's history, the former term had

Table 5.1 Presidents of the State Historical Society of Missouri, 1959–1998

E. L. Dale, Carthage	1959–1962
Roy D. Williams, Boonville	1962–1965
Leo J. Rozier, Perryville	1965–1968
T. Ballard Watters, Marshfield	1968–1971
William Aull III, Lexington	1971–1974
Elmer Ellis, Columbia	1974–1977
William R. Denslow, Trenton	1977–1980
Lewis E. Atherton, Columbia	1980–1983
Francis M. Barnes, Kirkwood	1983–1986
Joseph Webber, St. Louis	1986–1989
Robert C. Smith, Columbia	1989–1992
Avis Green Tucker, Warrensburg	1992–1995
H. Riley Bock, New Madrid	1995–1998

Table 5.2 New Nonpresidential Members of the Finance/Executive Committee, 1960–1997

Jean Tyree Hamilton, Marshall
James C. Olson, Kansas City
Blanche M. Touhill, St. Louis
Virginia Garton Young, Columbia
Lawrence O. Christensen, Rolla
Vera Faurot Burk, Kirksville

been attached to a large, but relatively inactive, group consisting of all the trustees, elected and ex officio. They numbered thirty-six persons in October 1987. At the 1989 business meeting, the society's membership approved an amendment increasing the size of the executive committee from six to eight members. President Joseph Webber had initiated that change as a way "to get more people involved in the management of the society." Beginning in January 1990, the executive committee, which exercises active oversight of the society's business, consisted of eight elected trustees plus the society's president.

More interesting and important than organizational structures are the people who fill them. Salient facts from their individual biographies form a collective profile of the society's top volunteers, as well as reveal the special talents they brought to the agency charged with preserving the record of Missouri's history. The most dramatic change in the nature of the society's personnel was that, under Brownlee and Goodrich, women participated as leaders for the first time. When the 1970 annual meeting elected Avis Green Tucker fifth vice president, she became the first female officer in the society's seventy-two-year history. Twenty-two years later, Tucker became the organization's first woman president. Jean Tyree Hamilton, in December 1986, was the first woman to join the finance committee. Virginia Garton Young was another pioneer. Prior to her service as interim director in 1985, she had served as a trustee and officer since the mid-1970s. In 1989, Young and Blanche M. Touhill became members of the executive committee. Vera Faurot Burk joined it in 1996.

A more subtle change began during the 1980s. Starting with Executive Director Goodrich himself, the society drew on the talents of individuals born in the 1930s or later, who came of age after World War II. That generalization applies to Lawrence O. Christensen, H. Riley Bock, and Blanche Touhill. A majority of the society's leaders, however, were of Richard Brownlee's generation or older. The society's fourth director (Brownlee), plus Leo Rozier, William Denslow, William Aull III, Joseph Webber, Francis M. Barnes, James Olson, Elmer Ellis, and Robert Smith, had all served in the Armed Forces during World War II; Smith also participated in the Korean conflict. Vera Burk worked for the Coded Messages Division, Office of War Information in Washington, D.C., in 1944–1945. Lewis Atherton, E. L. Dale, Ballard Watters, Roy Williams, and Jean Hamilton were born prior to 1910, while Burk, Virginia Young, Avis Tucker, and James Olson followed in the twentieth-century's second decade. With their personal experience spanning that century and in some cases reaching back into the nineteenth, those who charted the society's course during these years drew on collective personal histories as deep as the society's own.

As the biographies of the society's elected leaders during earlier decades have shown, some who acquired a substantial interest in Missouri history were not native to the state. That also was true of James Olson, an Iowan; Elmer Ellis, born in North Dakota; and Avis Green Tucker, from Kansas. As the only Kansas native to rise to high office in the State Historical Society of Missouri, Tucker may serve as a symbol of reconciliation between two states that, as Richard Brownlee's scholarship dramatically demonstrated, have not always behaved with civility toward one another. On the other side of the matter, some recent presidents and executive committee members represent families with roots planted firmly in nineteenth-century Missouri. The first members of Albert Price's and Robert Smith's families to reside in Boone County and Columbia in the antebellum period originated in Virginia and Kentucky. Price's great-grandfather, banker Robert Beverly Price Sr., was a patron of artist George Caleb Bingham. In 1864, when Confederate guerrillas threatened Columbia, Price protected his bank's gold by burying it.

Leo Rozier was a member of the same pioneering French family as his brother George. William Aull's mother was born a Goodman in Virginia, while his father and grandfather earned law degrees from that state's university in Charlottesville. All settled in Missouri. Jean Hamilton's paternal grandfather, William Pleasant Tyree, came to Lafayette County in 1837 from Tennessee. His wife, Kate, was a cousin of President James K. Polk. William Tyree sought treasure in the California gold fields and fought in the Mexican War and Civil War. Fortunately, nativity is not a prerequisite to skill in narrating and interpreting Missouri history. Lawrence O. Christensen, one of the most able of his generation of scholars, was born in Montana.

During the Brownlee and Goodrich eras, the state's two major metropolitan areas received a greater representation in the society's leadership councils than had been true before 1960. Joseph Webber, born in Kansas City, became a corporate executive in the photographic industry in St. Louis after World War II. Both Bud Barnes and Blanche Touhill were St. Louis natives. The careers that brought them recognition by the society—government service and university administration—were based in the St. Louis area. James C. Olson, chancellor of the University of Missouri–Kansas City in the late 1960s and early 1970s, retired to that city after serving as University of Missouri system president between 1976 and 1984. Avis Tucker attended high school in Kansas City, lived in that community with her journalist husband for some years, and retained business interests there after moving to Warrensburg. Bob Smith, Virginia Young, and Albert Price call Columbia their home, although Young was born in Mountain View and grew up in Springfield.

Small Missouri towns also supplied the society with a large proportion of its leadership, creating a balanced urban-rural representation fairly well reflective of the state's demography and varied interests. Larry Christensen grew up in Glasgow in Howard County and taught in Rolla, while Riley Bock lived in New Madrid. The historic Missouri River town of Lexington was home to William Aull III. William Denslow was a native and longtime resident of Trenton in northwest Missouri. Jean Hamilton of Marshall and Avis Tucker of Warrensburg, communities in the west-central region of the state, and Leo Rozier from Perryville in southeast Missouri, also represented small-town and rural areas. It was places like these that Professor Lewis Atherton wrote about—with a blend of loving care and scholarly detachment—in his book *Main Street on the Middle Border* (1954). Born in Bosworth in 1905, Atherton also lived on a farm in Carroll County and graduated from Carrollton High School.

The most significant information about the individuals listed in Tables 5.1 and 5.2 is the nature of their preparation for leadership of the state historical society. They brought to their jobs a variety of talents enriched with experience and training relevant to the historical society's mission. One group, almost entirely absent from the corps of elected leaders who served with Floyd Shoemaker, consisted of academically trained historians. Society presidents Elmer Ellis and Lewis Atherton held the Ph.D., published respected works of scholarly history, and taught in the University of Missouri's history department. Their elevation to prominence in the society by Richard Brownlee was a part of that director's effort to apply professional standards to the ongoing work of the society. Dr. Noble E. Cunningham and Dr. Arvarh Strickland, also of the university's history faculty, both served as trustees, with Cunningham also serving as a vice president under Brownlee and Jim Goodrich. Before receiving his doctorate from the university in 1972, Lawrence Christensen gained teaching experience in public schools located in three states. While pursuing his degree, Christensen served as a graduate assistant in the WHMC and a teaching assistant for the history department. During a lengthy career at the University of Missouri–Rolla, his specialties included Missouri history.

Both Blanche Touhill and James Olson were professors of history as well as university administrators. Touhill, who became chancellor of the University of Missouri–St. Louis in 1991, received her Ph.D. from

St. Louis University in 1962. Her expertise was in Irish and British history. Olson's experience as director of the Nebraska State Historical Society from 1945 to 1956 gave him a unique preparation to play a policy-making role on the executive committee. Olson also taught history and chaired his department at the University of Nebraska, where he had been awarded the doctorate in 1942. His lengthy list of publications included a sesquicentennial history of the University of Missouri, written with his wife, Vera Olson. When the Nebraska society dedicated its James C. Olson Research Library in October 1988, Dr. Olson received the highest form of recognition a scholar can earn: a library named in his honor. The society's Elmer Ellis also achieved that distinction.

As in earlier years, lawyers and journalists were prominent in the society's leadership. Among the lawyers were four who graduated from the University of Missouri's School of Law in Columbia—Aull, Bock, Rozier, and Smith—and another, Barnes, who received his law degree from Washington University in St. Louis. Barnes, Rozier, and Smith also had been multiterm members of the Missouri House of Representatives. William Denslow earned his B.J. degree from the School of Journalism in 1938. He was not the publisher of a Missouri newspaper, but, rather, applied his training to radio broadcasting and magazine publishing. From 1948 to 1979, Denslow was business manager and then editor of the *Royal Arch Mason Magazine* and active in many civic organizations. His books included the *Centennial History of Grundy County, Missouri,* and *Freemasonry and the American Indian.* Avis Tucker published the *Warrensburg Daily Star-Journal* with her husband, William C., from 1947 until his death in 1966. She continues to publish the newspaper and operate radio stations. Tucker served as a president of the Missouri Press Association. For nearly thirty years, Vera Faurot Burk, with her husband, Samuel A., ran radio stations in Kirksville.

Together, these volunteers' collective professional résumé included impressive credentials. When Bud Barnes retired from the General Assembly in May 1992, a *St. Louis Post-Dispatch* reporter commented that "he will never retire as a historian." During his sixteen years as a Republican lawmaker, Barnes worked to restore and display battle flags carried by Missourians during the Civil War and obtained appropriations to repair the Missouri marker at the Vicksburg, Mississippi, battlefield site and to restore the Thomas Hart Benton mural in the capitol. Beginning in 1980, he edited the journal of the Kirkwood Historical Society and contributed frequently to it. Business executive Joseph Webber promoted the cause of historical understanding in several ways. An Army historian in Europe during World War II, he coauthored a battle history that appeared in 1946: *Bastogne: The Story of the First Eight Days.* Webber was a book collector and a friend of the society's reference library and the university's Ellis Library. Over a period of years, he donated hundreds of volumes to both institutions.

Virginia Young was a trained librarian, and therefore of eminent usefulness to the society, which was the second largest specialized library in Missouri by the 1980s. Holder of the M.L.S. degree from the University of Oklahoma, Young built a national and international reputation in her field. When she received the American Library Association's (ALA) honorary life membership in July 1985, she was only the eighty-sixth person to hold the award in the association's 111-year history. Young's book, *The Library Trustee,* published by the ALA in a fifth edition in 1995, was the authority on its subject. She served on the National Committee for the White House conferences on libraries in 1979 and 1991. Vera Burk, too, devoted her energies to supporting Missouri libraries. She was, for example, president of the Friends of the University of Missouri Libraries in 1976–1978 and a member of the steering committees of the Governor's Conference on Libraries in 1978 when delegates were chosen for the White House Conference on Libraries held in 1979.

Both Virginia Young and Avis Tucker served on Missouri's Coordinating Board for Higher Education, Young as its first chair beginning in 1975. The society's appropriation requests came to this body after state government reorganization created it in 1974. The board also had the responsibility of creating and updating a master plan for the state's system of higher education. Board experience was useful to leaders of the historical society after it joined with the university for budget-making purposes. Avis Tucker also served as a University of Missouri and Westminster College curator, while Robert C. Smith offered his services as a trustee to Stephens College for some thirty-five years.

Another historian by avocation was H. Riley Bock. While still a law student in 1979, he edited "One Year at War: Letters of Captain George W. Dawson, C.S.A.," a two-part article that appeared in the *Missouri Historical Review.* In 1992, Secretary of the Interior Manuel

Lujan Jr. appointed Bock a member of the Trail of Tears National Historic Trail Advisory Council. Jean Tyree Hamilton took graduate courses in history at the University of Missouri–Columbia and, with her husband, Henry, was very active in the cause of historic preservation. They were prime movers over a period of several decades in the Missouri Archaeological Society and the Friends of Arrow Rock. Jean Hamilton's article, "Mr. Bingham's Tombstone," appeared in the *Review* in 1979.

Table 5.3 lists the recipients of the State Historical Society of Missouri's highest honor, the Distinguished Service Award and Medallion. Secretary Shoemaker had designated as trustees and honorary life members persons who had rendered meritorious service to the agency. Richard Brownlee's creation of the Distinguished Service Award in 1968, however, made annual and public the recognition of honorees, who accepted their awards at the society's fall luncheon. The recipients included four staff members: besides Shoemaker and Brownlee, they were Marie Woods, administrative assistant, and Sidney Larson, curator of the art collection. Lewis Atherton, Elmer Ellis, and William Francis English represented the society's relationship with the university history department. The 1979, 1981, and 1986 awards recognized other academic historians in Missouri colleges, one of them from a private institution.

The presence of three legislators and Secretary of State James Kirkpatrick on the list of award winners represented the historical society's obligation to the many friends in state government who stood with it during appropriations deliberations and at other critical times. The largest group of those who earned the Distinguished Service Award consisted of past presidents and other members of the finance/executive committee. They worked with administrators Shoemaker, Brownlee, and Goodrich from the 1930s, in the cases of Edward Swain and Roy Williams, to the 1990s, in the cases of Robert Smith and Avis Tucker. Their devoted labor proudly summarized two-thirds of the society's history. The contribution of some recipients is unique. The society's collection of Thomas Hart Benton's works attests to the artist's generosity from the mid-1940s to the mid-1970s. The two Prices who received the Distinguished Service Award—R. B. Jr. and his nephew, Albert Price—served as the society's treasurers from 1923 until the present, while R. B. Price Sr. had held that important position from 1901 to 1923. Friends like Anna Tibbe of St. Louis, the 1988 recipient,

H. Riley Bock (left) served as president of the society during the final years of its first century. A native of New Madrid and a lawyer, Bock was elected to the presidency in 1995. He is shown here with Judge Stephen N. Limbaugh, the speaker at the society's 1996 annual meeting.

expanded the scope of the society's collections. She and her late husband, Anton, had donated, among other resources, her father Charles Trefts's photographic collection.

All of the awardees possessed a trait ascribed by President Riley Bock to Avis Tucker at the 1996 annual luncheon: "uncommon energy." And not a few displayed the old-fashioned Missouri gumption that Virginia Botts, the 1980 winner, often expressed. At Richard Brownlee's first annual meeting, held in October 1960, Botts "asked for clarification as to whether . . . women might be officers and trustees" of the society, and she urged their appointment to leadership positions. The director assured his friend and neighbor that the society maintained no restrictions on women in leadership roles. Rocking the boat ever so slightly was a distinguished service to an agency that sometimes needed encouragement to change.

Jim Goodrich's promotion to the society's directorship left vacant the position of associate director, one to which, within a few years, he appointed women. At their December 7, 1985, meeting, members of the finance committee authorized the new director, in compliance with the university's affirmative action guidelines, to recruit an associate director. On July 1, 1986, R. Douglas Hurt, a staff member of the Ohio Historical Society since 1983, began his duties as associate director. At the same time Mary K. (Kathy) Dains became the society's assistant

Table 5.3 Recipients of the Distinguished Service Award and Medallion

1968	**Floyd C. Shoemaker**, Columbia, Retired Secretary of the Society
1969	**Thomas Hart Benton**, Kansas City, Artist
1970	**Edward E. Swain**, Kirksville, Publisher and Veteran Society Officer
1971	**Judge Roy D. Williams**, Boonville, Veteran Society Officer
1972	**George A. Rozier**, Jefferson City, Veteran Society Officer
1973	**T. Ballard Watters**, Marshfield, Veteran Society Officer
1974	**Marie Woods**, Columbia, Member of the Society's Office Staff since 1943
1975	**William Aull III**, Lexington, Veteran Society Officer
1976	**Dr. William Francis English**, Columbia, Missouri Historian and Director of Western Historical Manuscript Collection
1977	**R. B. Price**, Columbia, Banker and the Society's Treasurer and Financial Adviser, 1923–1968
1978	**Dr. Elmer Ellis**, Columbia, Friend of the Society in Several Capacities and Veteran Society Officer
1979	**Dr. John C. Crighton**, Columbia, Missouri Historian and Professor at Stephens College
1980	**Virginia Botts**, Columbia, Friend of the Society
1981	**Dr. David D. March**, Kirksville, Missouri Historian and Professor at Northeast Missouri State University
1982	**Honorable Robert Ellis Young**, 136th District Member of the Missouri House of Representatives and Friend of the Society
1983	**William R. Denslow**, Trenton, Veteran Society Officer
1984	**Dr. Lewis Atherton**, Columbia, Missouri Historian, Veteran Society Officer, and Friend of the Society in Several Capacities
1985	**Dr. Richard S. Brownlee**, Columbia, Retiring Director of the Society
1986	**Dr. Leslie Anders**, Warrensburg, Missouri Historian and Professor of History at Central Missouri State University
1987	**Honorable Francis M. Barnes**, Kirkwood, 96th District Member of the Missouri House of Representatives, Veteran Society Officer, and Friend of the Society
1988	**Anna Tibbe**, St. Louis, Friend of the Society
1989	**Sidney Larson**, Columbia, Professor of Art at Columbia College and Curator of the Society's Art Collection
1990	**Joseph Webber**, St. Louis, Veteran Society Officer and Friend of the Society
1991	Two Award Recipients: **Jean Tyree Hamilton**, Marshall, Veteran Trustee and Friend of the Society **James C. Kirkpatrick**, Newspaper Publisher and Missouri Secretary of State

1992	**Dr. Adolf E. and Rebecca Schroeder**, Columbia, Preservationists of Missouri's Folk and Ethnic Heritage
1993	**Robert C. Smith**, Columbia, Veteran Society Officer
1994	**Honorable Thomas F. Eagleton**, St. Louis, United States Senator (retired), Promoter of the Cause of History in the State and Nation
1995	Two Award Recipients:
	Rush Limbaugh Sr., Cape Girardeau, Veteran Society Officer
	Albert M. Price, Columbia, Banker and Society Treasurer since 1968
1996	Two Award Recipients:
	Avis Green Tucker, Warrensburg, Veteran Society Officer
	Honorable Emory Melton, Cassville, 29th District State Senator and Friend of the Society
1997	Two Award Recipients:
	Dr. Noble E. Cunningham, Columbia, Professor Emeritus of History, University of Missouri–Columbia, Veteran Society Officer and Friend of the Society
	Dr. Arvarh E. Strickland, Columbia, Professor Emeritus of History, University of Missouri–Columbia, Trustee and Friend of the Society

director. Dains and Hurt also served as associate editors of the *Missouri Historical Review.* After Doug Hurt left the society in July 1989, Dains, as of February 1, 1990, became Goodrich's associate director. Lynn Wolf Gentzler, who on that date moved over from WHMC to become the society's assistant director, assumed the duties of associate director on September 15, 1991, following Kathy Dains's retirement. Gentzler also became associate editor of the quarterly.

As was true of the society's presidents and executive committee members, the professional résumés of key staff members also revealed their relevant qualifications and important contributions to the work of the agency. In 1991, Gentzler, who had earned her master's degree in history from the university's Columbia campus in 1973, assumed the day-to-day leadership of the editorial staff. The same institution had awarded senior reference specialist Laurel E. Boeckman, who had been in charge of the reference library for seventeen years in 1998, her degrees in library science. Some department heads acquired their expertise on the job. Senior reference specialist in the newspaper library beginning in December 1995, Ara L. Kaye, came to the society in 1986 from the fields of retailing and nursing. Nancy Lankford, associate director of the joint manuscript collection on the Columbia campus in the 1990s, received her graduate training at the University of Missouri–Columbia. First employed by the Columbia facility of WHMC in 1966, Lankford began her administration of its operations in 1982. Sidney Larson brought a rare and needed expertise to the society nearly two decades after it had seriously begun to acquire a fine arts collection. Professor of art at Columbia College since 1951, he became curator of the society's collection on a part-time basis ten years later. Larson was one of Dick Brownlee's first professional appointments and remained one of Jim Goodrich's valued advisers.

While the society continued to employ qualified and imaginative personnel such as these in its established departments, it also enlisted specialists to develop new projects. Goodrich announced to the annual meeting's membership in October 1996 that the Missouri General Assembly had funded a long-desired position. The society would hire a photographic specialist to better organize, preserve, and improve the accessibility of the more than one hundred thousand photographs in its collection. By that date, two oral historians had joined the staff. The society hired Will Sarvis in 1995 to build a collection of oral history interviews on Missouri's post–World War II political history. Sarvis had taught history at Radford University in Virginia and served as an oral historian for the U.S. Forest Service. C. Ray Brassieur, the society's original oral historian, who had earned an M.A. degree from Louisiana State University and was a veteran of the staff of the Missouri Cultural Heritage Center, came to the society in 1993.

One achievement of the society's staff was to increase patron accessibility to the society's collections. Under Laurel Boeckman's direction, reference library staff members compiled several finding aids to unindexed materials of interest to genealogical and other researchers. These included indexes to Union and Confederate death rolls. In the 1990s, a WHMC senior manuscript specialist, Randy Roberts, created similar guides to that collection's holdings in religion and folklore. The newspaper library staff added over three thousand catalog and index cards to its finding aids in 1988. Earlier, staff members had prepared slide shows for use by local historical societies and other groups. "A Visit to Your State Historical Society" explained the agency's facilities and services in a fifteen-minute presentation. A longer program, "Missouri Women in History," informed citizens of the state about that thriving research field.

Staff specialists were contributing members of professional organizations. Lynn Gentzler began her service as Missouri state chair for the annual awards program of the AASLH in 1992, a position Jim Goodrich had held the previous ten years. She became a regional chair for the AASLH awards in 1996. She also read papers and chaired sessions for several conferences, including the Missouri Conference on History. That group, which held meetings each spring, also has involved Nancy Lankford, Randy Roberts, and Jim Goodrich. During the 1990s, the society's director served as a member of the conference's steering committee and chaired the book prize committee.

Genealogical research brought increasing numbers of patrons to the society's collections. Early in 1990, Goodrich reported to the executive committee that he had made a "concerted attempt" during his tenure as director "to collect genealogical materials, since it has become readily apparent that people interested in genealogy have become the largest segment of the society's users." James W. Goodrich sent staff out for after-hours engagements. In June 1987, for example, Laurel Boeckman joined Kay Pettit of the newspaper library to present information on the society's resources to a workshop, held in Kansas City, entitled "Resources in Genealogy." In May 1992, reference librarian Marie Concannon spoke about the society's genealogical resources to librarians in Kansas City, Kansas. She also attended the Federation of Genealogical Societies' conference in Seattle in 1995. Ara Kaye of the newspaper library and Christine Montgomery of the editorial staff also spoke to groups interested in family history. The preservation of buildings, as well as of family records, continued to interest staff members long after Dorothy Caldwell's retirement. In 1996, reference librarian Linda Brown-Kubisch accepted membership on Columbia's Historical Preservation Exploratory Committee.

Publications during the Goodrich era continued to measure the professional attainments of some of the society's personnel. Employing research that he accomplished while a Missouri resident, R. Douglas Hurt published *Agriculture and Slavery in Missouri's Little Dixie* with the University of Missouri Press in 1992. Mary K. Dains pursued her work in the field of Missouri women's history in articles published in the *Review.* Brown-Kubisch published some results of her research on the black experience in the Canadian province of Ontario in 1996.

In addition to her writing for the quarterly, Lynn Gentzler prepared entries for *American National Biography* and the *Dictionary of Missouri Biography* in the mid-1990s. Randy Roberts's publications included a coauthored chapter in a 1993 book about American towns that refused to accept Carnegie libraries early in the twentieth century.

Art curator Sidney Larson, like his mentor Thomas Hart Benton, created works of art that employed local historical subject matter, as well as wrote about Missouri art. Two of his murals, located in the Guitar Building and the Boone County Courthouse, depict the history of Columbia and the county, while another historical mural of Larson's is found in the city building in Jefferson City. An accomplished and recognized art conservator, Larson restored works by Benton, Bingham, and other American artists located within and beyond Missouri, including some in the society's collection. Columbia College, in 1996, named its new art gallery for Sid Larson, one of the most notable of the many honors that the society's curator has earned.

II

During the state historical society's first nine decades, those who guided its destinies found little need for self-reflection. As Jim Goodrich observed to William Aull in April 1987: "To my knowledge, no 'official' review of the scope or mission of the society has ever taken place." About to embark on such a study, the society still used as its mission statements the constitution adopted by the Missouri Press Association in 1898 and the legislation of the following year making the society a trustee of the state. One of its original charges disappeared in 1987, when the society revised its bylaws. The agency had never explored the archaeology of Missouri or the Midwest or operated "an ethnological and historical museum." After October 1987, its formal statement of purpose matched its practice.

While the historical society's leadership shared, over decades of time, a remarkably consistent understanding of the organization's mission, only rarely did outsiders question that consensus. The state audit of the society's finances for the period January 1969 through June 1971 included one of the few recorded doubts about the agency's success in achieving its stated goals. The audit team praised the society for fulfilling its purpose of acquiring and preserving historical collections. "However, in the dissemination of information the society directly serves only a small number of Missourians." They included in that number scholarly researchers, educators, its own members, and other agencies of state government. The auditors' report asked the society's leaders to "consider ways of expanding services to include all Missourians" and suggested some: filmed presentations; recorded programs, presumably for radio broadcast; and the sale of materials on microfilm.

The auditors' report did not cause a reexamination of the society's goals or programs. Nevertheless, the examiners raised issues central to the life of the organization. The challenge of how best to assign limited resources to a range of possibilities was implicit in countless decisions made by the society's leaders. While the auditors underestimated the society's reach in 1972—many of the "members" who received the *Review,* for example, were schools whose history classes made use of the quarterly's features—as a tax-supported agency it needed to ask how effectively it served its publics and how well it achieved its goals. Its decision-makers needed to identify the most appropriate evidence to measure growth toward desired outcomes.

As financial analysts, representatives of the state auditor's office made the natural assumption that they could quantify success. If the society's programs directly reached a majority of the state's residents, the institution attained a greater degree of success than if they served only a minority of citizens. The history of the State Historical Society of Missouri suggests that, while quantitative measurements are valid, they do not stand alone. A historical society is more like a municipal symphony orchestra than a state highway department. The latter builds and maintains a tangible asset, the value of which administrators can easily quantify: the construction of new mileage, the number of vehicles using highways during a given time, the reduction of accidents through elimination of hazards, and so on. Although a historical agency deals in quantities of books and manuscripts, what it preserves through them is the heritage of millions of people, most of whose names or families' stories do not appear in the written record. That only a small portion of a city's people hears an orchestra perform does not mean that the musicians and the conductor fail to serve the entire population by keeping alive a musical heritage. The same is true of the work of archivists, preservationists, librarians, and historians.

The clearly articulated assumption of Missouri's editors and legislators at the close of the nineteenth century was that some agency must preserve the state's historical record before it disappeared, regardless of whether anyone made immediate use of that record. Francis Sampson, during his years as a collector of Missouriana, and Elmer Ellis, when he founded the Western Historical Manuscript Collection, understood what the quantifiers of usage did not: preservation is self-justifying, quite apart from use. The measure of worth of Sampson's collecting was not how many readers he served in his own time, but that he merely saved what other Missourians neglected and discarded, so that as people eventually found a use for his pamphlets and books these resources would reside in a central depository to which all citizens had free access. Although few of his contemporaries knew what this bibliophile was about, he in fact served them all, and their descendants as well.

Late-nineteenth-century Missourians made the decision to preserve the record of the past. And since the day that Isidor Loeb opened the society's first reading room, and that Sampson edited the first issue of the *Missouri Historical Review,* the society *has* sought ways to reach increasing numbers of Missourians with the information that it conserved. While "success" has a significant qualitative dimension, it is also quantitative. Evidence from the late 1980s and 1990s reveals both numerical growth toward, and decline from, the goal of disseminating Missouri's history to the largest possible audience.

As Table 5.4 reveals, the society's state appropriation grew to unprecedented levels during the Goodrich administration. The decade from 1985–1986 to 1994–1995 witnessed a 44 percent increase in available state funds. That figure would have been larger had the state's finances not required withholding a portion of the General Assembly's grant of funds in six of the ten fiscal years. Careful management, which included postponing the replacement of departed personnel and delaying equipment purchases, prevented serious reductions in programs. But withheld funds and small appropriations increases also resulted in no salary enhancements in some years and a failure to keep up with inflationary cost increases. Goodrich cited an example of the latter in the executive committee's meeting of September 18, 1992. Forty-three titles of periodicals on microfilm, which cost $690.13 in 1988, had risen to a total of $988.79, a greater than 40 percent increase.

Table 5.4 State Appropriations for the State Historical Society of
Missouri, 1985–1986 to 1994–1995

	General Assembly's Appropriation and Amount Withheld	Net Appropriation	Percent Change over Previous Year
1985–86	$532,468	$532,468	+12%
1986–87	609,379 −18,281 (3%)	591,098	+11%
1987–88	635,345	635,345	+ 7%
1988–89	658,625 −38,819 (3%)	619,806	− 2%
1989–90	732,117 −21,964 (3%)	710,153	+15%
1990–91	784,292 −43,136 (5%)	741,156	+ 4%
1991–92	754,669 −60,373 (8%)	694,296	− 6%
1992–93	759,169 −22,775 (3%)	736,394	+ 6%
1993–94	748,223	748,223	+ 2%
1994–95	793,181 −23,795 (3%)	769,386	+ 3%

Source: Biennial reports to the governor.

The society's budgets could not show the number of persons served
by its programs, but they did reveal the organization's priorities. Of
the total state funds disbursed during fiscal year 1989, 79.4 percent,
or $507,501 of the $638,866, fell into the categories of salary/wages
and staff benefits. The employees paid with these funds, of course,
represented all of the society's service programs. By assisting patrons
who visited the society's collections, by responding to researchers who
mailed or telephoned their requests for information, by appearing before
groups throughout the state, by preparing issues of the *Review*—in these

and many more ways, the society's specialists involved a wide range of history-minded Missourians in its programs. After the investment in people, the budget's largest categories were those necessary to publish four issues of the quarterly, the printing of which alone cost $57,500 in fiscal year 1989, and the microfilming of resources, especially newspapers. Supplementary monies from the Membership Trust Fund helped to pay for these and other ongoing programs.

The society's collections provided Missourians with the most comprehensive set of resources on the state's history available anywhere. At each annual meeting, the director reported the number of researchers, genealogical and scholarly, who had visited the collections during each preceding fiscal year. In her 1985 report, Virginia Young stated that over 30,000 researchers had come to the society's quarters between July 1, 1984, and June 30, 1985. And another 22,000 Missourians had requested assistance by telephone or by mail. In 1994–1995, Jim Goodrich revealed in his October 1995 report, over 56,000 patrons had utilized the society's and WHMC's collections in personal visits or through mail and telephone contacts. Beginning in September 1993, distant researchers made use of a toll-free phone number to reach the society's staff.

In the biennial editions of the *Official Manual of the State of Missouri*, Executive Director Goodrich reported the extent of the various collections for those who sought evidence of sheer physical size and quantitative growth. Most dramatic was the increase in the newspaper collection on microfilm: from over 27.4 million pages in 1985–1986 to more than 36 million pages ten years later. Annually, the society microfilmed 500,000 pages of newspapers in the mid-1990s. The executive director's considered opinion in 1996 was that the society's most valuable and significant resource was its imposing collection of newspapers, the largest aggregation of any state's newspapers in the United States. The agency's map collection numbered more than 2,600 items in 1996. It held in excess of 450,000 books, pamphlets, and official state publications in 1995–1996, an increase of 15,000 in a decade. The joint manuscript collection administered 500,000 society manuscript items and 700 reels of society microfilmed documents.

If some quantitative indexes of the society's well-being registered growth, one revealed continued decline. The erosion of membership numbers persisted after 1985. Slipping under the ten-thousand-member threshold by the 1991–1992 fiscal year, membership stabilized at around eight thousand beginning in 1993–1994. Each year the society recorded the names of its new members. The data in Table 5.5 report those totals, offering another perspective on the dominant trend in the society's membership over an extended time span.

A possible cause of the decline was the increased cost of membership. Following the recommendation of the executive committee and the endorsement of the trustees in the autumn of 1990, a special meeting of members, held on May 11, 1991, approved a doubling of the annual member dues from $5 to $10. In 1988, the society had boosted life memberships from $100 to $250. Perhaps because Missourians, from the days of Floyd Shoemaker's leadership, had come to expect low-cost membership in their state historical society, the 1991 price increase appeared extravagant. As a notice in the *Review* pointed out, however, with its new fee, "Missouri still would rank forty-eighth [in membership costs] of the forty-nine states that have state historical societies charging membership dues."

In fact, no one could locate with precision the causes of membership decline. One result of it was clear. Beginning in 1984, while Dick Brownlee continued as director, the society made a concerted effort to better publicize the society's programs with a view to building its membership. Jim Goodrich oversaw this public relations campaign both before and after he became executive director. From 1984 to the mid-1990s, the society employed James F. Wolfe of Jefferson City, a professional publicist, to promote an interest in Missouri history and a public awareness of what the society offered to Missourians. In 1985, Wolfe devised a history quiz entitled "Missouri, the Know-Me State." Submitted to 287 state newspapers, by late May 1987, 103 of them ran the brief feature. By the spring of the following year, 149 papers carried it, two-thirds of those receiving it. Jim Wolfe also prepared news releases on material published in the *Review,* as well as information about the annual meeting and luncheon and other special events, including art exhibits.

The society took other initiatives to increase knowledge of its work and promote membership. In January 1992, at the suggestion of President Robert Smith, the executive committee revived a tactic that Shoemaker had used fifty years earlier. Armed with membership application forms, trustees actively solicited new members in their local areas. In

Table 5.5 New Members, Fiscal Years 1971–1972 to 1993–1994

1971–72	1,158	1983–84	771
1972–73	1,209	1984–85	533
1973–74	1,079	1985–86	550
1974–75	1,009	1986–87	627
1975–76	961	1987–88	484
1976–77	1,024	1988–89	568
1977–78	1,069	1989–90	446
1978–79	1,032	1990–91	480
1979–80	1,049	1991–92	334
1980–81	1,235	1992–93	371
1981–82	728	1993–94	466
1982–83	516		

Note: Fiscal year is July 1–June 30 each year; includes all membership categories.

the first half of the 1990s, membership flyers in the pay envelopes of university employees, a Christmas letter to members promoting gift memberships, a new society brochure, and advertisements on Bob Priddy's syndicated radio program, *Across Our Wide Missouri,* expressed the society's "more aggressive approach to membership growth," as the January 10, 1992, executive committee's minutes expressed the policy.

Membership erosion was one factor that convinced the society's leadership to initiate an organizational planning process in 1988. Reasons of a more general nature also argued for institutional planning. Data on the society's strengths and needs would assist the administration and the executive committee in reaffirming or reassessing familiar goals, establishing new ones, and allocating the resources to reach them. The American Association for State and Local History, of which the society had long been a member, encouraged the leaders of societies nationwide to appreciate the benefits of assessing strengths and weaknesses and re-examining goals. President Joseph Webber distributed copies of the association's "Technical Report 11: Institutional Master Planning for Historical Organizations and Museums" at the executive committee's meeting of March 20, 1987. Since the society recently had acquired a new executive director and president and had revised its bylaws, Webber explained in late May, now was "a propitious time . . . to explore the possibilities for the future." On October 3, 1987, Jim Goodrich attended a daylong AASLH workshop on master planning, after which he placed before the committee the benefits that might accrue to the society from a self-study and the procedures recommended by the national association's specialists. Having thus carefully considered the matter, the executive committee voted at its March 25, 1988, meeting to authorize the creation of a master plan for the State Historical Society of Missouri.

Fifteen months later, in June 1989, Associate Director Douglas Hurt issued his summary report of the self-study. The AASLH's advice that neither a society's chief executive nor a trustee direct such a project, and the committee's decision not to employ an outside consultant to conduct it, had pointed to Hurt as the obvious choice as study director. Observing guidelines such as that the process should be "open . . . with no hidden agendas," and that "self-study should not be conducted to affirm the status quo," Hurt worked with department heads to initiate self-evaluations within each of the agency's major functional units. "Specifically," Hurt reported to Goodrich during the assessment process, "each department is identifying the audience or public that it serves. Each is asking: 'Are we serving the public?' and 'How can we serve the public better?' " By mid-March 1989, the departments had submitted their reports to Hurt, and he was in the midst of interviews with individual staff members to elicit additional information and opinions. On July 15, 1989, Goodrich distributed copies of Hurt's summary report to members of the executive committee.

The report contained numerous suggestions for change. Some of them urged an expansion of the society's publics and therefore a reinterpretation of how administrators, staff, and elected leaders understood its mission. Proposals for significant change, Hurt wrote, had as their goal increasing "the visibility and prestige of the institution" and "substantially improving its public programming." The report, based on staff recommendations, in effect agreed with the 1972 auditors' report: "The society needs to become far more public service oriented. It must actively seek ways to offer its resources and expertise to its members and to the general public." One way to do that would be to sponsor tours of, for example, the state's Civil War battlefields or historic buildings. An annual lecture series on themes such as the role of Native Americans and women in Missouri history; an oral history program that would gather recollections from citizens representing an array of backgrounds and experiences; and an expanded publications program that might include a handbook of Missouri history and a magazine for young adults—these and other projects together could give state residents reasons to join the society and "help turn the tide of decreasing memberships." The report also proposed a docent program, speakers of national reputation for the annual luncheon, a regular spring meeting held in cities other than Columbia, and a major fellowship to bring an established scholar to the society for an extended period of research and public lectures—all of which would "enhance the image of the society," fulfill its mission, and serve greater numbers of state citizens.

Other themes threaded through the individual departments' evaluations, which originated in the reference and newspaper libraries, the editorial and art/acquisitions departments, cataloging, and manuscripts. Staff members stressed the need for new personnel to help handle existing workloads and make possible such projects as the creation of additional finding aids to assist patrons. They called attention to salaries that still lagged behind the compensation paid to comparable university personnel and urged the society to subsidize their attendance at regional and national professional meetings. Portions of the report suggested the need for effective security procedures to protect library resources and better temperature and humidity controls to conserve the art properties. Several departments called for enhanced computer capabilities to render daily tasks more efficient. The society's quarterly, the report suggested, ought to eliminate some features and place a renewed emphasis on scholarship. In no area of the society's activities did the self-study report recommend the deletion or reduction of programs or services.

The executive committee met in a special daylong session on October 27, 1989, to discuss the report. Since the committee had to fund whichever of the proposals its members accepted, the committee's decisions would in fact constitute the society's actual plan for future action. Trustee William Aull neatly summarized the committee's alternatives in a letter of October 26: increase the budget "drastically" to accomplish much at once, or establish a list of priorities that available funds could address over time. Although the society's records include no minutes of the discussion session, the committee clearly favored the second approach. Members instructed Executive Director Goodrich to formulate his version of the society's mission statement in the wake of the self-study and to list his top priorities for the society's next few years.

Goodrich's response, dated November 27, both strongly reaffirmed the unique nature and mission of the society as both had evolved since the turn of the century and promised innovation when "adequate staffing and funding are available":

> The State Historical Society of Missouri is a specialized research library with historical collections and genealogical materials that are available for the use of patrons who either write, telephone or visit the society in search of historical or genealogical information. It is directed by state statute to collect, preserve, make accessible and publish materials regarding the history of the state and western America.

Floyd Shoemaker and Dick Brownlee could easily have made the same statement.

The executive director's top priority was to maintain continuity with the past. The society must continue to strengthen that which had made it unique: its reference, newspaper, and manuscript collections, and its fine arts and publications programs. Goodrich set specific goals in his response to the committee's request. He recommended the compilation and publication of a cumulative index to the *Missouri Historical Review* for the volumes published after 1951. Goodrich endorsed the Hurt report's recommendations, not original to it, that the society develop an oral history program, and that it help to finance professional employees' travel to meetings in their fields. He committed the society to increasing its support of the History Day program and called attention to the fiscal year 1991 appropriations request for a photographic specialist staff position.

Since the days when the finance committee had to remind Francis Sampson that his book-collecting travel expenses were straining the society's resources, all directors and trustees had lived within the confines of limited financial means. That same constraint governed the society's response to the report of the self-study project. The planning process of 1988–1989 was a positive experience for the society as an institution. No one challenged the viability of established functions or collections, suggesting, for example, that fine art was marginal to fulfillment of the society's mission. The self-study report provided staff members, professionals and nonprofessionals alike, with a risk-free means of sharing their experience-based perspectives, experience that the trustees could not duplicate. The staff's vision of what the society's future might be, as summarized in Doug Hurt's report, reminded all who knew the society well what they probably already knew: that it could easily find creative ways to reach greater numbers of Missourians with its resources and services. But Jim Goodrich and the committee reminded all concerned what they knew better than others: money controlled dreams and set limits on planning. Some of the dreams of 1988–1989 came to fruition; others remained for future decision-makers to revive and supplement.

III

The growth of the state historical society's collections during the administration of James W. Goodrich demonstrated the essential support that donors have given to the agency's programs. Unable by law to set a price on many items, the society could not assign a cash value to the gifts it received. But those contributions were a significant supplement to the state appropriation and the Membership Trust Fund's accumulation of dues and other income.

Each issue of the *Missouri Historical Review* included a section listing recent gifts of Missouri-related research materials to the society. The July 1996 issue, for example, recognized the donors of telephone directories from St. Louis, Fulton, and Concordia; a college and a high school yearbook from 1917 and 1922, respectively; the records of a school district in Mississippi County covering the years 1893–1908; several genealogical studies; the Arthur Allee manuscript collection; a master's thesis on the drawing of the state's boundaries; the 1991 Neosho Historical Buildings Survey; photographs pertaining to Neosho's favorite son, Thomas Hart Benton; a program from the lecture appearance of former British Prime Minister Margaret Thatcher at Westminster College in 1996; and a postcard view of a street scene in Stanberry, ca. 1909. Executive Director Goodrich regularly reported cash gifts, large and small, to the executive committee. The Clifford W. Gaylord Foundation made several of the larger grants, including five thousand dollars in 1995 for the purchase of the Francis Scheidegger photograph collection. Some of the society's friends remembered it in their wills. The donor of a 1989 bequest of ten thousand dollars intended that it support the enhancement and maintenance of the collections.

As it had under Richard Brownlee's direction, the fine arts collection grew significantly during the Goodrich years. Most of the art gallery's newsworthy events after 1985 involved George Caleb Bingham's works. In 1985 and 1986, Mrs. Marshall S. Woodson of Thomasville, Georgia, donated Bingham's portraits of Robert S. Barr and Mary Barr Singleton, and Mrs. E. Sydney Stephens of Columbia gave the artist's portraits of James Leachman Stephens and Amelia Hockaday Stephens. All four subjects had been members of central Missouri families active in business and civic affairs. Thornton Hough, a descendant of General Alexander W. Doniphan, gave the society four Bingham portraits of Doniphan family members in May 1990. A few months earlier, the society had purchased the artist's portrait of Mrs. Jacob Fortney Wyan as a memorial to Richard Brownlee. In 1991, it bought the artist's likeness of General Odon Guitar and received as the gift of William C. Black of Kansas City Bingham's portrait of Judge Francis Marion Black. With these acquisitions, the society owned more than twenty-five Bingham works.

An 1878 Bingham painting attracted special interest in two of the society's gallery exhibits. The first, which visitors viewed between March and July 1991, featured what its owner, Nelson A. Rieger of Colorado Springs, believed was one of Bingham's relatively few landscapes. *Colorado Landscape, View of Pike's Peak from Greenland* offered a panorama of the Colorado Rockies in the vicinity of that famed mountain. In 1992, however, the society's gallery curator, Sidney Larson, proved that Bingham had copied part of his work from another artist's 1872 painting of Mount Washington, New Hampshire. Larson's discovery in this Bingham work of a common practice among nineteenth-century artists caused the title of Rieger's property to revert to the original *Mountain Landscape, 1878.* In addition to providing the expertise to unravel an artistic puzzle, the society hosted Nelson A. and Susan Rieger's *Western America: Landscapes and Indians,* a traveling exhibit of twenty-seven works from their personal art collection in 1994. One of the paintings was the Bingham landscape.

Art from the society's collection appeared in numerous exhibits during the Goodrich years. In 1987, editorial cartoons from the Daniel R. Fitzpatrick collection not previously featured appeared in the Corridor

Gallery, while the Art Gallery featured maps from the society's files. Exhibited in 1995 in the society's facilities were some of Edward S. Curtis's nineteenth-century photographs of Native Americans, Thomas Hart Benton's series *The Year of Peril,* and Louis Kurz and Alexander Allison's Civil War prints. The society sent some of its significant art holdings to other locations. "Missouri Artists: Then and Now," a feature of the 1990 state fair in Sedalia viewed by thousands of people, included a number of its paintings. Fifty Benton lithographs traveled with a large collection of the artist's work to sites in twelve states in 1986, and two Fred Shane paintings joined a tour of six museums in the same year. The governor's mansion in Jefferson City displayed Bingham's *Watching the Cargo* for twelve months in 1986–1987, and Greta Kempton's *Truman Family* has been prominently displayed there since 1993.

Through Sidney Larson, the society continued to solicit contributions to its collection of contemporary artists. The society unveiled Larson's portrait of former director Richard Brownlee in a May 1991 ceremony. In 1992, Claire Shane Lohnes donated over 90 artworks done by her father, Fred Shane, and over 250 of his sketches and drawings three years later. The wildlife drawings of Charles Schwartz broadened the subject matter of works in the art collection. In 1987, he and his wife, Elizabeth, added working sketches of the mural panels that Schwartz had painted for the headquarters building of the Missouri Department of Conservation to the collection of wildlife studies they had donated in the 1960s. The editorial cartoon collection also grew, first through the donation in 1987 of 150 Jesse T. Cargill cartoons by his granddaughter, Catherine Cargill Blake. In 1990, the family of L. Mitchell White gave the society his collection of original editorial cartoons. Thus the personal favorites of the man who had originated the society's large file of newspaper cartoons came to rest in its archives.

The reference library's acquisition of books and pamphlets numbered in the hundreds each year. Among the purchased and donated items were some valuable rare volumes, such as Thomas L. McKenney's *History of the Indian Tribes of North America.* That work was part of R. E. "Bud" Lucas's 1986 gift of books. Next door to the reference library, the editorial department administered the growing collection of photographs. As the editorial staff revised the illustrated *Historic Missouri* in 1987, it urged readers of the *Review* to donate photographs as part of "an active effort to expand its contemporary collection and bring it

James W. Goodrich, society president Avis Tucker, Claire Shane Lohnes, society art curator Sidney Larson, and past society president Robert C. Smith stand in front of a Fred Shane self-portrait during the society's 1992 annual meeting, which featured an exhibit of the artist's works. Tucker was the first woman to be elected president of the society.

up to the 1980s." Not contemporary, but of great value to historians of eastern Missouri, especially the St. Charles area, was the John J. Buse collection, given by John L. Buse in 1991. Gathered from a variety of sources, the collection included thousands of historic photographs with accompanying captions.

The Missouri Newspaper Project (MNP), funded by the National Endowment for the Humanities, allowed the newspaper librarians to move closer to goals set by the state's editors in the 1890s. Announced by Executive Director Goodrich at the October 1987 annual meeting as Missouri's share of a nationwide effort, the project sought to locate, catalog, and preserve on microfilm as many as possible of all the newspapers ever published in the state. Staff members entered cataloging data into the Online Computer Library Center's (OCLC) national database. The newspaper project was also a fulfillment of a priority that

Goodrich had set in his November 1989 response to the society's self-study: "to pursue joint ventures with other state agencies or institutions." The society's partner in the MNP was the University of Missouri–Kansas City and its Miller Nichols Library.

Although the society had collected newspapers for ninety years, its librarians knew of gaps in their holdings of a number of papers. The MNP in the early 1990s allowed for the borrowing from editors, private collectors, and other libraries, and the microfilming of issues of numerous Missouri newspapers. Society newspaper librarians who assisted the MNP staff, Mark Thomas and Kay Pettit, traveled to the southeastern Missouri towns of Perryville, Jackson, and Steele in August 1989, for example, to transport safely to Columbia copies of newspapers dated as early as 1897. In January 1990, they returned these papers, which totaled some 26,000 pages. In September 1990, Thomas drove to Canton, Milan, and Iowa City, Iowa. Editors in the two Missouri communities loaned issues of their newspapers to the society, while the State Historical Society of Iowa donated its holdings of several Missouri titles. In the late 1980s and early 1990s, the society microfilmed newspapers in the files of the Mercantile Library in St. Louis and the Kansas State Historical Society. During the early 1990s, issues of the *Review* routinely reported on additional automobile trips by staff members to borrow papers not yet part of the society's collection. Funds provided by the Missouri Newspaper Project clearly strengthened an already large and useful newspaper collection as it made the society's holdings known to researchers nationwide. The newspaper library also obtained, in August 1992, an essential resource for genealogists and historians: the just-released census of 1920.

As impressive as were the additions to the historical society's art and newspaper collections during Jim Goodrich's administration, perhaps more imposing were the four-campus manuscript collection's acquisitions. Important collections seemed to flow into the manuscript facilities, not the least of which were the papers of Republican Senator John C. Danforth after his retirement in 1994. In 1989, the third member of the *Mexico Ledger* publishing family to be closely associated with the society, trustee Robert M. White II, donated his personal papers to the society. The children of Joseph Byrne made a gift of the extensive records of their father's St. Louis–based fur and wool company, covering years in the early twentieth century, in 1991. At the September 1991 annual meeting, Jim Goodrich announced the acquisition of other collections, which pertained to the Katy Railroad, the American Royal horse show in Kansas City, the Gaslight Square neighborhood of St. Louis, and Marlin Perkins, naturalist, zoo administrator, and television personality. In 1992–1993, branches of the Western Historical Manuscript Collection acquired the papers of former St. Louis mayor Vincent Schoemel and the records of the Greater Kansas City Chamber of Commerce, among other collections. The papers of former member of the U.S. House of Representatives Alan Wheat and longtime Lincoln University professor of history Lorenzo Greene appeared on the list of manuscript acquisitions during fiscal year 1995.

Oral history techniques offered a unique, qualitatively different means of assembling the record of Missouri's past than those long used by the society. Since oral history tapped memory for unwritten accounts of events and interpretations of experience, some of it in the realm of folk culture, it went beyond the society's traditional goal of preserving knowledge. Interacting in an atmosphere of trust, a skilled interviewer and a participant in a sense created knowledge, as together they reconstructed the past.

Although Executive Director Goodrich, with the active support of the executive committee, made the addition of an oral history program a society priority in 1989 and began requesting funds to hire a trained specialist as early as 1990 for fiscal year 1992, the legislature did not fund the project at once. Prior to C. Ray Brassieur's arrival in 1993, the executive committee discussed several potential projects, including interviews with Civilian Conservation Corps participants in the 1930s, veteran Missouri newspaper publishers, and World War II veterans. Brassieur's first in-depth project, however, was compatible with work he had done in his previous position with the Missouri Cultural Heritage Center. The Bootheel Project was another of the society's cooperative efforts, linking it with the University of Missouri's Folk Art Program and the Museum of Art and Archaeology. The project enjoyed the financial support of the National Endowment for the Humanities and the Missouri Arts Council.

Brassieur's contributions to this multidisciplinary team study included an interview with farm manager Maxwell Williams, which appeared in the *Missouri Historical Review* in October 1996. Williams, who came to the state's southeastern corner in 1930, offered insight into a variety of agriculture-related subjects. Visitors to the society's 1996 annual meeting experienced a second product of the Bootheel Project. A compact exhibit designed for travel to sites around the state displayed visual and audial evidence of the "Art and Heritage of the Missouri Bootheel," the display's title. The exhibit and the published interview demonstrated that the society's oral history program possessed the potential to reach a large audience with fascinating information.

Devoting much of its effort to collecting historical materials, the society necessarily committed other resources to managing and conserving the collections it held in trust for the people of Missouri. The staff and administration learned anew during the 1980s and 1990s that hazards both predictable and unexpected jeopardized irreplaceable properties. Although the executive committee decided, in September 1986 and September 1992, not to purchase an electronic book security system "in view of the society's low percentage of book loss," the theft of an 1830 first edition of *The Book of Mormon* in 1993 prompted change. By the autumn of 1994, the society allowed patrons to bring into the reference library only items necessary for conducting research and provided coin-operated storage lockers for personal belongings. Time, use, and moisture took their toll on other valuable resources. A Gaylord Foundation grant in 1986 paid for conservation work on several Thomas Hart Benton paintings. Earlier that year, condensation buildup caused when construction workers neglected to reactivate the air circulation system caused "substantial damage" to Benton's *Exterminate* and other works. Insurance covered most of the nearly twenty-thousand-dollar cost of restoration.

The extensive microfilming program preserved other materials besides deteriorating newsprint. These included some heavily used manuscript collections and the historic sites files assembled in the 1950s and early 1960s. The Membership Trust Fund paid two student assistants in 1986 to mend and prepare for microfilming nearly 90,000 pages of newspapers collected years before. In the following year, forty-two thousand dollars from the same fund permitted the filming of 281,000 pages "of old papers which are in desperate condition and literally crumbling away." The newspaper library also replaced reels of microfilmed papers damaged through repeated use. The reference library, in 1991, requested deacidification and encapsulation of several plat books "to prevent further deterioration of the loose pages which are chipping and crumbling." Members' dues proved essential in these and similar acts of preservation.

In addition to the staff's printing of finding aids, other actions occurred to improve patron access to the collections. Beginning November 1, 1986, the reference and newspaper libraries offered seven and one-half hours of service on Saturday. Over 175 patrons used the facilities during the first five days of weekend service. "Access" also meant offering materials to researchers in the most easily usable format. Technicians cleaned and microfilmed the Maximilian E. Schmidt collection of glass negatives in 1996. The process made available positive images to researchers. Equipment wore out in the course of normal use, as in the case of eight microfilm readers retired late in 1989. Among their replacements were two coin-operated microfilm reader-printer copiers, equipment that increased the efficiency both of researchers and staff members.

During the Goodrich years, a much more sophisticated form of technology, computers, promised other advantages beside enhanced efficiency. Through gift and purchase, the society added personal computers in several departments, including Arthur V. Nebel's contribution of two units to the Columbia branch of the joint manuscript collection in 1987, in honor of Elmer Ellis and W. Francis English. Along with the administrative office, which employed computers in such routine functions as renewing memberships, the society's editorial department and the Western Historical Manuscript Collection used the new technology the most extensively by the late 1990s. In 1996, for example, WHMC's Columbia branch established a site on the World Wide Web. From anywhere in the world, users of the Internet could obtain information on manuscript collections, the oral history program, and History Day, as well as visit the web sites of the other three branches of the manuscript archive. A year later, the society's World Wide Web site appeared, providing information about the organization, its holdings, and programs.

The society was less successful in placing the contents of its reference library in the University of Missouri's on-line computer catalog. The university libraries installed two such systems. In 1996, MERLIN—Missouri Education and Research Libraries Information Network—replaced the earlier LUMIN, or Libraries of the University of Missouri Information Network. One impetus to integrating with the university's catalog all or part of the reference library's titles, including the Bay Collection, was the positive recommendation of a 1991 consultant's study, which Lynn Wolf Gentzler oversaw. That report also advised listing the society's book and pamphlet holdings nationally with OCLC.

As early as 1986, Jim Goodrich sought funds from the university itself or from the General Assembly to pay for these projects. Included in the society's fiscal year 1994 program improvement requests, proposed two years earlier, was over $165,000 for the complete automation of the reference collection's card catalog. The society made a similar request for fiscal year 1995, but in both cases the legislature objected. By 1996, about 2 percent of the society's book collection appeared in MERLIN. Its cataloging of acquisitions was also done on-line. The fact that it was not a lending library, as well as the vigorous competition of many worthy programs for limited funds, helped to explain why the society had not made greater progress in computerizing its catalog as its one hundredth anniversary arrived.

As the state historical society sustained its traditional functions of acquiring new resources and managing the existing ones, under Jim Goodrich it also gave unprecedented support to the teaching of Missouri history. Occasionally Floyd Shoemaker had sought ways to link the society's activities and secondary school libraries and classrooms. But he never moved far beyond urging school districts to become members of the society and discover instructional uses for the *Missouri Historical Review*. In February 1935, for example, Shoemaker informed an official of the St. Louis city schools that he had mailed the quarterly's most recent issue to each building in the district. Now he desired to send "suggestions . . . which might be helpful in exploiting the educational possibilities of our magazine." Under Richard Brownlee, with the society occupying its new quarters, many school groups visited the various collections for tours and work on research projects. An opportunity to support history education unavailable to Brownlee or Shoemaker, the History Day program emerged in the 1980s, and by the following decade the society was its major financial sponsor in Missouri.

In his November 1989 memorandum to the executive committee listing his priorities for the society, Goodrich placed a "high priority" on the History Day activities. He noted that "thousands of students, along with hundreds of teachers, participate at the local, regional and state levels." Part of a national effort to involve young scholars and their instructors in research topics centered on an annual theme, and then sharing their findings in written reports, three-dimensional projects, media presentations, and performances, Missouri's competition culminated each spring in Columbia. Laura S. Bullion of the Western Historical Manuscript Collection led the Missouri project. The University of Missouri, the State Historical Society of Missouri, and the Missouri Committee for the Humanities (MCH) were early sponsors, with grants from the latter providing most of the initial funding.

The MCH, its seed money having firmly established the state's History Day program, encouraged a greater administrative and financial role for the historical society beginning in 1987. Over several years, Goodrich and the executive committee responded in two ways. They sought funds in the society's state appropriation for History Day in Missouri, and by the 1993–1994 fiscal year that line item amounted to nearly fifteen thousand dollars. The society also made grants to History Day from the Brownlee Fund, which the committee had established upon the former director's retirement. In September 1989, for example, the executive committee voted to spend five thousand dollars from the fund for partial support of the program. When money from other sources appeared problematic early in 1992, the committee unanimously passed a motion "guarantee[ing] funding by the society for History Day 1993."

In the 1990s, private funds also became essential to the financial success of History Day activities. Most of the gifts originated with individual members of the society's executive committee. Former president Bud Barnes obtained ten thousand dollars from the Clifford W. Gaylord Foundation to help meet the costs of the 1990 competition, the same year that the Allen P. and Joseph B. Green Foundation of Mexico contributed two thousand dollars. Thanks to trustee Avis Tucker, the Kemper Foundation of Kansas City donated twenty-five hundred dollars in 1992. Before he died in 1994, former president Joseph Webber had created an endowed fund to generate an annual History Day teacher award. Maryann Shephard, a social studies teacher at Brentwood High School in St. Louis County, won the initial Missouri History Day Teacher of Merit Award in 1995.

Teachers like Shephard from across the state mentored the hundreds of students who participated annually in History Day activities. Taking part in the April 11, 1992, state competition were 418 students and

84 teachers from 74 schools, who submitted 221 separate entries. Missouri students compiled an excellent record in national competition. In June 1992, at the University of Maryland in College Park, four of the fifty-four Missouri students who attended National History Day reached the finals. In Washington, D.C., in 1994, students from Joplin, Sarcoxie, and Rolla schools won monetary awards for their projects.

Sixteen-year-old Sharon Baker of rural Atlanta, Missouri, received a special award at the 1989 nationals for creating the best project in women's history: a slide program on local resident Edna Crawford. Crawford had served in Europe during World War I and still resided in Atlanta seventy years later. Baker's enthusiastic endorsement of History Day cited her increased confidence while appearing before audiences and her skills as a researcher. "History Day is a great thing for kids, and I hope it continues. . . . I love History Day!" The society recognized Laura Bullion's contribution to the success of Missouri's program in the certificate of appreciation that it gave her at the 1993 annual meeting. At the annual meeting three years later, Jim Goodrich characterized the society's sponsorship of History Day in Missouri as "one of the best things that we do."

The society launched another teaching program at the October 17, 1987, annual meeting. Workshops, attended by seventy members, offered advice on researching genealogy and family history, writing local history, and accomplishing historic preservation. Over the last dozen years of the society's first century, this outreach program provided practical assistance to highly motivated audiences of adult learners, many of whom came to Columbia specifically for the workshop sessions rather than for the annual meeting or luncheon. Interesting sessions included "Museum Techniques for Local Museums and Local Historical Societies," taught by Martin Shay, director of the State Museum, in 1988. Meeting in an adjacent room that day was a class conducted by society and WHMC staff members on "History Day for Classroom Teachers." Sanford Rikoon spoke on oral history in 1990, while Linda Benedict instructed her workshop participants on "How to Do a Newsletter that Gets Read." The tenth year's schedule of workshops, offered on October 5, 1996, included sessions on "Tracing African-American Ancestry" and "Project Planning for Local Historical Societies." In their first twelve years, the annual meeting day workshops drew over nine

Daniel Brown (left) and William "Beau" Kostedt (right) were two of the History Day in Missouri students who competed at National History Day in 1996. They displayed their award-winning three-dimensional project at the society's 1996 annual meeting.

hundred participants. They and the History Day activities proved to be useful and creative ways to actively involve state residents in the study of Missouri history.

IV

The Richard S. Brownlee Fund was the State Historical Society of Missouri's first program of financial grants to scholarship-in-progress. A $25,000 gift from the Clifford W. Gaylord Foundation, announced by President Barnes in September 1985, inaugurated the endowment. The finance committee added monies from the Membership Trust Fund to the gifts contributed in honor of the retired director to establish the fund's initial principal at $50,000 in December of that year. Broad guidelines, liberally interpreted, encouraged potential applicants. Persons or organizations without regard to place of residence were eligible for grants. They must "have made or propose to make publications or contributions of any kind whatever to the history of the state of Missouri and its citizens, past, present or future." In September 1986, finance committee members voted to increase the fund's principal to $100,000. In 1996, the executive committee approximately doubled the account's balance to nearly $235,000 and nearly doubled the number of awards as well.

While the Brownlee Fund did support History Day on an interim basis, other grants during the first eleven years of its existence underwrote

Historic preservation consultant Debbie Sheals presented a workshop entitled "House Genealogy: Tracing the History of a Building" at the society's 1995 annual meeting.

the work of mature scholars. Those projects revealed the variety of research on Missouri history in the late twentieth century. Three separate grants, the first in 1992, supported the preparation of the *Dictionary of Missouri Biography*. The fund's subsidy of research in the state's antebellum history included William Foley's and David Rice's work on the Chouteau family (a 1991 grant), Dick Steward's on dueling in Missouri (1991), Carl J. Ekberg's on the Valle family of Ste. Genevieve (1993), R. Douglas Hurt's biography of Nathan Boone (1994), and Christopher Phillip's biography of Claiborne Fox Jackson (1995). Brownlee Fund support of Lewis O. Saum's research on Eugene Field resulted in two articles in the *Missouri Historical Review* by October 1996 and the 1991 annual luncheon address. Projects that covered the broad sweep of Missouri history, including John C. Crighton's on health services in

St. Louis and Mark Stauter's on the metal trade in the state, also won financial support.

The first recipients of Brownlee Awards, in 1986, were Larry Christensen and Gary Kremer, to underwrite their work on volume 4 of the Missouri Sesquicentennial History, which was published in 1997. The fund's support of projects in twentieth-century Missouri history included Bonnie Stepenoff's study of the deforestation of the Bootheel region (1992 and 1997), James N. Giglio's biography of baseball professional Stan Musial (1992), Henry Lewis Suggs's work on Chester A. Franklin and the *Kansas City Call* (1993), and Virginia Laas's research on writer and political figure Emily Newell Blair (1995). The Missouri Division of the American Association of University Women, the Vernon County Historical Society, the Kirkwood Historical Society, and the Friends of Arrow Rock were among the organizations that won Brownlee grants. Along with the historical society's support of History Day for school-age students of Missouri history, its Brownlee Fund proved to be one of its most influential innovations during James Goodrich's administration.

The historical society recognized completed research by means of its awards program and its selection of luncheon speakers. The new Donald W. Reynolds Alumni and Visitor Center on the university campus first hosted the annual business meeting and luncheon on October 15, 1994. Columbia's two hotels had been the sites of these gatherings until the university constructed suitable facilities after World War II. Failing to obtain its own auditorium in the late 1950s library construction project, the society instead used meeting and dining facilities in the nearby Fine Arts Building and Memorial Union through 1993. Floyd Shoemaker had scheduled many of the early annual meetings and dinners in April. The Goodrich administration confirmed a long-standing precedent, however, when it arranged the business meeting and luncheon around Missouri Tiger football games in the autumn months. Beginning in 1992, the society shortened the luncheon agenda by presenting Brownlee awards and certificates of appreciation to retiring trustees at the business meeting. Luncheon guests witnessed other recognitions, including special awards. One of these was a citation of achievement from the American Association for State and Local History earned by Bob Priddy in 1989, for his *Across Our Wide Missouri* radio series and his book on Thomas Hart Benton's state capitol mural.

Annually, a committee of three professional historians selected the outstanding *Review* article. In the thirteen years from 1985 to 1997, six college and university professors of history, one professor of German, another of communication and fine arts, three Ph.D. candidates in history, a museum curator, and a librarian-archivist received article awards. These authors' subjects, too, celebrated the diversity of Missouri history, a variety that would have astonished the quarterly's readers of earlier years. Four of the thirteen essays demonstrated the flourishing interest in Missouri women's history that marked the 1980s and 1990s. Bonnie Stepenoff won the 1991 award for her analysis of anarchist Emma Goldman and socialist Kate Richards O'Hare as inmates of the state penitentiary in 1917–1920. Two of the prize articles dealt with acts of violence: Larry D. Ball's "Federal Justice on the Santa Fe Trail: The Murder of Antonio José Chavez" (1987 award) and Thomas G. Dyer's "'A Most Unexampled Exhibition of Madness and Brutality': Judge Lynch in Saline County, Missouri, 1859" (1995). The 1861 Battle of Boonville, child labor in the mining industry of Washington County, and Harry Truman's racial views were the subjects of other prizewinning essays. The best article in the *Review*'s volume 90, "'This Magnificent New World': [Senator] Thomas Hart Benton's Westward Vision Reconsidered," by John D. Morton, also won the Western Historical Association's prestigious Ray Allen Billington Award.

In 1992, the executive committee endorsed former President Barnes's proposal to annually recognize the best book in Missouri history. Former associate director R. Douglas Hurt won the first stipend and citation in 1993 for his *Agriculture and Slavery in Missouri's Little Dixie*. Three biographies were among the first five award winners: Sally M. Miller's of Kate Richards O'Hare (1994), Robert H. Ferrell's of Harry S. Truman (1995), and Kenneth C. Kaufman's of Roswell M. Field (1997). Trustee Virginia Young received the 1996 Missouri History Book Award for her late husband Raymond's *Cultivating Cooperation: A History of the Missouri Farmers Association*. A longtime officer in MFA and president of the MFA Oil Company, Young represented a large number of authors of merit who were not academics.

The Floyd C. Shoemaker Award continued to identify high school seniors and college students who wrote outstanding essays on the state's history. Andy Collins's "To the Victor Belongs the Spoils," the 1985 award winner, appeared in the January 1986 issue of the *Missouri*

Historical Review. But after granting the prize in 1987 and 1989, the society received no applications in 1990. Joining an award it wished to retain with a program it increasingly supported, the executive committee in that year decided to honor the former secretary by recognizing the best essay on Missouri history entered in the History Day competition. The 1993 recipient, Amber R. Clifford, published her essay on the Southern Tenant Farmers' Union in the October issue of the *Review.*

Speakers at the annual luncheon also demonstrated the vitality of interest in the state's history. Among the academics appearing were Richard S. Kirkendall in 1986, who addressed the topic "Truman and Missouri"; James I. Robertson in 1992, who explained "Why the Civil War Still Lives"; and Margaret Ripley Wolfe in 1997, who discussed "Rumors of a Little Rebellion in Dixie: Real Women and Their Region." A majority of the speakers between 1985 and 1997 were not professional historians. Representing journalism, politics, and the law, most of them spoke from personal experience as participants in the events upon which they commented. James J. Fisher in 1985 and Ron Powers in 1990 both reflected on history from journalists' perspectives. Another newspaperman, sports editor emeritus Bob Broeg of the *St. Louis Post-Dispatch,* in 1993 spoke on one of his favorite subjects: University of Missouri football. Speaking on contemporary politics, Lisa Myers, an NBC-TV broadcast journalist, commanded a large audience in 1994. In 1995, retired Democratic Senator Thomas F. Eagleton spoke about U.S. Senator Harry S. Truman's elevation to the vice presidency in 1944. Lyman Field, a Kansas City lawyer and Thomas Hart Benton's friend, "remembered" the artist in 1989. And U.S. District Judge Stephen N. Limbaugh, in the 1996 address, recalled his and his father, Rush Limbaugh Sr.'s, involvement in the creation of the Ozark National Scenic Riverways in southeast Missouri.

Jim Goodrich liked to call the *Missouri Historical Review* the journal of record of the state's history. That, indeed, was its distinction. The *Review* completed its ninety-first volume with the issue of July 1997—the 364th issue since Francis Sampson had edited the first one, published in October 1906. Goodrich organized one special collection of essays, for the October 1989 *Review,* to observe the University of Missouri's sesquicentennial. He dedicated that issue to the late Lewis Atherton. The quarterly similarly honored Elmer Ellis and Richard Brownlee in January and July 1990, respectively. In 1986, his first year with full

Noted Civil War historian James I. Robertson (left) was the speaker at the society's annual meeting luncheon in 1992. Francis M. "Bud" Barnes (right), a trustee since 1978, served as president of the society from 1986 to 1989.

responsibility for the journal, Goodrich named a board of editors. Thus the *Review* became a refereed journal. Susan M. Hartmann, a specialist in women's history at the University of Missouri–St. Louis and later Ohio State University, and Arvarh Strickland, of the Columbia campus, were among the board members who served into the late 1990s.

As editor, Goodrich enjoyed the talents of several associate editors. Mary K. Dains served in that capacity through October 1991, and Doug Hurt was her coassociate editor for volumes 81 (1986–1987) through 83 (1988–1989). Lynn Wolf Gentzler replaced him beginning with the April 1990 issue and remained associate editor after Dains's retirement. Research assistants Leona S. Morris, Ann L. Rogers, Christine Montgomery, Kristin Kolb, and Lisa Frick ably facilitated the production process of the quarterly and the society's other publications.

For the first time since Floyd Shoemaker's editorship, the *Review* acquired a new physical appearance with volume 90 (1995–1996). Each of the volume's four issues arrived in members' mailboxes with a color background surrounding the cover photo, disorienting, perhaps, for those accustomed to the photo laid against a white background. The information on the title page, rearranged and in larger type, also accommodated readers. As had long been true, front covers in the late twentieth century provided a gallery, of sorts, for the society's collections of visual sources. World War I posters and postcard views of Missouri communities were among the pictorial representations of the past that invited readers to survey the articles inside. Three times in volumes 80 through 90 (July 1987, October 1993, and April 1994), covers carried photographs of New Deal projects and sharecropper evictions in southeast Missouri during the late 1930s. They and articles accompanying them provided background to the Bootheel Project of which the society's oral history program was a part. Paintings appeared on many of the *Review's* front covers. The April 1991 issue displayed Nelson and Susan Rieger's Bingham painting, *Mountain Landscape 1878,* while the October 1991 cover presented Sidney Larson's portrait of Richard Brownlee. The four issues of volume 80 carried Thomas Hart Benton color illustrations from a series he had painted for a 1944 edition of Twain's *Life on the Mississippi.* Although the original works in the society's fine art collections reached a restricted audience, the *Review's* reproductions exposed some of them to a large public.

Volumes 80 through 90 (1985–1986 through 1995–1996) published 171 articles and edited documents. While some of them bridged two or more broad chronological periods, most fell into five distinct eras of historical specialization. Sixty-six articles represented scholars' research in Missouri history to 1875. Thirty of these were on antebellum topics, ranging from Native Americans to the Civil War's immediate background, while the remaining thirty-six dealt with the most intensely studied years of the state's past, 1861–1875. Thirty-nine articles in these eleven *Review* volumes treated events in the 1876–1932 time span. Although only three contributions investigated topics in the period after 1960, twenty-eight fell within the chronological limits 1933–1959. In its distribution of articles over the whole sweep of Missouri history, the *Missouri Historical Review* satisfied readers of varied interests.

Every volume of the quarterly from 1985–1986 to 1995–1996 carried at least one article on the Civil War, but the published essays clustered around other fields of interest also. Even at a time when social history attracted much of the interest of historians nationwide, political history remained a vital concern of those who wrote Missouri history. One reason was Harry Truman. Nine articles on the former president appeared in the eleven volumes surveyed. While subject areas of former strength, such as business history and the trans-Mississippi West, retained a moderate presence in the quarterly's pages under Goodrich's editorial supervision, historians actively researched the fields of ethnic and gender history. Twelve pieces on African American topics and fourteen on

European ethnic groups, most on Missourians of German extraction, appeared in these volumes. Three authors discussed the contributions of both Germans and Italians to viticulture in Missouri. The increasing vitality of women's history found expression in fifteen articles. Four contributions by Lawrence Christensen on Missouri's World War I experience revealed, as never before, the importance of that subject. The Rolla historian published a total of nine articles in the *Review* between April 1986 and July 1996.

Following the scholarship, readers rediscovered a long-familiar feature, the "Historical Notes and Comments" section. The 1988 self-study had suggested that the news items that had appeared in the last one-third of a typical issue since the Shoemaker era be broadcast in a newsletter instead. But at the close of the society's first century, these informative items remained in the journal.

"Historical Notes and Comments" not only carried news of the state historical society itself, but also of local societies' activities. While some readers undoubtedly ignored what may have seemed items of purely local interest, this quarterly survey represented at least two significant truths. Thoughtful readers knew that the pursuit of historical understanding and the celebration of the past flourished at the grassroots level, without benefit of a state appropriation or the work of full-time professionals. Further, by publishing local news the State Historical Society of Missouri fulfilled one of its commitments: to encourage the growth of, maintain contact with, and serve as a clearinghouse for the interests and activities of town and county societies.

After listing recent gifts of books and other tangible resources, "Historical Notes and Comments" presented two bibliographies: articles on Missouri history in newspapers and in magazines. As publishers of a journal of record, dedicated to the comprehensive coverage of the state's history, the editors of the *Review* felt obligated to note all available published sources on the state's history. The quarterly's complete record of sources also included full book reviews of major publications and "book notes" on other volumes.

In all of its features, from cover to cover, the *Missouri Historical Review* continued to accomplish the goal that Richard Brownlee had set: It simultaneously addressed an audience of professional scholars and a much larger public of avocational historians. That was a challenging task, but both those whose work was the study of history, and those who read history after their day's work had ended, found features of value and interest. During Jim Goodrich's editorial years, several series of vignettes appearing inside the back cover seemed designed to appeal to both audiences. Reflecting research and conveying useful data, the several paragraphs accompanied by an illustration caught the general reader's interest. Volumes 80 through 82 showcased a number of Missouri's local historical museums and societies. Volumes 85 and 86 presented a series on Missouri National Register of Historic Places attractions, which included the Laura Ingalls Wilder House in Mansfield. The digest presentations in volumes 87 through 89 looked at several Missouri colleges that had ceased to operate. "Contributors to Missouri Culture," a series beginning in the October 1995 issue, featured individuals such as James Langston Hughes, a Joplin native and later the "Poet-Laureate of Harlem," and institutions such as Ste. Genevieve's Summer School of Art.

The society also intended to serve both the scholarly community and a general readership through its other publications. One such title was *The Directory of Local Historical, Museum, and Genealogical Agencies in Missouri.* The 1994–1995 edition, for example, was a 106-page softcover reference work with information on more than 375 organizations across the state. A very different book was *My Road to Emeritus,* the memoirs of a man who had significantly affected the society's life. Elmer Ellis had printed his recollections privately in 1988. The following year, upon Jim Goodrich's recommendation, the executive committee published the volume with the University of Missouri Press. The office of Haskell Monroe, Columbia campus chancellor, shared the publication costs. Appropriately, Ellis's rendition of his long association with the university appeared during the institution's sesquicentennial year, 1989.

The society issued the second edition of its popular *Historic Missouri: A Pictorial Narrative* in 1988. The editorial process extended from late 1986 into early 1988, as staff members simultaneously prepared two other books and an issue of the *Review* every third month. The ninety-four-page booklet included three hundred illustrations—reproductions of photographs, drawings, paintings, and maps—eight in color. A panel of a Thomas Hart Benton mural depicted a major theme of the state's early history, the westward movement, on the front cover. The Gaylord Foundation provided a grant to partially cover production costs. The "narrative" half of the subtitle was informative, if secondary to the illustrative material, appearing as several lead paragraphs in each of the nine chapters and as substantive captions with each illustration. Most of the pictorial material came from the society's collections, making this widely distributed publication another showcase for its visual resources.

The 1977 edition of *Historic Missouri* had originated in the special U.S. bicentennial issue of the *Missouri Historical Review.* The 1989 publication, *Thomas Hart Benton: Artist, Writer, Intellectual,* grew from a similar concept. In the spring of 1987, Goodrich and the editorial staff planned "a special Benton issue of the . . . *Review,*" whose essays by "four top Benton scholars" would recognize the centennial of the artist's birth in 1989. By late 1987, however, the staff had proposed a book rather than a Benton issue of the quarterly, with eight instead of four contributors. The interdisciplinary team of essayists included four art historians, two professors of English, a journalist, and a practicing artist. The latter was Sidney Larson, the society's art curator and Benton's friend and assistant on several projects, including the mural at the Truman Library in Independence. The journalist was Bob Priddy, whose subject was Benton's mural in the Missouri state capitol and the controversy it had caused.

Thomas Hart Benton "is probably better known in the public mind for the controversy he stirred up during his lifetime than for his artistic production," wrote contributor Douglas Wixson. Readers of his and other essays learned a good deal about both subjects. Of all its readers, those already conversant with movements in twentieth-century European and American art and politics found *Thomas Hart Benton* to be the most rewarding. In its pages they encountered a many-sided Benton: the young New York modernist rebelling against traditional artistic modes, and the older Midwestern regionalist painter of public art; the Marxist-influenced critic of American institutions, and the alleged reactionary who harbored anti-Semitic and misogynist views; the artist who trafficked in ideas as well as paint and palette; and the supreme egoist, and the selfless teacher and benefactor.

The Benton book extended well beyond what the society's holdings and activities had traditionally defined as Missouri history, but that was its intention. When the executive committee approved the project in January 1988, Goodrich spoke of its potential as "a substantial contribution to knowledge about one of Missouri's most important sons." As had been true of only a few of the society's book publications since Floyd Shoemaker brought out the first one after World War I, *Thomas Hart Benton* appealed to specialists in the national scholarly community, not only historians of Missouri who resided largely within the state. The same had been true of *Ozark Folksongs* in the 1940s and 1950s, and of Gottfried Duden's *Report* in 1980.

The Benton essays made clear to nonspecialists that an enduring controversy about the artist's work was whether its achievement was aesthetic—and therefore occupied an important and enduring place in the history of art—or merely "cultural," as one hostile critic phrased the matter in 1987. But even if only the latter, those interested in Missouri's history were not troubled. The State Historical Society of Missouri collected art as cultural artifact—because it reflected the experience of people—just as did manuscript letters, newspapers, and reference works. While it taught its readers a good deal more, *Thomas Hart Benton* reminded the society's members and friends of that important truth.

Conclusion

*O*ne way to summarize the operations and programs of the State Historical Society of Missouri's first century is to reflect on the agency's experience in light of the concept of "public history." A product of the changes that transformed the study of history in the United States during the late 1960s and the 1970s, the public history movement most visibly expresses itself through the work of the National Council on Public History. In 1997, that organization's journal, *The Public Historian,* was in its nineteenth year of publication, while its newsletter, *Public History News,* was in its seventeenth. The council's statement of purpose announces that it "promotes the application of historical scholarship outside the university in government, business, historical societies, preservation organizations, archives, libraries, professional associations, and public interest groups." Those who promote public history encourage the use of source materials other than written documents; reach out to a broader public than academics and their traditional college-age students; include practitioners who have other occupations than university or college teaching; and employ methodologies of study that allow access to archaeological, mass media, and other nontraditional sources.

Although they did not always have this relatively recent term to describe what they were about, historical societies have consistently practiced public history. In programs and activities made possible by the financial support of state government and its members, the State Historical Society of Missouri has been a public history agency since

1898. Its subject matter, its audience, its method of study, and the media through which it has disseminated information and interpretation always have spilled beyond the boundaries traditionally recognized by the university-based historical profession. That expansiveness, reach, and innovation, over a period of one hundred years of service to the people of Missouri, is the reason for celebration in 1998.

During the 1930s, in its U.S. Highway 36 project in north Missouri, the society was a national pioneer in erecting highway historic markers, a means of reaching a mobile audience with historical information later expanded to the entire state in the 1950s and 1960s. Although the society lacked the financial means to restore, maintain, and exhibit historic Missouri sites, it did prepare a valuable inventory of such places, which it published in 1963. Public history encourages the use of folk materials. In another innovative effort, after World War II the society published four volumes of Vance Randolph's collected Ozark folk songs. Beginning in the 1920s, Floyd Shoemaker used the society's close ties with Missouri newspaper editors to offer for publication the "This Week in Missouri History" series. These brief articles reached thousands of Missourians who otherwise might have had no informed, structured contact with their state's past. In its leadership of commemorations such as the state's centennial in 1920–1921 and the Platte Purchase celebration in the 1930s, the society also reached out to large audiences of citizens, a practice repeated in the 1980s when it became the main sponsor of Missouri History Day, one of its most popular programs.

For a century the members and leaders of the State Historical Society of Missouri have come from all walks of life. They have been avocational historians, the sorts of people without whose interest and support the study of history can become a narrow discipline, its insights uncommunicable to average citizens and therefore meaningless except to a few specialists. Any effort to study the past of a people that cuts itself off from the people themselves can become a self-defeating endeavor, indeed. Beginning with Francis Sampson, the lawyer, skilled amateur natural scientist, and collector who became the society's first paid administrator, the society has drawn upon the talents of hundreds of such persons. U.S. District Judge Stephen N. Limbaugh delivered the address to the society's annual meeting in October 1996; state legislator Francis "Bud" Barnes has provided key leadership from the 1970s to the present day; journalist Walter Williams was a source of strength in earlier decades;

librarian Virginia Garton Young, in addition to her ongoing service as a trustee, stepped in as acting director following Richard Brownlee's retirement and continues to serve on the executive committee, as does Barnes. The list of examples is long and impressive.

For decades, in its publications, the society has defined history as much more than past politics, diplomacy, and wars. A browser of the *Review*'s indexes will find articles from an early date on such subjects as nineteenth-century taverns, Missouri agriculture, the works of the state's writers, house design and construction, the theater and other amusements, and additional topics in vogue at the end of the twentieth century. Since its beginning, the society has collected and preserved the state's newspapers, not only for their political and historical news, but also for their value to genealogists and mundane content such as want ads, comic strips, and reports from traffic court. Beginning in the 1920s, the agency acquired works of visual art—because they constituted source material for understanding the past, as well as represented aesthetic achievement in Missouri. The same can be said of the society's vast and priceless collection of editorial cartoons.

In the second half of the nineteenth century, the State Historical Society of Wisconsin modeled two paths of development for other state-supported societies. One was as a collector of rare documents and books in fields well beyond that state's history, a precedent that Missouri's official state historical society chose to follow. For example, among its acquisitions, the J. Christian Bay Collection represented the regional history of the middle western United States, of which Missouri was a part. The Wisconsin society's other precedent, also followed by the State Historical Society of Missouri, was its role as a public agency in service to the state's people. For a century, Missouri's tax-supported historical agency has pursued the mission of collecting, preserving, and disseminating the history of the state's people, for the people of Missouri.

Any issue of the *Missouri Historical Review* printed toward the end of the society's first century carries clear signs that public history is the agency's business. The July 1997 *Review* (volume 91, number 4) provided an example. On the cover, to accompany one of the scholarly articles inside, was an 1880s photo of the St. Louis Browns professional baseball club. In addition to an article about a Confederate army officer, other essays discussed nineteenth-century grape production for wine-making and a turn-of-the-century political couple, Governor Lon and

Margaret Stephens. The "Historical Notes and Comments" section of this issue highlighted visual historical source materials, including the recent gift of a portrait by George Caleb Bingham and the contents of the Maximilian E. Schmidt Photograph Collection, the work of a Boonville jeweler-*cum*-photographer. A sketch inside the back cover reported the career of Belle Johnson, an accomplished Monroe City photographer. Keeping readers in touch with grassroots historical efforts, "Historical Notes and Comments" also summarized the recent activities of 104 local Missouri historical societies and listed articles on the state's history that recently had appeared in newspapers and magazines. It also presented reviews and brief notes of books whose authors were both professionally trained and amateur historians. Each issue of the journal reports an active record of ongoing service to the state.

While its century-old mission has, in a sense, quietly challenged the notion that academic historians alone should define the nature of historical research and study, the State Historical Society of Missouri has contributed to, as well as respected, the work of university-based professional historians. A fundamental theme of this state society's development has been its interaction with the University of Missouri and a close association with members of its history department. Of great importance is the university's assurance that the society will always have a home on the Columbia campus. The cooperation between the two entities led to the merger in the 1960s of the university's and the society's manuscript resources in the Western Historical Manuscript Collection. The history department's participation as trustees of the society, as members of special committees, as workers in the state History Day contest, and as conduits to historical manuscripts, plus the adjunct professorship and the special assignments given to the society's executive director, are ample precedents for future joint efforts with the academic home of Lewis Atherton and Elmer Ellis. The dual goal of the *Missouri Historical Review* to serve both the scholarly and the avocational communities of Missouri historians symbolizes the society's larger mission. It must maintain high professional standards in its publications and in the management of its collections for the benefit of Ph.D.s as well as for armchair historians. This goal it has met for much of its history.

As the society enters its second century, resolve must temper self-congratulation. A proud past record will not guarantee a successful future. Careful planning, prudent spending, occasional risk-taking by the society's leadership, combined with the continued high quality of its professional staff and the loyalty of its members, will assure a future that will match the society's past. Justice Felix Frankfurter meant exactly that when he told Floyd Shoemaker to "make the future worthy of the past." The persons who constitute the State Historical Society of Missouri in the next one hundred years will carry with them a distinguished record of achievement that will require hard work to maintain.

A Note on Sources

In place of elaborate scholarly documentation and an extensive formal bibliography, this history offers what should be, to most interested readers, a more useful guide to three types of sources. Appearing first is a discussion of the major sources on which the study rests. Second is a bibliography of the State Historical Society of Missouri's publications, from the first issue of the *Missouri Historical Review* in 1906–1907 to the present. Third is a compilation of selected titles of books and dissertations that grew from substantial research in the collections of the society and the Western Historical Manuscript Collection, operated cooperatively with the University of Missouri.

I

Abundant sources exist in the society's own collections upon which to ground a narrative and analysis of its development. Especially enlightening about the continuity of issues and detail of operations since 1901 are the minutes of the society's governing body, the finance committee, as it was known until 1987, and executive committee, its name since then. A second essential mine of information is the *Missouri Historical Review,* which is in its ninety-second volume during the society's centennial year. The biennial reports prepared by the society's directors since 1902 are quite useful retrospectives and a source of data on finances, membership, annual meetings, publications, and numerous other subjects. A good source of information on and interpretation of the society's first half-century is Floyd Shoemaker's *Semicentennial History,* cited below. On the seventy-fifth anniversary, the *Review* published "The State Historical

261

Society of Missouri, 1898–1973: A Brief History," by Richard S. Brownlee, James W. Goodrich, and Mary K. Dains. Director Richard S. Brownlee's 1972 annual report to the society's members includes an informative tribute to the many contributions of Floyd C. Shoemaker, who died that year. Brownlee's 1973 report to the annual meeting, which observed the society's seventy-fifth anniversary, is a useful capsule history of the organization.

As valuable as these sources are, however, the richest resources for a study of the society's day-to-day institutional life, as well as its long-term significance and accomplishments, are a number of manuscript collections held by the Columbia campus branch of the Western Historical Manuscript Collection. The collections of papers and records that I examined are uneven in their coverage of topics and particular eras, allowing the most complete understanding of the society's operations from about 1930 to the mid-1970s. The bulk of Francis Sampson's and Floyd Shoemaker's correspondence prior to the early 1920s appears not to have been preserved, and what remains of the latter's from the 1920s is of limited value. Dick Brownlee and Jim Goodrich made less use of correspondence than their predecessors, relying more on the telephone, the fax machine, and other forms of communication that leave a less distinct trail of paper than that spread by Shoemaker.

Of the various manuscript collections, the most extensive (and amazing) is the main body of the State Historical Society of Missouri's records. Contained in nearly two hundred large storage boxes, the collection remains unprocessed and therefore without the degree of organization that researchers might ideally expect, but it is nevertheless very useful for those willing to dig and read extensively. The society has supplemented this archive with other record collections, including one of Richard Brownlee's scrapbooks. Also of particular value to this study were several collections of Floyd C. Shoemaker papers and the papers of George A. Rozier, William Francis English, Walter Barlow Stevens, the Viles-Hosmer families, Francis Asbury Sampson, Elmer Ellis, and Lewis E. Atherton.

I did not make extensive use of interviews but did enjoy and profit considerably from conversations with the current executive director, James W. Goodrich, and with trustee Virginia Young.

II

Regarding the society's own publications, it is important to note that it is in the nature of historical research and changing interpretations that some of the older sources are not the last word on their subjects. Nevertheless, the list presented here represents a proud record of accomplishment and is one of the tangible monuments left behind by scores of staff members for later generations to use and admire.

Debates of the Missouri Constitutional Convention of 1875. Edited by Isidor Loeb and Floyd C. Shoemaker. 12 volumes, 1930–1944.
Historic Missouri. 1959.
Historic Missouri: A Pictorial Narrative. 1977; 2d edition, 1988.
Journal of the Missouri Constitutional Convention of 1875. Edited by Isidor Loeb and Floyd C. Shoemaker. 2 volumes, 1920.
Messages and Proclamations of the Governors of the State of Missouri. 20 volumes, 1922–1965.
Missouri, Day by Day. Edited by Floyd C. Shoemaker. 2 volumes, 1942–1943.
Missouri Historical Review, Volumes 1– , 1906– (published quarterly).
Missouri Historic Sites Catalog. Edited by Dorothy J. Caldwell. 1963.
Missouri Newspapers: When and Where, 1808–1963. By William Howard Taft. 1964.
My Road to Emeritus. By Elmer Ellis. 1989.
Ozark Folksongs. Collected and edited by Vance Randolph; edited for the society by Floyd C. Shoemaker and Frances G. Emberson. 4 volumes, 1946–1950.
Report on a Journey to the Western States of North America and a Story of Seven Years along the Missouri. By Gottfried Duden. English translation: general editor, James W. Goodrich. 1980.
The State Historical Society of Missouri: A Semicentennial History, 1898–1948. By Floyd C. Shoemaker. 1948.
Thomas Hart Benton: Artist, Writer, and Intellectual. Edited by R. Douglas Hurt and Mary K. Dains. 1988.

III

The following is a selection of books and Ph.D. dissertations in Missouri history based on substantial research in the collections of the State Historical Society of Missouri, including various sites of the Western Historical Manuscript Collection. This list is representative of a large amount of scholarship but is not comprehensive.

Anders, Leslie. *The Eighteenth Missouri*. Indianapolis: Bobbs-Merrill, 1968.

———. *The Twenty-first Missouri: From Home Guard to Union Regiment*. Westport, Conn.: Greenwood Press, 1975.

Atherton, Lewis E. *The Frontier Merchant in Mid-America*. 1939. Reprint, Columbia: University of Missouri Press, 1971.

———. *Main Street on the Middle Border*. Bloomington: Indiana University Press, 1954.

Bellamy, Donnie D. "Slavery, Emancipation, and Racism in Missouri, 1850–1865." Ph.D. diss., University of Missouri, 1971.

Bloch, E. Maurice. *The Paintings of George Caleb Bingham: A Catalogue Raisonné*. Columbia: University of Missouri Press, 1986.

Brownlee, Richard S. *Gray Ghosts of the Confederacy: Guerrilla Warfare in the West, 1861–1865*. Baton Rouge: Louisiana State University Press, 1958.

Cain, Marvin R. *Lincoln's Attorney General: Edward Bates of Missouri*. Columbia: University of Missouri Press, 1965.

Cassity, Michael. *Defending a Way of Life: An American Community in the Nineteenth Century*. Albany: State University of New York Press, 1989.

Christensen, Lawrence O. "Black St. Louis: A Study in Race Relations, 1865–1916." Ph.D. diss., University of Missouri, 1972.

Christensen, Lawrence O., and Gary R. Kremer. *A History of Missouri: Volume 4, 1875 to 1919*. Columbia: University of Missouri Press, 1997.

Christensen, Lawrence O., and Jack B. Ridley. *UM-Rolla: A History of MSM-UMR*. Columbia: University of Missouri Printing Services, 1983.

Christ-Janer, Albert. *George Caleb Bingham of Missouri: The Story of an Artist*. With a preface by Thomas Hart Benton. New York: Dodd, Mead, and Co., 1940.

Clevenger, Homer. "Agrarian Politics in Missouri, 1880–1896." Ph.D. diss., University of Missouri, 1940.

Crighton, John C. *A History of Columbia and Boone County.* Columbia: Computer Color Graphics, 1987.

———. *The History of Health Services in Missouri.* Omaha: Barnhart Press, 1993.

Crockett, Norman L. *The Woolen Industry of the Midwest.* Lexington: University Press of Kentucky, 1970.

Curtis, Susan. *Dancing to a Black Man's Tune: A Life of Scott Joplin.* Missouri Biography Series, ed. William E. Foley. Columbia: University of Missouri Press, 1994.

Detjen, David W. *The Germans in Missouri, 1900–1918: Prohibition, Neutrality, and Assimilation.* Columbia: University of Missouri Press, 1985.

Dorsett, Lyle W. *The Pendergast Machine.* New York: Oxford University Press, 1968.

Duffner, Robert W. "Slavery in Missouri River Counties, 1820–1865." Ph.D. diss., University of Missouri, 1974.

Dunne, Gerald T. *The Missouri Supreme Court: From Dred Scott to Nancy Cruzan.* Columbia: University of Missouri Press, 1993.

Dwight, Margaret L. "Black Suffrage in Missouri, 1865–1877." Ph.D. diss., University of Missouri, 1978.

Fink, Gary M. *Labor's Search for Political Order: The Political Behavior of the Missouri Labor Movement, 1890–1940.* Columbia: University of Missouri Press, 1974.

Foley, William E. *The Genesis of Missouri: From Wilderness Outpost to Statehood.* Columbia: University of Missouri Press, 1989.

———. *A History of Missouri: Volume I, 1673 to 1820.* Columbia: University of Missouri Press, 1971.

———. "Territorial Politics in Frontier Missouri: 1804–1820." Ph.D. diss., University of Missouri, 1967.

Forderhase, Rudolph Eugene. "Jacksonianism in Missouri: From Predilection to Party, 1820–1836." Ph.D. diss., University of Missouri, 1968.

Geiger, Louis G. *Joseph W. Folk of Missouri.* University of Missouri Studies, vol. 25, no. 2. Columbia: Curators of the University of Missouri, 1953.

Gibbs, Christopher C. *The Great Silent Majority: Missouri's Resistance to World War I.* Columbia: University of Missouri Press, 1988.

Glauert, Ralph Edward. "Education and Society in Ante-Bellum Missouri." Ph.D. diss., University of Missouri, 1973.

Goodrich, James W. "The Waldo Brothers and the Westward Movement." Ph.D. diss., University of Missouri, 1974.

Gottschalk, Phil. *In Deadly Earnest: The History of the First Missouri Brigade, CSA.* Columbia: Missouri River Press, 1991.

Grenz, Suzanna M. "The Black Community in Boone County, Missouri, 1850–1900." Ph.D. diss., University of Missouri, 1979.

Grinder, Robert Dale. "The Anti-Smoke Crusades: Early Attempts to Reform the Urban Environment, 1893–1918." Ph.D. diss., University of Missouri, 1973.

Grothaus, Larry H. "The Negro in Missouri Politics, 1890–1941," Ph.D. diss., University of Missouri, 1970.

Holland, Antonio F. "Nathan B. Young and the Development of Black Higher Education." Ph.D. diss., University of Missouri, 1984.

Holmes, Harry D. "Socio-Economic Patterns of Non-Partisan Political Behavior in the Industrial Metropolis: St. Louis, 1895 to 1916." Ph.D. diss., University of Missouri, 1973.

Hurt, R. Douglas. *Agriculture and Slavery in Missouri's Little Dixie.* Columbia: University of Missouri Press, 1992.

Johnson, Ronald Wayne. "The Communist Issue in Missouri, 1946–1956." Ph.D. diss., University of Missouri, 1973.

Jones, Charles T. "George Champlin Sibley: The Prairie Puritan, 1782–1863." Ph.D. diss., University of Missouri, 1969.

Kellner, George H. "The German Element on the Urban Frontier: St. Louis, 1830–1860." Ph.D. diss., University of Missouri, 1973.

Kemper, Donald J. *Decade of Fear: Senator Hennings and Civil Liberties.* Columbia: University of Missouri Press, 1965.

Kirkendall, Richard S. *A History of Missouri: Volume V, 1919 to 1953.* Columbia: University of Missouri Press, 1986.

LeSueur, Stephen C. *The 1838 Mormon War in Missouri.* Columbia: University of Missouri Press, 1987.

Lyon, William Henry. *The Pioneer Editor in Missouri, 1808–1860.* Columbia: University of Missouri Press, 1965.

March, David D. *The History of Missouri.* 4 vols. New York: Lewis Historical Publishing Co., 1967.

McAllister, Paul E. "Missouri Voters: An Analysis of Ante-Bellum Voting

Behavior and Political Parties." Ph.D. diss., University of Missouri, 1976.

McCandless, Perry. *A History of Missouri: Volume II, 1820 to 1860.* Columbia: University of Missouri Press, 1972.

———. "Thomas H. Benton, His Source of Political Strength in Missouri from 1815 to 1838." Ph.D. diss., University of Missouri, 1953.

McCurdy, Frances Lee. *Stump, Bar, and Pulpit: Speechmaking on the Missouri Frontier.* Columbia: University of Missouri Press, 1969.

Mering, John V. "The Whig Party in Missouri." Ph.D. diss., University of Missouri, 1960.

Mitchell, Franklin D. *Embattled Democracy: Missouri Democratic Politics, 1919–1932.* Columbia: University of Missouri Press, 1968.

Norris, James D. *Frontier Iron: The Maramec Iron Works, 1826–1876.* Madison: State Historical Society of Wisconsin, 1964.

Ogilvie, Leon P. "The Development of the Southeast Missouri Lowlands." Ph.D. diss., University of Missouri, 1967.

Olson, James, and Vera Olson. *The University of Missouri: An Illustrated History.* Columbia: University of Missouri Press, 1988.

Oster, Donald B. "Community Image in the History of Saint Louis and Kansas City." Ph.D. diss., University of Missouri, 1969.

Parham, Byron Andrew Powell. "Isolationism in Missouri, 1935–1941." Ph.D. diss., University of Missouri, 1972.

Parrish, William E. *David Rice Atchison of Missouri, Border Politician.* Columbia: University of Missouri Press, 1961.

———. *A History of Missouri: Volume III, 1860 to 1875.* Columbia: University of Missouri Press, 1973.

———. *Missouri under Radical Rule, 1865–1870.* Columbia: University of Missouri Press, 1965.

Piott, Steven L. "From Dissolution to Regulation: The Popular Movement against Trusts and Monopoly in the Midwest, 1887–1913." Ph.D. diss., University of Missouri, 1979.

———. *Holy Joe: Joseph W. Folk and the Missouri Idea.* Missouri Biography Series, ed. William E. Foley. Columbia: University of Missouri Press, 1997.

Primm, James Neal. *Economic Policy in the Development of a Western State: Missouri, 1820–1860.* Cambridge: Harvard University Press, 1954.

Rash, Nancy. *The Painting and Politics of George Caleb Bingham.* New Haven: Yale University Press, 1991.

Rosen, Wilbert H. "Hamilton Rowan Gamble, Missouri's Civil War Governor." Ph.D. diss., University of Missouri, 1960.

Saum, Lewis O. *The Fur Trader and the Indian.* Seattle: University of Washington Press, 1965.

Scarpino, Philip V. *Great River: An Environmental History of the Upper Mississippi, 1890–1945.* Columbia: University of Missouri Press, 1985.

Schmidtlein, Gene F. "Truman the Senator." Ph.D. diss., University of Missouri, 1962.

Scroggins, Albert Taylor, Jr. "Nathaniel Patten, Jr., and *The Missouri Intelligencer and Boon's Lick Advertiser.*" Ph.D. diss., University of Missouri, 1961.

Sellars, Richard West. "Early Promotion and Development of Missouri's Natural Resources." Ph.D. diss., University of Missouri, 1972.

Settle, William A., Jr. *Jesse James Was His Name: Or, Fact and Fiction Concerning the Careers of the Notorious James Brothers of Missouri.* Columbia: University of Missouri Press, 1966.

Shalhope, Robert E. *Sterling Price: Portrait of a Southerner.* Columbia: University of Missouri Press, 1971.

Shoemaker, Floyd Calvin. *A History of Missouri and Missourians.* Columbia: Lucas Brothers, 1927.

———. *Missouri and Missourians: Land of Contrasts and People of Achievements.* Volumes 1 & 2. Chicago: Lewis Publishing Co., 1943.

———. *Missouri's Hall of Fame: Lives of Eminent Missourians.* Columbia: Missouri Book Co., 1918.

Slavens, George Everett. "A History of the Missouri Negro Press." Ph.D. diss., University of Missouri, 1969.

Soapes, Thomas F. "Republican Leadership and the New Deal Coalition: Missouri Republican Politics, 1937–1952." Ph.D. diss., University of Missouri, 1973.

Steffen, Jerome Orville. *William Clark: Jeffersonian Man on the Frontier.* Norman: University of Oklahoma Press, 1977.

Stephens, Frank F. *A History of the University of Missouri.* Columbia: University of Missouri Press, 1962.

Thelen, David. *Paths of Resistance: Tradition and Dignity in Industrializing Missouri.* New York: Oxford University Press, 1986. Reprint, with new introduction, as *Paths of Resistance: Tradition and Democracy in Industrializing Missouri,* Columbia: University of Missouri Press, 1991.

Trexler, Harrison Anthony. *Slavery in Missouri, 1804–1865.* Johns Hopkins University Studies in Historical and Political Science, series 32, no. 2. Baltimore: Johns Hopkins University Press, 1914.

Viles, Jonas, et al. *The University of Missouri: A Centennial History.* Columbia: University of Missouri, 1939.

Index

Notes: Page numbers in italics refer to photos. *Society* refers to "State Historical Society" and *University* refers to "University of Missouri."

African American history, 11, 52; in *Missouri Historical Review*, 182, 251–52; in research materials, 52, 175–76

Alvord, Clarence W., 36

American Association for State and Local History (AASLH), 13–14, 208–9, 223, 230–31; awards by, 142, 148, 149, 247

American Historical Association (AHA), 13, 15, 50

Annual meetings, 35–36, 63, 72–74, 115, 247; activities at, 63–64, 111; amendments to constitution at, 27, 83; location of, 65, 232; speakers at, 180–81, 249; workshops at, 244–45, *246*

Anthropology, and state historical societies, 14, 22–23

Archaeology, in mission, 22–23, 224

Archives, of state government, 16–19, 67–68, 183

Art collections, 196–97; acquisitions, 87, 106, 195–97, 235–36; care of, 191–92, 224, 240; contemporary artists in, 196, 236; rationale for, 194–95, 258; space for, 167, 172; uses of, 190, 251, 253–54; value of, 193–94

Atherton, Lewis, 42, *126,* 128, 149, 152, 168–69, 181, 185, 204, 205; background of, 213, 215; contributions of, 138, 155, 164, 199, 218; and manuscript collections, 124–25, 172–73; and University, 170, 175

Audit, of Society finances, 224–25

Audubon, John J., engravings of, 191–92

Aull, William, III, 204, 213; background of, 214, 215, 216; on finance committee, 24, 176, 232

Bailey, Elizabeth, 210

Baker, Sam A., 81–82

Baker, Sharon, 244

Ball, Larry D., 248

Barnes, Francis M. "Bud," 204, 211, 213, 248, *250,* 257–58; background of, 214, 216–17; on finance committee, 24, 243, 245

Barrett, Jesse W., 87

Batterson, Polly, 148

Bay Collection, J. Christian, 3, 106–13, *112,* 167; additions to, 111, 118; value of, 193–94

Bek, William G., 36, 57, 184

Bell, Whitfield J., Jr., 181

Bellamy, Donnie D., 175

Benedict, Linda, 244
Benson, Susan Porter, 175
Benton, Thomas Hart, 117, *197,* 218;
  publications about, 254–55
—works by, 3, 106, 118–19, 195–96;
  care of, 192, 240; exhibits of, 236;
  Exterminate, 192; lithographs of,
  191–92, 195; space for, 110–11; uses
  of, 37, 251; *The Year of Peril,* 113–15
Biennial reports, 46, 55–56, 111;
  finances in, 82, 86
Bingham, George Caleb: works by, 3,
  118–19, 193–94, 195, 235; *Order No.
  11,* 87, 112–13, 116–17, 179, 192;
  uses of works by, 37, 251
Black, William C., 235
Blake, Catherine Cargill, 236
Bock, H. Riley, 213, 219, *219;*
  background of, 215, 216, 217–18
Boeckman, Laurel E., 221, 222
Boeker, Mrs. Roy, *145*
Bond, Christopher "Kit," 162
Book of the Pageant (Shoemaker), 64
Book reviews: in *Missouri Historical
  Review,* 94, 252; of *Ozark Folksongs,*
  134–35
Books. *See* Collections; Publications
Boone County Historical Society, 19
Bootheel Project, 239–40
Botts, Virginia, 219
Boucher, Euphrates, 42
Brassieur, C. Ray, 222, 239
Breckenridge, William Clark, 17, 89
Briggs, Frank, 116
Broeg, Bob, 249
Brown, Daniel, *245*
Brown, Everett, 201
Brown, Sally, 131
Brown-Kubisch, Linda, 223
Brownlee, Richard S., II, 5, 48, *155, 199,*
  199–200, 204, 208, 218, 236; and
  acquisitions, 150–51, 196; activities as
  secretary, 157–60, 189–90, 192–93,
  198; background of, 154–56; goals
  for Society, 186–87, 188, 242; and
  manuscript collections, 172–73;

Missouri Historical Review, 179–82,
  182, 252; on need for more space,
  167–69; and publications, 136,
  183–84; publications by, 178–79,
  182; retirement of, 202, 204; in
  succession process, 152–53, 202–3
Brownlee Fund, Richard S., 243, 245–47
Budgets. *See* Finances
Bugg, James L., Jr., 173, 175
Bullion, Laura, 198, 243, 244
Burk, Vera Faurot, 213, 216, 217
Buse, John J., 237
Bylaws, revision of, 211, 224

Caldwell, Dorothy, 148, 183, 187
Cataloging, 44, 81, 163, 198, 237–38,
  241–42
Census records, 88, 199
Centennial celebrations: Civil War,
  3, 160, 178; Mark Twain, 64–65;
  Missouri, 3, 59–64, 90; Platte
  Purchase, 59–60, 65–67
Chandler, Mrs. Orville, *145*
Christensen, Lawrence O., 176, 213,
  214–15, 247
Christ-Janer, Albert, 51–52
Civil War, 175, 251; Brownlee's expertise
  in, 154, 156, 178–79; centennial, 3,
  160, 178; effects of, 10–11, 18
Civil Works Administration, 68
Clemens, Samuel L. *See* Twain, Mark
Clifford, Amber R., 249
Cockrell, Francis Marion, 124
Collections, 2, 92, 188; books, 192, 228;
  care of, 165, 188, 190, 193, 240–41;
  cartoons, 106, 110–11, 115–16, 119,
  235–36; items turned down, 118,
  122–23; maps, 26, 192, 228, 236;
  in mission of Society, 3, 16–19, 23;
  photographs, 26, 222, 233, 234,
  236–37; as role of state historical
  societies, 13–14, 16; Sampson's,
  17, 31–33, 86; Twainiana, 71, 86,
  112–13, 118–19; uses of, 10, 250–51,
  253; value of, 193–94; variety in,
  228, 258. *See also* Art collections; Bay

Collection, J. Christian; Libraries;
Manuscript collections; Newspapers
—accessibility of, 163, 191, 204; finding
aids, 222, 232; longer hours, 52, 241
—acquisitions, 39–40, 120–23, 150; of
books, 88–89, 111, 163–64, 199, 217,
236–37; purchases of, 108, 133–36,
162, 194, 234; soliciting, 26, 40–42,
44–45, 85, 236–37; during World
War II, 106, 117–18
Collins, Andy, 248–49
Columbia, Missouri, 11, 128; as Society
location, 9–10, 20, 25
Computers, 232, 237, 241
Concannon, Marie, 223
Constitution, State Historical Society,
21–24, 30, 211; amendments to, 27,
83
"Contribution of the State Historical
Society . . . to the Constitutional
Convention," 129–30
Copyright claims, for *Ozark Folksongs,*
135–36
Cornish, Dudley B., 179
Correspondence: handled by staff,
52–53, 158, 190–91; preservation of
120–21, 122; Shoemaker's, 48–49
County historical societies. *See* Local
historical societies
County records, Sampson's search for, 42
Crighton, John C., 246–47
Crouse, Emmett J., 65–66
Crowder, Enoch, 92
Croy, Homer, 197–98
Culmer, Frederic A., 51, 87, 124
Cunningham, Noble E., Jr., 175, 215

Dains, Mary K. (Kathy): publications by,
182, 223; roles of, 187, 219–21, 250
Dale, E. L., 104, 106, 213
Dalton, John M., 160, 167, 197–98
Davidson, Clarissa Start, 181
Davis, Allen F., 175
Davis, Thomas M., 184–85
*Debates of the Missouri Constitutional
Convention of 1875,* 91, 128–30

Denny, James M., 180
Denslow, William R., 168, 213, 215,
216
Depression, effects of, 55–56, 56–57,
78–81, 94
Dew, Charles B., 175
Dexter, Patrick J., 180
*Directory of Local Historical, Museum,
and Genealogical Agencies in Missouri,
The,* 253
Directory of Local Historical Societies,
185–86
Displays. *See* Exhibits
Donnell, Forrest C., 131
Dooley, Tom, 197–98
Dorsett, Lyle W., 175
Draper, Lyman C., 45, 198
Dry, Morris E., 198
Duden, Gottfried, 184–85
Dwight, Margaret L., 176
Dyer, Thomas G., 248

Eagleton, Thomas F., 249
Education, 225–26, 242; by Society, 21,
102. *See also* Schools.
Edwards, Mary E., 44
Ekberg, Carl J., 246
Ellis, Elmer, *103,* 111, 128, 140, 184,
204, 218, 226, 253; background of,
213, 215; and executive directors, 152,
205; on finance committee, 101–2,
125, 127, 158; influence of, 96, 164;
and manuscript collections, 121–23,
125, 172; and need for more space,
165–66, 168–70
Emberson, Frances, 134
Engelhardt, Tom, 196
English, W. Francis, 54, 125–27, 138,
152, 172, 175, 218
Epperson, Ivan H., 92–93
Equipment, 88, 190–91; replacement of,
192, 241
Executive committee, 101, 141, 229–31,
239, 243, 245, 248; on mission of
Society, 69–70, 232; retitling finance
committee to, 211–12. *See also*
Finance committee

Executive directors, 16; changes of title, 150, 211; and finance committee, 29, 43–44; leadership by, 3–4, 24–25, 150–51, 177; transitions between, 44, 149–54, 202–5. *See also* specific directors

Exhibits, 51; of art, 195, 235–36; of Bootheel Project, 240; for centennial celebrations, 64, 65; at fairs, 36, 64

Facilities: dedication of, 166–67; inadequacies of, 38–39, 51, 94–96, *95,* 165, 167–68, 192; new, 39, 46, 157–58, *168;* planning for, 209–10, 232; and relations with University, 2–3, 26–27, 164–66; for special collections, 110–11, 115, 123; storage, 94–96, 167, 192

Federal government. *See* New Deal programs

Federal Writers' Project, 68–69

Ferrell, Robert H., 248

Field, Lyman, 249

Field work, 14, 42, 120

Finance committee, 86, 139–40, 158, 176; and acquisitions, 106, 108–9, 112–13, 196; care of collections, 191–93; and costs of membership growth, 199–200; and executive directors, 3, 150, 157–58; and facilities, 94–96, 166; funding for special projects, 142–43, 245; leadership by, 24–25, 75–76, 104, 211–12; and limited funding, 2, 82; and manuscript collections, 121, 126–27, 172; membership of, 27, 29, 99–101, 164; protecting private funding, 83–85; and publications, 90–91, 131, 135, 179, 183, 184; retitled executive committee, 211–12, 248; and Sampson as executive director, 29, 42, 43–44; and Shoemaker as executive director, 29, 99, 151–52, 153; support for Society's mission, 69–70, 146. *See also* Executive committee

Finances, 81; of added membership, 59, 199–200; audit of, 224–25; budget

decisions, 158, 176, 227–28, 233–34; managing limited resources, 167, 192–93, 226; of *Missouri Historical Review,* 91, 138–39. *See also* Finance committee; Funding

Fink, Gary M., 175

Fires, 16–17, 165

Fisher, James J., 249

Fitzgerald, Irene, 199

Fitzpatrick, Daniel: cartoons by, 106, 110–11, 115–16, 119, 235–36

Fitzpatrick, W. H., 66

Flader, Susan L., 175

Foley, William E., 175, 181, 246

Forderhase, Eugene, 175

Frankfurter, Felix, 5

Frick, Lisa, 250

Frizzell, Robert W., 180

Funding, 65, 190–91, 243; for additional staff, 190–91, 222, 233, 239; and limits on projects, 2, 122–23, 232; for new facilities, 38–39, 165–66, 168–69, 192, 210; private, 82–85, 97, 110, 162–64, 245–47; for publications, 90, 185; for purchases, 109–10, 121–22; relationship to mission, 70, 141, 146; sources of, 55, 160, 200–201; for special projects, 210, 237–38, 239. *See also* Membership Trust Fund; specific projects

—state, 15–16, 21–22, 39–40, 141–42, 158, 160–64, 200–201, 242; for historical commemorations, 59–60, 62, 64, 65, 67; inadequacies of, 26, 62, 78–80, 200–201; increases in, 97, 226–27

Gardner, Frederick D., 62, 81

Gaylord Foundation, Clifford W., 234; uses of, 240, 243, 245–47, 253

Genealogy, 14, 223; finding aids for, 222; information requests on, 53, 190

Gentry, North Todd, 93

Gentzler, Lynn Wolf, 208, 223, 224, 242; roles of, 221, 250

George, G. Houston, 197

George, Melvin D., 171
German-American Experience in Missouri, The (Marshall and Goodrich), 208
Giffen, Jerena East, 181–82
Gifts/donations, 101, 180, 194, 243; of art, 87, 113–16, 195, 235; asking for, 109–10, 121; of books, 163–64, 199, 217; and independence of Society, 70, 72; of materials, 41, 86; of newspapers, 85, 87–88, 118; recognition of, 86, 234, 252; and tax-exempt status, 163–64
Giglio, James N., 247
Glassberg, David, 12
Glauert, Ralph E., 175
Goebels, Gert, 184–85
Goodrich, James W., 5, 159, 175, *207*, 228, *237;* and acquisitions, 223, 238–39; activities as executive director, 208–9, 223; background of, 206–8; and funding, 234, 242; goals for Society, 203–4, 232–33, 238; on mission of Society, 224, 232–33; planning by, 171–72, 231; and publications, 184, 185, 187, 250, 254; publications of, 182, 208; and special projects, 222, 237–38, 242–44
Gray Ghosts of the Confederacy (Brownlee), 156, 178–79
Green, A. P., 146
Green, Fletcher M., 52
Gregg, Kate L., 75, 93–94
Gribben, John, 167
Grothaus, Larry H., 176
Gubernatorial papers, decision to stop publishing, 183
Guitar, Odon, 89
Guitar, Sarah, 123; as librarian, 51, 52–54; work of, 90, 91, 131

Hamilton, Jean Tyree, 199, 204; background of, 213, 214, 215, 218
Hart, Albert Bushnell, 38
Hartley, Elizabeth Anne, 131
Hartmann, Susan M., 250
Hatcher, Joyce, 131

Haymes, Lon S., 144
Hedgepeth, Mrs. Leo, *145*
Hesse, Don, 196
Hetherington, Sue, 131
Hewitt, W. C. (William Cresap), 101, 103–4
Highway department, and marker program, 142, 188–89
Highway markers. *See* Historic markers
Historical commemorations, 3, 139, 158–59, 181, 182, 257. *See also* Centennial celebrations
Historical pageants, 12, 64, 67
Historical reenactments, 12
Historical societies. *See* Local historical societies; State historical societies; State Historical Society of Missouri
Historic markers, 3, 12, 71–72, 140–44, *145*, 188–89, 257
Historic Missouri, 130, 183–84
Historic Missouri: A Pictorial Narrative, 183–84, 253–54
Historic sites, 11–12, 144–48, 189; inventory of, 140, 148. *See also* Historic markers
History: making meanings from, 8–12; public perspectives on, 60
History Day, 233, 241, *245,* 249; success of, 242–44, 257
History of Adair, Sullivan, Putnam, and Schuyler Counties, 9
History of Boone County (Switzler), 9
History of Missouri and Missourians (Shoemaker), 48
History of the University of Missouri (Stephens), 9
Holland, Antonio F., 176
Holmes, Kenneth, 183
Holt, Ivan Lee, 197–98
Hough, Thornton, 235
Howard, Benjamin, 87
Hunter, Mrs. S. L., *145*
Hurt, R. Douglas, 223, 246, 248; evaluation report by, 231–34; roles of, 219–21, 250
Hyde, Arthur M., 64

Independence of Society, 2, 67–70; and
state legislature, 83–85, 144–46; and
University, 125–28, 176–77
Indexing, 81–82, 163, 173; of *Missouri
Historical Review,* 92, 233
Insurance on collections, 39, 193–94,
240

Jaeger, Joseph, 189–90
Jameson, J. Franklin, 13–15
Jesse, Richard H., 19
Jewett, W. O. L., 19–20
Johnson, Charles S., 52
Johnson, Richard, 71–72
Johnson, Ronald W., 175
Jolly, B. H., 75
Jones, Charles T., Jr., 175
Jones, Dorothy V., 180
Journalists, 155, 209; on finance
committee, 101, 104; importance to
Society, 27, 30–31, 140
*Journal of the Missouri Constitutional
Convention of 1875, The,* 63, 90,
128–30

Karr, Fred, 66
Kaufman, Kenneth C., 248
Kaye, Ara L., 221, 223
Kellner, George H., 175, 185
Kemper, William T., 58
Kennard, J. B., 125
King, Roy T., 131
Kingsbury, Lilburn, 75
Kirby, Rollin, 197
Kirkendall, Richard S., 175, 249
Kirkpatrick, James C., 176, 218
Kolb, Kristin, 250
Kostedt, William "Beau," *245*
Kremer, Gary, 247

Laas, Virginia, 247
Lankford, Nancy, 205, 221–22, 223
Larson, Sidney, 196, 218, 222, 236, *237,*
254; art of, 204, 224, 251; expertise
on Bingham, 195, 235
Legislature, Missouri, 72; and centennial
celebrations, 59–62, 64–66, 160, 178;

and mission of Society, 2, 60, 62, 67,
69–70, 144–45
Leonard, Abiel, 86–87, 124
Lesueur, A. A., 20
Lewis Publishing Company, 91, 132–33
Libraries, 31–32, 41–42; purchases for,
81, 82, 89; in role of state historical
societies, 14, 16, 23
—University and Society, 26–27, 96,
165–66, 167–72, 236–37; expansion
plans for, 38–39, 41–42, 172, 209–10;
on-line catalogs of, 241–42
Limbaugh, Stephen N., *219,* 249, 257
Limbaugh, Rush H., Sr., 4, 51, 104–6,
157
Little, B. M., 73
Litton, Jerry, 197–98
Local historical societies, 35, 146; and
annual meetings, 74–75; directory of,
185–86, 253; in *Missouri Historical
Review,* 137, 181, 252; Society support
for, 3, 63, 157, 159, 247
Local histories, publication of, 9
Loeb, Isidor, 24, *30,* 37, 66, 94–96,
115; and acquisitions, 109–10, 113,
114; contributions of, 26, 29–30; on
finance committee, 24, 26, 75–76, 80,
83–85, 99–101; publications by, 63,
90, 91, 129; roles of, 3, 9, 21, 36, 104;
and Sampson, 33, 43; and Shoemaker,
43, 47–48, 132–33
Lohnes, Claire Shane, 236, *237*
Lucas, R. E. "Bud," 236

Maasdorf, Friedel, 184–85
Magrath, C. Peter, 171
Mahan, George A., 55–56, 57, 65, 68,
73, 93, 124; contributions of, 70–72,
86
Mahan Memorial Mark Twain
Collection, 71, 86
Mandel, Estelle, 113–14
Manuscript collections, 2, 193, 241;
acquisitions for, 41–42, 51, 86–87, 89,
118, 122–25, 197–98, 238–39; extent
of, 171, 228; merger of, 172–74; use

of, 174–76, 190. *See also* Western Historical Manuscript Collection

March, David, 181

Marshall, Howard Wight, 208

Martin, Frank L., 54

Mayo Collection, Peter, 196–97

McAllister, Paul E., 176

McCandless, Perry, 179

McCausland, Susan A. Arnold, 37

McClure, Clarence H., 73

McCown, Pearle, 91, 108, 111

McCutcheon, John T., 196–97

McNeil, W. K., 136

McNutt, J. Scott, 101

McReynolds, Allen, 77, 124, 129–30; on finance committee, 66, 75–76; as president, 58, 76; speeches by, 73–74, 140

Membership: decrease in, 200–201, 228–30; growth of, 35, 82, 97, 188, 199–200; trying to increase, 3, 42, 54–59, 231–34; variety of backgrounds in, 252–53, 257–58

Membership dues, 27, 99; increase in, 200–201, 229; uses of, 80, 83, 241; waivers of, 23–24, 56–57

Membership Trust Fund, 82–85, 97; uses of, 110, 162–63, 180, 192, 228, 240, 245–47

Mering, John V., 175

Messages and Proclamations of the Governors of the State of Missouri, The, 90–91, 128–29

Microfilm, 192, 198–99, 228; newspapers on, 88, 163, 192–93, 237–38, 240–41

Middlebush, Frederick A., 96

Miller, Sally M., 248

Minorities, 61; on historic markers, 143–44; in *Missouri Historical Review,* 182, 251–52

Mississippi Valley Historical Association, 34–35, 72–73

Missouri: centennial of, 3, 59–64, 90; economy of, 51, 62; finances of, 83, 85; sesquicentennial of, 181

Missouri: A Guide to the "Show Me" State (van Ravenswaay), 51, 146

Missouri, Day by Day, 130–31

Missouri, Mother of the West (Shoemaker), 48, 91; sales of, 51

Missouri and Missourians: Land of Contrasts and People of Achievements (Shoemaker), 131–33

Missouri Committee for the Humanities (MCH), 243

Missouri Constitutional Convention, 1943–1944, 117–18, 129–30

Missouri Historical Review, 3, 63, 91–92; articles in, 53, 93, 120, 140, 184, 208, 248–49, 258–59; associate editors of, 187, 206, 219–21, 250; cost of, 37, 99, 158, 162, 200; editors of, 37, 48, 157, 179–82, 250–53; evolution of, 37, 232, 249–50; features in, 86, 94, 143, 181–82, 234; index to, 92, 233; scholarship in, 157, 232; style of, 93, 137–39, 250–53; uses of, 57, 242

Missouri Historical Society, 13, 25, 88, 147–48, 177

Missouri Historic Sites Catalog (Caldwell), 148, 183

Missouri History Day Teacher of Merit Award, 243

Missouri Law Enforcement Memorial Foundation, 210

Missouri Newspaper Project (MNP), 237–38

Missouri Newspapers: When and Where (Taft), 183

Missouri Press Association (MPA), 62–63, 149, 181; and founding of Society, 4, 8, 19–26, *22;* membership of, 30, 31, 76, 103, 104, 106; support for Society, 18, 39–40, 139–40

Missouri's Struggle for Statehood (Shoemaker), 48

Missouri State Park Board, managing historic sites, 144, 146, 189–90

Mitchell, Franklin D., 175

Moll, Justus R., 58, 74

Montgomery, Christine, 223, 250

Moore, W. K., 182
Morris, Leona S., 250
Morse Mark Twain Collection, 112–13
Morton, John D., 248
Moss, James E., 187
Muench, Friedrich, 184–85
Museums, 2, 14, 23
Myers, Lisa, 249
My Road to Emeritus (Ellis), 253

Naeter, George A., 54
Nagel, Elsa, 185
Nasatir, A. P., 89
Nast, Thomas, 196–97
National Trust for Historic Preservation, 148
Nebel, Arthur V., 241
New Deal programs, 67–69, 94–95, 251
Newspaper editors, 9, 14, 18, 31, 76, 193, 238; membership in Society, 35, 55, 103–4
Newspapers: acquisitions of, 35, 42, 50, 87–88, 118; art from, 106, 196–97, 235–36; collection of, 228, 229, 258; management of collection, 81, 82–83, 94, 163, 183, 222; on microfilm, 88, 118, 192–93, 198–99; in mission of Society, 3, 23–24; Missouri Newspaper Project, 237–38; "This Week in Missouri History" column for, 89–90, 130, 138
Nixon, William H., 123
Norris, James D., 175
Not-for-profit status, 163–64

Officers, 25, 140; backgrounds of, 75–78, 212–21, 257–58; contributions of, 58, 211–12
O'Hare, Kate Richards, 248
Olson, James C., 181, 199, 204; background of, 213, 214, 215–16; and need for more space, 168–71
Omnibus State Reorganization Act of 1974, 170, 176
Online Computer Library Center, 237
Oral history program, 222, 239–40, 241; for new outreach, 231–33

Organ, Minnie K., *28, 36*; role of, 27–28, 42–43
Oster, Donald B., 12, 208
Owen, Mary A., 36
Ozark Folksongs (Randolph), 106, 130, 133–36; significance of, 255, 257

Painter, William R., 61–62
Park, Guy B., 73
Parker, Ralph, *199*
Parrish, William, 179, 181
Patrons: correspondence with, 52–53, 158, 190–91; disseminating information to, 1, 225–26, 231–33; use of collections by, 37–38, 51–52, 163, 174–76, 190–91, 228, 259
Payne, Moses U., 124
Peritore, Laura, 195
Pettit, Kay, 223, 238
Photostat machine, copying newspapers with, 81, 83, 88
Pioneer Merchant in Mid-America, The (Atherton), 124
Platte Purchase centennial, 59–60, 65–67
Portraits: donations of, 87, 195, 235; of executive directors, 149, 204, 236. *See also* Art collections
Powers, Ron, 249
Preservation, 18; microfilming for, 240–41; in mission of Society, 22–23, 148, 226; of Ste. Genevieve records, 198
Presidents, Society, 104, 211–12. *See also* Officers; specific individuals
Prewitt, Nancy C., 172, 176
Price, Albert M., *199*, 211, 214, 218
Price, R. B., Jr., 218
Price, R. B., Sr., 218
Priddy, Bob, 247, 254
Primm, James Neal, 172
Professional staff, 38, 43–44, 53, 67–68, 241; contributions of, 221–24; effect of low funding on, 81–82, 162, 190–91; ideas in Hurt report, 231–34; numbers of, 44, 190–91; praise for,

52–54, 157–58, 176; in publications, 90–91, 130–31, 136, 137; standards of, 3, 186–88
Publications, 63, 151, 183–85, 228, 248, 252–53; expansion of, 89–94, 130, 232; in the 1940s, 128–40; by staff members, 48, 223–24; by state historical societies, 5, 14. *See also Missouri Historical Review*
Public history movement, 256–59
Public Works Administration (PWA), 94–95

Quaife, Milo M., 140

Rader, Perry S., 20, 27, 29
Randolph, Vance, 53, 119; *Ozark Folksongs* by, 106, 130, 133–36, 255, 257
Ratchford, C. Brice, 176, 180–81
Ray, S. J., 196
Reading room, *40,* 165; art in, 86, 87, 116; users of, 37–38, 51–52, 190–91, 228
Report on a Journey to the Western States . . . (Duden), 184–85, 255
Research, 166; in mission of Society, 23, 140; in Society publications, 131, 180; by staff, 72, 158, 210. *See also* Patrons
Rice, David, 246
Rieger, Nelson A., 235
Rikoon, Sanford, 244
Road to Santa Fe, The (Gregg), 93–94
Roberts, Randy, 222, 223, 224
Robertson, James I., 249, *250*
Robinett, Paul M., 141
Robins, Ruby M., 143
Robinson, H. E., 20, 36
Rockefeller Foundation grant, 122, 125, 127–28
Roediger, David, 175
Rogers, Ann L., 250
Rollins family, 195; and Bingham materials, 87, 116–17, 195
Rollins manuscript collection, James S., 51, 124
Rosen, Wilbert H., 175

Rost, Mrs. Vincent, Jr., *145*
Roth, James, 117
Rozier, George A., 58–59, 65, 115, 148, 156, 172, 211; and acquisitions, 109, 135, 150; background of, 77–78, 214, 215, 216; on finance committee, 24, 76, 101, 158; as president, 78, 104
Rozier, Helen Elizabeth McReynolds, 77–78
Rozier, Leo, 213
Russell, George, 210

Salaries, 32, 36; funding for, 39–40, 82, 186–87, 227–28; levels of, 81, 232
Sales: of publications, 90–91, 131; of unnecessary materials, 82–83, 85
Sampson, Francis Asbury, 4, 5–6, 11, *34,* 226; acquisitions by, 32–33, 35, 40–42; collections of, 17, 31–33, 86; and finance committee, 29, 42, 43–44; and *Missouri Historical Review,* 37, 182; roles of, 26, 31–35, 44–45
Sappington, John, 124, 145–46
Sarvis, Will, 222
Saum, Lewis O., 175, 246
Scholarship-in-progress grants, 245–47
Scholes, Walter, 175
Schools, 3, 63; History Day in, 242–44; history instruction in, 9, 50, 242; publications in, 57, 136
Schroeder, Adolf, 185
Schwartz, Charles and Elizabeth, 236
Scott, Mary Semple, 92
Security systems, 193–94, 232, 240
Semicentennial History (Shoemaker), 113
Settle, William A., Jr., 179
Severance, Henry O., 41, 96
Shackelford, Thomas, 37
Shalhope, Robert E., 175
Shaughnessy, Thomas W., 204
Shay, Martin, 244
Sheals, Debbie, *246*
Shelby, Joseph O., 195
Shephard, Maryann, 243
Shoemaker, Floyd C., 5–6, *49, 74–75, 112,* 115; and acquisitions, 42, 85,

89, 107–13, 114, 135; activities
as secretary, 48–51, 151–52, 177;
assistant for, 152–53, 187; background
of, 46–47; contributions of, 4–5,
180, 218, 248–49; as editor of
Missouri Historical Review, 92, 93–94,
137–39; and finance committee,
29, 99, 151–52, 153; and historical
commemorations, 59–61, 65–66; and
historic marker program, 141–43;
and manuscript collections, 121–27;
membership initiatives by, 54–59,
97–99; and Missouri war letters
project, 120–21; and need for more
space, 94–96, 165–66; and newspaper
collections, 87, 88; protecting
independence of Society, 68–69,
144–46; and publications, 130, 242;
publications by, 63, 64, 89–90, 91,
113, 129, 132–33, 139–40, 181,
257; relationships of, 30, 43–44,
45, 53–54, 78, 146–48; retirement
of, 149, 153–54, 156; and Society
funding, 2, 80, 83–85
Shoemaker Award, Floyd C., for student
essays, 248–49
Silvestro, Clement L., 153
Slavens, George Everett, 176
Slavery, 52, 181–82
Smith, Forrest, 145
Smith, Robert C., 211, 218, 229–30,
237; background of, 213, 214, 216,
217
Smith, Thomas K., 58, 117
Snyder, J. E., 36
Source materials, publication of, 90
Southern, William N., 90
Speaking engagements, 232; by
Brownlee, 157–60; by Goodrich,
208–9; by Shoemaker, 50, 157–58
Spencer, Mr. and Mrs. R. Perry, 124
Stark, Lloyd C., 65–67, 143; papers of,
122–23, 126
State. *See* Legislature; Missouri
State historical societies, 5–6, 12–15,
258; comparison of memberships, 55,

58–59, 97–99, 137, 200; cooperation
among, 35, 50, 238; funding for,
15–16, 80–81, 158, 229; projects by,
2, 23
State Historical Society of Missouri, 8,
16–19; anniversaries of, 139–40, 182;
awards by, 204, 218–19, 247–48;
at end of Shoemaker directorship,
148–52, 156–57; evaluation of and
planning for, 171, 230–34, 242;
founding of, 4, 19–26; increasing
professionalism of, 151, 157, 177–78,
186–88, 245–47; independence of,
65–69, 176–77; and public history
movement, 256–59; as trustee of state,
21–22, 83
—mission of, 22–23, 194–95; continuity
of, 203–4, 259; interpretation of by
executive directors, 157, 232–33;
limiting projects to, 1–2, 68–70,
144–46, 150–51; review of, 140–41,
224–25
*State Historical Society of Missouri:
A Semicentennial History, The*
(Shoemaker), 139–40
State Historical Society of Wisconsin, as
model, 13, 15, 20, 45, 258
Statehood, Missouri's. *See* Centennial
celebrations
Stauter, Mark, 247
Steffen, Jerome O., 175
Ste. Genevieve, 64–65, 198
Stepenoff, Bonnie, 247, 248
Stephens, Edwin W., 9–10, *20,* 24,
30–31, 90; and founding of Society,
18, 19–26, 30
Stephens, Frank F., 9
Stephens, Lon, 21
Stephens, Mrs. E. Sydney, 235
Stephens College, 50–51
Stevens, Walter B., 61, 76–77; writing
by, 90, 93
Steward, Dick, 246
Stewart, Cindy, 198
St. Louis World's Fair, 1904, 3, 36

Strickland, Arvarh E., 175, 181–82, 204, 215, 250
Stucky, Duane, 169–70
Students, as staff, 38, 67–68
Suggs, Henry Lewis, 247
Swain, Edward Everett, 67, 104, 115, 135, 218; on finance committee, 75–76, 99–101
Switzler, William F., 9–10, 35–36
Symington, Stuart, 197–98, *199*

Taft, William H., 18, 183
Talbert, Mrs. J. T., 69
Tax-exempt status, 163–64
Taylor, Maxwell D., 180
Technological advances, 118. *See also* Equipment; Microfilm
Thelen, David P., 175
"This Week in Missouri History" (essay series), 89–90, 130, 138, 257
Thomas, Mark, 238
Thomas Hart Benton: Artist, Writer, Intellectual, 254–55
Thwaites, Reuben Gold, 13–15, 27, 45, 88–89
Tibbe, Anna, 218–19
Torrey, Jay L., 61
Touhill, Blanche M., 213–16
Trail, E. B., 198
Translations, 163, 184–85
Treasurers, 27, 211, 218
Trefts, Charles, 197, 219
Trexler, Harrison Anthony, 38
Truman, Harry S., 148; in *Missouri Historical Review,* 182, 251; presidential library of, 119, 128
Trustees, of Society, 27, 140, 167, 204; backgrounds of, 104, 212–21, 257–58; limiting mission by, 69–70; roles of, 25, 58, 101, 204, 211–12
Tucker, Avis Green, 24–25, 218, 219, *237,* 243; background of, 213–14, 215, 216, 217
Twain, Mark (Samuel L. Clemens): centennial celebration, 64–65; donation by, 41; materials, 71, 86, 112–13, 118–19

Uehling, Barbara, 169–70
University of Missouri, 149, 243; comparison of Society to, 177, 186–87; and cooperation of libraries, 26–27, 85, 241–42; history department of, 5, 9, 102, 127, 138, 152, 174–76; history of, 10, 11–12, 31; and manuscript collections, 121–22, 124, 127, 173–76, 238; sharing facilities with, 38–39, 95–96, 164–72, 209–10
—relationship of Society with, 2–3, 20–21, 102, 125, 210, 259; under Brownlee, 150, 154–56, 170–72, 176–77
University of Missouri Press, 185, 253
Usher, Roland G., 73

Van Ravenswaay, Charles, 51, 75, 146–48
Viles, Jonas, 9, 10, 16–17, 37, 67, 72–73, 123; roles of, 35–36, 43, 70

Watters, T. (Theron) Ballard, 153, 213; on finance committee, 101, 103–4
Watts, Steven, 175
Webber, Joseph, 212, 213, 217, 230, 243
Welliver, Warren, 168
Welsh, Donald H., 152–53, 187
Western Historical Manuscript Collection (WHMC), 121–28, *174,* 193, 206, 241; acquisitions for, 124–25, 239; consolidation of, 2–3, 172–74
White, L. M. (Leander Mitchell) "Mitch," 104, 114, 128, 135, 146, 148, 177, 211; and cartoons, 115, 196, 236; and executive directors, 151–54, 156–57; on finance committee, 101, 102–3
White, R. M. (Robert Morgan), 25–26, 33, 58, 60–61, 76; contributions of, 29, 31; on finance committee, 24, 27, 40
White, Robert M., II, 238
Whitton, Rex M., 142
Williams, Maxwell, 239–40

Williams, Roy D., 76, 109, 147, 213, 218; on finance committee, 75–76, 99–101

Williams, Sarah, 52

Williams, Walter, 9–10, 43, 61, 86, 257–58; contributions of, 29–31; on finance committee, 24, 27, 75; in founding of Society, 20–21, 30; and publications, 37, 91

Williamson, Hugh P., 180

Withers, Ethel, 75

Wixson, Douglas, 254

Wolfe, James E., 229

Wolfe, Margaret Ripley, 249

Women, 61; history of, 52, 92, 143–44, 181–82, 251–52; in leadership of Society, 213, 219

Wood, James Madison, 36

Woodman, Harold D., 175

Woods, Charles L., 58

Woods, Marie, 188, 218

Woodson, Mrs. Marshall S., 235

Workshops at annual meetings, 244–45, *246*

Works Progress Administration (WPA), 51, 146; Historical Records Survey, 18, 68

World War I, 92–93, 252

World War II, 106, 120, 122; Missouri war letters project, 120–21; service of Society personnel in, 103, 104, 155, 213

World Wide Web sites, 241

Wright, Purd B., 61, 86

Wyllie, Irvin H., 153

Young, Raymond, 248

Young, Virginia, 3, 158, 228; background of, 213, 214, 217, 258; leadership by, 24, 205, 213

Zwick, G. L. (Galius Lawton), 104–6